Organizational Encounters with Risk

Organizational encounters with risk range from errors and anomalies to outright disasters. In a world of increasing interdependence and technological sophistication, the problem of understanding and managing such risks has grown ever more complex. Organizations and their participants must often reform and re-organize themselves in response to major events and crises, dealing with the paradox of managing the potentially unmanageable. Organizational responses are influenced by many factors, such as the representational capacity of information systems and concerns with legal liability.

In this collection, leading experts on risk management from a variety of disciplines address these complex features of organizational encounters with risk. They raise critical questions about how risk can be understood and conceived by organizations, and whether it can be 'managed' in any realistic sense at all. This book is an important reminder that the organizational management of risk involves much more than the cool application of statistical method.

BRIDGET HUTTER is Peacock Chair of Risk Management at the London School of Economics and Political Science and Director of the ESRC Centre for Analysis of Risk and Regulation (CARR) at the London School of Economics and Political Science.

MICHAEL POWER is Professor of Accounting and a Director of the ESRC Centre for Analysis of Risk and Regulation (CARR) at the London School of Economics and Political Science.

Organizational Encounters with Risk

Edited by

BRIDGET HUTTER AND MICHAEL POWER

CAMBRIDGE
UNIVERSITY PRESS

CAMBRIDGE UNIVERSITY PRESS
Cambridge, New York, Melbourne, Madrid, Cape Town, Singapore, São Paulo

CAMBRIDGE UNIVERSITY PRESS
The Edinburgh Building, Cambridge CB2 2RU, UK

Published in the United States of America by Cambridge University Press, New York

www.cambridge.org
Information on this title: www.cambridge.org/9780521609289

First published 2005

Printed in the United Kingdom at the University Press, Cambridge

A catalogue record for this book is available from the British Library

ISBN-13 978-0-521-84680-6 hardback
ISBN-10 0-521-84680-3 hardback
ISBN-13 978-0-521-60928-9 paperback
ISBN-10 0-521-60928-3 paperback

Contents

Tables

Contributors

TIMOTHY BESLEY is Professor of Economics and Political Science at the London School of Economics and Political Science, working mainly in the fields of Development Economics, Public Economics and Political Economy. He is a Fellow of the British Academy, the Econometric Society and the European Economics Association. He is a founding board member and the first elected President of the Bureau for Research and Economic Analysis of Development (BREAD). He is also a past co-editor of the *American Economic Review* and has served regularly as a consultant to the World Bank and to HM Treasury.

REBECCA CULYBA is a PhD candidate in the Department of Sociology at Northwestern University and a Research Assistant at the American Bar Foundation, where she works on Carol Heimer's project on 'clinic-level law'. Her dissertation examines the relationship between classification systems and authority in medicine in the United States over the last seventy years. She also chairs the board of directors for a local non-profit organization in Athens, Georgia, offering social services to people infected with AIDS and HIV-prevention programmes to the community.

MAITREESH GHATAK is Professor of Economics at the London School of Economics and Political Science, working mainly in the areas of Development Economics and Public Economics. He is Director of the Programme for the Study of Economic Organisation and Public Policy (EOPP) based in STICERD. He is a senior fellow of the Bureau for Research and Economic Analysis of Development (BREAD). He is also an editor of the *Review of Economic Studies* and co-editor of the *Economics of Transition*.

GEOFFREY HEAL is Garrett Professor of Public Policy and Corporate Responsibility at Columbia University's Graduate School of Business. He is a member of a number of policy committees including being chair of the National Academy/National Research Council's Committee on the Valuation of Ecosystem Services and a member of the Environmental Protection Agency's Science Advisory Board. He is a Fellow of the Econometric Society and his research includes the securitization of catastrophic risks, risks associated with the growth of derivative markets, the economic aspects of security in highly inter-dependent systems, and the interaction between society and its natural resource base. He is author of a number of books including *Valuing the Future* (Columbia University Press, 1998).

CAROL A. HEIMER is Professor of Sociology at Northwestern University and Senior Research Fellow at the American Bar Foundation. Her research interests address risk and insurance and organization theory, medical sociology and sociology of law. She is author of *Reactive Risk and Rational Action* (University of California Press, 1985), *Organization Theory and Project Management* (Norwegian University Press and Oxford University Press, 1985) and *For the Sake of the Children* (University of Chicago Press, 1998). She is a winner of both the theory and medical sociology prizes of the American Sociological Association. Her current project, 'Clinic-level law: the "legalization" of medicine in AIDS treatment and research', is a National Science Foundation-funded comparative study of the role of law in medicine.

BRIDGET HUTTER is Peacock Chair of Risk Management at the London School of Economics and Political Science and co-director of the ESRC Centre for Analysis of Risk and Regulation (CARR). Her research concerns the sociology of regulation and risk management; the regulation of economic life with particular reference to regulatory enforcement and corporate responses to regulation; and the social control of organizations. She is author of numerous publications on the subject of regulation, including *Compliance* (Clarendon Press, 1997) and *Risk and Regulation* (Oxford University Press, 2001). She is also the editor of the *British Journal of Sociology*.

SHEILA JASANOFF is Pforzheimer Professor of Science and Technology Studies at Harvard University. She has held academic appointments at several universities, including Cornell, Yale, Oxford and Kyoto, the Institute for Advanced Study, Berlin and the Rockefeller Foundation's study centre in Bellagio. Her research concerns the role of science and technology in the political structures of modern democratic societies, with a particular focus on the use of science in law and public policy. She is author of *Controlling Chemicals* (Cornell University Press, 1985), *The Fifth Branch* (Harvard University Press, 1990), *Science at the Bar* (Harvard University Press, 1995) and *Designs on Nature* (Princeton University Press, 2005). She has served on the board of directors of the American Association for the Advancement of Science and as President of the Society for Social Studies of Science.

HOWARD KUNREUTHER is the Cecilia Yen Koo Professor of Decision Sciences and Public Policy at the Wharton School, University of Pennsylvania and co-director of the Wharton Risk Management and Decision Processes Center. His research interests concern the management of low probability – high consequence events. He is a member of the National Research Council (NRC) Board on Radioactive Waste Management and a Distinguished Fellow of the Society for Risk Analysis (receiving the Society's Distinguished Achievement Award in 2001). He is the co-author of *Managing Environmental Risk Through Insurance* (Kluwer Academic Publishers, 1997) and a recipient of the Elizur Wright Award for contributions to the literature of insurance. He is co-editor of *Catastrophe Modelling: A New Approach to Managing Risk* (Springer, 2005).

DONALD MACKENZIE holds a personal chair in Sociology at Edinburgh University, where he has taught since 1975. His first book was *Statistics in Britain, 1865–1930: The social construction of scientific knowledge* (Edinburgh University Press, 1981); his most recent is *Mechanizing Proof: computing, risk, and trust* (MIT Press, 2001). He currently holds an ESRC professorial fellowship to work on social studies of finance.

JULEIGH COLEMAN PETTY is a PhD candidate in the Department of Sociology at Northwestern University and a Research Assistant at the American Bar Foundation. Her dissertation topic, 'Mastering medicine: scientific authority and clinical expertise', is a study of medicine and science as competing institutions, drawing on evidence from infectious disease (particularly HIV/AIDS) and pain management. She also works on Carol Heimer's project on 'clinic-level law'.

MICHAEL POWER is Professor of Accounting and a co-director of the ESRC Centre for Analysis of Risk and Regulation (CARR) at the London School of Economics and Political Science, where he has worked since 1987. He is a Fellow of the Institute of Chartered

Accountants in England and Wales, has held visiting fellowships at the Institute for Advanced Study, Berlin (1996/6) and at All Souls College, Oxford (2000). He is author of *The Audit Society: rituals of verification* (Oxford University Press, 1999) and *The Risk Management of Everything* (Demos, 2004).

DIANE VAUGHAN is Professor of Sociology and International and Public Affairs, Columbia University. She is the author of *Controlling Unlawful Organizational Behavior* (University of Chicago Press, 1983), *Uncoupling: turning points in intimate relationships* (Oxford University Press, 1986) and *The Challenger Launch Decision* (University of Chicago Press, 1996). Much of her research has investigated the dark side of organizations: mistake, misconduct and disaster. She was a researcher on the staff of the *Columbia* Accident Investigation board and is currently at work on *Dead Reckoning: Air Traffic Control in the Early 21st Century*.

Acknowledgements

The editors are grateful to the UK Economic and Social Research Council (ESRC) for the financial support of the Centre for Analysis of Risk and Regulation (CARR) at the London School of Economics and Political Science. Bridget Hutter wishes to thank Michael Peacock and the Michael Peacock Charitable Foundation for supporting her chair and for seeding the establishment of CARR. Michael Power wishes to thank the trustees of the P. D. Leake Trust and the Institute of Chartered Accountants in England and Wales for supporting his chair and programme of work. Thanks are also extended to Pauline Khng for her patience and diligent copy-editing.

Abbreviations and acronyms

AGREE	Appraisal of Guidelines Research and Evaluation
AHRQ	Agency for Healthcare Research and Quality
AIDS	Acquired Immunodeficiency Syndrome
AIRMIC	Association of Insurance and Risk Managers
AMA	American Medical Association
ARENA	Applied Research Ethics National Association
CDC	Centers for Disease Control and Prevention
CEO	Chief Executive Officer
CFO	Chief Financial Officer
CFR	Code of Federal Regulations
CIO	Chief Information Officer
COO	Chief Operating Officer
COSO	Committee of Sponsoring Organizations of the Treadway Commission
CPG	Clinical Practice Guidelines
CRO	Chief Risk Officer
DHHS	United States Department of Health and Human Services
DMC	Data Monitoring Committee
DRG	Diagnostic Related Groups
ERISA	Employee Retirement Income Security Act
ERM	Enterprise Risk Management
FDA	United States Food and Drug Administration
GAO	Government Accountability Office (formerly General Accounting Office)
GARP	Global Association of Risk Professionals
HIPAA	Health Insurance Portability and Accountability Act of 1996 (PL 104–191)
HIV	Human Immunodeficiency Virus
HMO	Health Maintenance Organization
IIA	Institute of Internal Auditors
IOM	Institute of Medicine

IRB	Institutional Review Board
JCAHO	Joint Commission on Accreditation of Healthcare Organizations
NBAC	National Bioethics Advisory Commission
NIH	National Institutes of Health
OHRP	Office for Human Research Protections
OPRR	Office for Protection from Research Risks
PRIM&R	Public Responsibility in Medicine and Research
PRMIA	Professional Risk Managers International Association
PSRO	Professional Standards Review Organization
RAROC	Risk-Adjusted Rate of Return On Capital
RIMS	Risk and Insurance Managers Society
SRA	Society for Risk Analysis
VAR	Value at Risk

1 | Organizational encounters with risk: an introduction

BRIDGET HUTTER AND MICHAEL POWER

Organizing and risking

CONTEMPORARY discussions of risk routinely point to the paradox of science and technology. On the one hand great advances have been made in health and welfare; on the other hand such advances also give rise to new problems and vulnerabilities, e.g. the benefits of increased longevity in Western societies have given rise to difficulties in pension and social security systems. This is the essence of Beck's (1992) famous 'risk society' thesis; the risks we face today are largely 'manufactured', potentially fatal by-products of an industrial machine which demands a new politics to control it. In this collection of essays, we retain a focus on this paradox but we shift the analytical focus from science and technology to organizations and organizing.

Organizations, rather than individuals, are the critical agents of any so-called risk society because it is primarily 'in these contexts that hazards and their attendant risks are conceptualized, measured and managed' (Short 1992: 4). Organizations are both centres for processing and handling risks and potential producers and exporters of risk. Efforts to manage risk involve the creation of organizational networks for that purpose, and these risk regulation 'regimes' (Hood et al. 2001) themselves give rise to new side effects and risks – risks of risk management. Above all, there is widespread recognition that disasters and accidents are in a very important sense *organized* (cf. Beamish 2002; Perrow 1984; Turner and Pidgeon 1997; Vaughan 1996).

Management orthodoxy suggests that organizations represent co-operative endeavours which seek to process and manage different sources of uncertainty in the pursuit of a goal, e.g. profit. Accounting and information systems, strategic planning processes, human resource and marketing functions, regulatory compliance and procurement processes are all components of this management of uncertainty in its

1

broadest sense. While specific 'risk management' practices may exist
and take a variety of forms in many different settings (e.g. health and
safety, finance, operations), the managing of risk in general is a constitutive feature of organization and is not some accidental feature of it.
For example, as the contribution by Besley and Ghatak in Chapter 6 in
this volume shows, the principal agent relationship and the risks to
each party in this relation are widely recognized as a fundamental
feature of organizational design. This is not to say that organizations
necessarily know or understand the risks they take, or that they always
invest in optimal or efficient formal risk management systems. Indeed,
there are good reasons for doubting this. It is simply to suggest that
'organizing' and 'risking' are two sides of the same coin.

Empirically, this intimate relationship between risk, management
and organization is most evident in so-called 'high-reliability' organizations where risk management is manifestly a core organizing principle (e.g. NASA, the nuclear industry, aviation and large petro-chemical
sites). However, the claim is also a generic conceptual one; formally
organized activity inextricably implies some form of uncertainty processing and some version of the management of risk. It follows that
'organizational encounters with risk' are as much about how organizations – such as corporations and states – experience the nature and
limits of their own capacity to organize as they are about external
shocks and disturbances in the environment. In different ways, all the
essays in this volume deal with this issue.

It is often assumed that organizations exist in, but are ontologically
separate from, their environments. The ideal typical concept of risk
management is often represented as cybernetic in form, involving the
sequential collection of information about these environmental uncertainties, the formulation of policy, the making of decisions and the
processing of feedback from implementation processes. However, the
view that managers deal with risk by first calculating and then choosing
alternative risk-return combinations is highly questionable (March and
Shapira 1987), and framing theory provides a reminder of the importance of context, sequence, attention capacity and many other variables
which shape decision making (e.g. Kahneman and Tversky 1979). How
managers actually respond to uncertainties also depends on the social
definition of management roles and on collective beliefs about risk
taking and related possibilities for control. In such settings the imposition of rational decision theory can be counterproductive, if not risky

itself (March and Shapira 1987). Rational organizational blueprints not only misdescribe decision making but may, if institutionalized as norms, have perverse organizational effects. Accordingly, the simplistic duality of organization and environment must be challenged: organizational responses to risk are shaped by their institutional environments, and this organizing process is itself a source of risk for individuals, for other organizations and for wider environments. Notorious examples are the steam explosion and leakage of radiation across Europe from Chernobyl in the USSR in 1986, the gas leak from the Bhopal chemical plant in India in 1984 (see Jasanoff, Chapter 9 in this volume), and the failure in 1984–91 of more than 1,400 Savings and Loan banks in the USA. On this view of organizations, they are actively engaged in the 'manufacture of risk' (Beck 1992).

The organizational origins of many disasters have become well established (Perrow 1984; Turner and Pidgeon 1997; Vaughan 1996). Even apparently natural events have had distributional consequences which are organizational in origin, e.g. substandard practice in the construction industry seems to have amplified effects of the Turkish earthquake in 1999. So the environment within which organizations operate is not some Hobbesian state of nature but consists of a web of relationships with other organizations and with human communities more generally. It is this 'double moment' of organizations which mirrors that of science and technology, namely their pervasive duality as both producers and managers of risk. This makes formal organizations a critical point of reference in any project to understand and delineate the so-called risk society.

As Jasanoff (Chapter 9 in this volume) reminds us, the events of September 11 (2001) in many ways highlight the complex and inter-related difficulties in the way societies, and the organizations within them, recognize, assess, manage and create risks. To the obvious and awful scale, human cost and media drama of the event must be added myriad more specific and complex reactions and consequences. These include insurance systems (Ericson and Doyle 2004: Chapter 5), infrastructure concentration and business continuity, structural engineering and the future of tall buildings, emergency services and disaster planning, settlement systems in financial markets, and notions of 'homeland security' and preventative war. As we write, we sense a growing proximity between regulatory and security issues and a blurring of traditional boundaries between policing and risk management. But while September 11 reminds us that disasters, when they crystallize, respect no disciplinary boundaries and call into question existing investments in expertise as never before, it also illustrates the duality described above. September 11, the 2004 bombings in Madrid, and the 2005 London bombings have served to constitute a managerial and political climate of 'security precaution', forcing organizations to think about both their environments in more security-conscious ways, and aspects of their own organizing which may create specific vulnerabilities, e.g. the concentration of command and control in a single centre. Business continuity consulting has thrived in the wake of these terrible events, suggesting that the production of fear is simultaneously functional for governments and the consulting industry. Indeed, such events may justify the introduction of otherwise unpopular surveillance measures without full regard to their efficacy, the case of identity cards in the United Kingdom being a notable example at the time of writing (Better Regulation Task Force 2004: 15).

The 9/11 Commission (2004) traced the 'organization-made' nature of security risks to structural weaknesses in the security services and to an apparent communication impasse between the organizations of the FBI and the CIA. These reflect generic organizational deficiencies already clearly identified in the work of Turner and Pidgeon (1997) and Vaughan (1996). Some also claim that US vulnerability of the kind witnessed on September 11, and not sufficiently imagined by its security agencies, is an unintended consequence of the country's foreign policy over many years. Whatever the truth of this, the generic message is clear: disasters, however great or small, are, in a very important sense, *organized*. And as Jasanoff (1994) has shown, the organization of various accounts and explanatory narratives of disaster constitutes the 'civic epistemologies' of risk.

The focus on organizations is not intended to belittle impact at the human level. Major events can undoubtedly have huge effects – over 3,000 people died in a few hours as a result of the events of September 11; Bhopal resulted in over 3,000 immediate deaths, not to mention countless long-term effects and injuries; and Chernobyl contaminated large areas of northern Europe with radioactive material. Financial disasters also cause widespread suffering and damage. The Savings and Loan crisis had resolution costs estimated at some 3–5 per cent of US gross national product and the collapse of Enron and Worldcom in 2002 resulted in the catastrophic loss of welfare for many employees and pensioners.

The scale of events can have seismic significance for entire systems of political and corporate governance in advanced economies. The Enron and Parmalat scandals have challenged the fabric of national and international risk regulation regimes in which auditors, both internal and external, non-executive directors and audit committees, state regulatory organizations and professional bodies, financial analysts and credit rating agencies have all lived in a delicately organized balance of compromises for many years. This complex assembly of agents and institutions is hardly a 'system' but has evolved slowly and in an ad-hoc manner, with occasional bursts of reform in the wake of scandals (e.g. Maxwell, BCCI, Barings in the UK). However, Enron triggered a more fundamental discourse about organizations in 'dis-organized' capitalism and has resulted in heavyweight legislation in the form of the Sarbanes-Oxley Act 2002 in the United States which is likely to have considerable international influence as a 'world-level blueprint' (Meyer et al. 1997). At the heart of this shaky edifice lies the role of accounting and accountants who epitomize the duality of organization in relation to risk – on the one hand they are critical for the smooth running of markets in making risks visible and transparent to those who would entrust their resources to entrepreneurs; on the other hand these intermediaries are also sources of risk to others and, via the drama of reputational meltdown visible in the demise of the firm Andersen, to themselves.

The impact of events and disasters depends on institutionalized forms of attention and social processes which amplify (or not) perceived dangers and consequences (Kasperson et al. 2003). It is argued that the long-term impact of Bhopal was at best ambivalent, with competing explanations being essentially unresolved (Jasanoff, Chapter 9 this volume). Indeed, some twenty years after the disaster, those living in proximity to the Union Carbide site are still being damaged by the effects and the site remains contaminated pending the outcome of legal proceedings. The very idea of impact can be contested by different affected groups and can vary greatly in duration. Major rail disasters in Britain have resulted in immediate media attention and political commitments that such events will never happen again, commitments which are often lost in the fullness of time (Hutter 2001). In addition to a number of rail crashes in the UK, the apparent failure of Swiss air traffic control to prevent a mid-air collision in July 2002, and the collapse of equity assets and the effects on pension funds, support claims that public confidence in the many and various institutions of risk management in developed economies is in decline. As organizational sources of risk are increasingly apparent, Beck's 'risk society' thesis, in which the authority of experts is called into question and in which each individual must take responsibility for his or her own actions in the face of risk, is becoming a more apparent empirical reality. Notwithstanding, and perhaps because of, the cultural plurality of risk perceptions, we are all our own risk managers now. In a cultural situation in which organizations become safer via their risk management processes, at the expense of citizens, it is hardly surprising that trust in institutions declines. Nor is it clear that reactively created certification and disclosure regimes, such as those required by the Sarbanes-Oxley legislation, have any capacity to create public trust (Power 2004a).

These reflections on the entanglement of organizations and risk are central to the collection of essays in this book. Each contribution addresses a dimension of the organization of risk and its management, a theme which we characterize by the motif of 'organizational encounters' with risk. In this introductory essay, we specify further why the metaphor of 'encounter' may be useful in moving forward the theoretical and empirical discussion of risk management. In the next section we focus again on the concepts of organization and organizing to re-emphasize the constitutive role of risk and its management for organizations. This is followed by an explication of the 'encounters' metaphor which identifies three coterminous perspectives or lenses. The first concerns the 'organization of attention', the second relates to forms of individual and institutional 'sense making' in the face of errors, accidents and anomalies, and the third relates to the 're-organizing' activity by which organization is constantly remade in the face of risk encounters. To repeat: these three moments are not to be taken as clear and distinct sequential stages; they characterize thematic aspects of complex empirical processes in which organizations and capacities to organize are rendered problematic.

Organizations and risk regulation

Large organizations occupy an increasingly prominent position in modern economic life and multinational organizations may even supplant the powers of the nation state (Braithwaite and Drahos 2000;

Sklair 2002). It is argued that new strategies of social control and regulation are required as these large organizations give rise to distinctive difficulties of risk detection, proof, responsibility and power (Reiss 1984). In particular, it is becoming a neo-liberal orthodoxy that large organizations must be 'recruited' as partners in regulatory programmes; as creators of risk, organizations are also being enlisted as co-regulators of risk (Clarke 1999: 182). Models of 'enforced self-regulation' (Ayres and Braithwaite 1992) posit the use of the self-observing and self-controlling capacities of organizations for regulatory purposes. In terms of principal-agent theory (Besley and Ghatak, this volume), regulators as principals increasingly seek to give incentives to organizations as agents to align themselves with regulatory objectives.

The capacity of organizations to be co-opted into broader risk regulation regimes will depend on their varying professional constituencies, hierarchical structures, operational norms and internal control cultures (Hutter, Chapter 3 this volume; Vaughan 1998: 53). Indeed, efforts to conceptualize large organizations as 'actors' in any unitary sense are constantly challenged by their internal complexity and diversity, features which constrain and shape their emerging role in the regulation of risk. The internal heterogeneity of organizations, the often temporary nature of the assemblies which constitute them, and the fuzzy operational boundaries between their 'inside' and 'outside' contrast with the legalistic and fictional identities which get stabilized for contracting purposes. These assemblies contain formal and informal information systems which provide the empirical conditions for the visibility and processing of uncertainties within risk management practices. Precisely how these internal informational systems and capacities shape organizational responses to risk is still poorly understood, often disguised in disembedded practitioner concepts, such as 'risk appetite'.

The traditional technical foundation of risk management is risk analysis, a discipline whose strength consists in its machine-like, engineering quality. Standard conceptions of risk analysis focus on identifying, measuring and evaluating possible outcomes from both natural and technological hazards. The concern is to estimate the probability and likely effects of specific events happening. The assumptions are essentially realist, assuming a world of risk which is discoverable, measurable, quantifiable and controllable (Gabe 1995), independently of the means by which such risks are framed and communicated.

However, in the tradition of science and technology studies, represented clearly by the contributions of MacKenzie and Jasanoff to this volume, the forms of abstraction inherent in technical risk analysis represent distinctive social constructions of risk knowledge, constructions which must be understood as part of the organization of risk cognition both at the level of specific professional cultures of knowing and at the cultural level of civic epistemology. Even the concept of probability, an apparently fundamental input to any technical risk calculus, involves the framing of uncertainty for a specific purpose and with a specific legitimizing function. Actual organizational decision making may operate at best in an informal 'probabilistic climate' where characterizations of likelihoods are often crude. Indeed, 'possible outcomes with very low probabilities seem to be ignored, regardless of their potential significance' (March and Shapira 1987: 1411), suggesting that the spectre of the high-impact, low-probability event, so important in the operational risk debate (Power 2005), is just a manner of framing ignorance or non-decidability in an acceptable way. However, low-probability high-impact events also characterize a 'space of fear' which can induce hyper-precautionary attention to risk and security. From this point of view rogue traders, fraudulent chief executive officers (CEOs) and terrorists are 'demonic' functional equivalents.

Once the analysis of risk and related forms of organizational decision making are understood as constructed in the setting of managerial behaviour and interests, variation in understandings of risk by organizational participants is elevated from the status of irrational noise to a matter of key importance. To date the risk perception literature has been mainly preoccupied with variations in perception between different lay groups and between lay publics and expert scientists. This literature has been criticized by 'constructivists' for taking risk as a culturally independent given around which perceptions may vary (Douglas 1987). The apparent 'problem' of variation in risk perception is not a function of ignorance with simple training remedies, but may reflect very different cultures of risk understanding even within a single organization. For example, directors of companies see risk in a way that is often not shared by staff who enact their programmes (cf. railway safety, Hutter 2001). Occupational subgroups, such as engineers and accountants, will have very different mental models of both the organization and its significant risks. In addition, the actual organizational 'appetite' for risk taking as revealed by concrete actions may be only very loosely coupled to official risk appetite policy inscribed in formal risk management manuals. In short, organizations as internal regulators of risk embody different and often incommensurable subcultures of risk understanding (Hutter, Chapter 3 in this volume), and the formal organization of risk management, such as an enterprise-wide risk management system, may not capture all the elements of these subcultures. The organization of risk management, including the role of specific agents such as risk officers (Power, Chapter 5 in this volume), can only ever be partially characterized by its ideal blueprints and this means that the role of large organizations as partners in regulatory processes is only as good as their ability to regulate themselves by securing internal commitment to a common 'mission' (Besley and Ghatak, Chapter 6 in this volume).

Having emphasized the importance of the organizational setting of risk management, it should not be forgotten how 'risk' itself functions as an 'organizing' category for management in general, a concept in whose name organizing and re-organizing activity is done. This reminds us that risk does not exist independently of management processes in organizations but that representations of risk, its management and the organizations which do the managing are *co-produced*. From this point of view, risk is not a 'thing', an independent object or set of imagined possibilities, to be managed, although it must be talked of in this way by practitioners. The management of something called 'risk' is also a constitutive *sense-making* project for management itself, defining the unity and identity of the array of practices undertaken by management. Risk language may also serve to 'amplify' risk representations within organizations themselves, something which may be desirable from the point of view of agendas for embedding risk management or undesirable because of the prospect of bringing about the 'timid' organization (Hunt 2003).

The explicit organizational framing of situations in terms of risk, the growing application of 'risk-talk', is therefore central to organizational encounters with risk. Luhmann (1993) suggests that there is no risk without decision making, but we might push the point further by suggesting that the growth of intra-organizational risk talk creates an expanded domain within which decisions are demanded (see also Holzer and Millo 2004). And if there is also no decision making without blame (Douglas 1987), then risk language functions as part of a web of normative framing practices in organizations in which risk management can be conceived as a moral technology for the attribution of responsibility (see also Baker and Simon 2002; Ericson and Doyle 2003).

In an introductory essay like this, it is tempting to offer a definition of risk. Indeed, many readers will expect this. We know of course of efforts to restrict the term 'risk' to calculative situations where the set of possible outcomes and their relative frequencies are known (Knight 1921), of attempts to distinguish risk from dangers, and of the use of risk within financial economics to denote variability of outcomes which may be judged either good or bad. Given this variation in meaning, casual use of the term 'risk' is potentially uninformative and incoherent. However, this collection suggests that we should study carefully the role of risk as part of an organizing narrative for organizations, a narrative which may serve some interests, e.g. those of risk managers, and not others. So we prefer, initially at least, to follow the term as it is used more loosely and more broadly in daily managerial practice. Indeed, for some managers it is not primarily a probability concept (March and Shapira 1987) and is used to refer to situations where the chance or probability that a threat or danger will result in adverse consequences cannot be formally calculated (Hutter and Lloyd-Bostock 1990). Rightly or wrongly, the concept of 'risk management' is, as a matter of empirical fact, being increasingly used to frame the processes by which organizations deal with many different kinds of uncertainty. And this fact alone deserves investigation.

Encountering risk: the organization of attention

Notwithstanding the title of this collection, we do not presume that the notion of 'encounter' is a developed and legitimate category for analysis. The concept is figurative, metaphorical and suggestive of a mode of empirical inquiry which is far from being fully developed but which sets a tentative methodological mood. The concept of encounter suggests a set of intellectual sensibilities about risk and the possible limits of management. Encounters may be characterized by a lack of clearly agreed or coherent data sets of historical event frequency in which judgements of probability are problematic and where the possibilities of rational calculation are limited, if they exist at all. Encounters with risk create demands for interpretations, not least for acceptable descriptions of the 'risk object' itself. Encounters with risk also suggest the problematic nature of organizational responses and reactions to risk which may, in formal terms, be knowable and calculable but which through ignorance or denial are attenuated and not processed by organizations. From this point of view, risk *incubation* is a form of pre-accident encounter where there is an organized suppression of risk intelligence (Turner and Pidgeon 1997). Equally, encounters with risk are not amenable to cool control but may spill over and have amplification effects within and beyond organizational boundaries (Kasperson et al. 2003).

In short, the concept of encounter challenges traditional accounts of the meaning and stability of risk management routines and practices. The terrorist attacks of September 11 are suggestive. The small possibility of aircraft flying into high buildings was known, calculable and part of insurance knowledge. This was processed as risk in a narrow, actuarial sense and scenarios had explicitly considered the resilience of the World Trade Center to impact of this kind. But the *intentional* flying of aircraft fully laden with fuel into high buildings was not calculated and could not even be properly imagined outside of the confines of horror movies. Organizational 'encounters' with risk properly belong in, and emerge from, the cracks in existing institutional thinking; they challenge what can be imagined, what currently makes sense and what is currently feared by insurance agencies and security organizations. From such encounters, attention to new hazard objects may emerge (Slovic 2002).

Encountering risk is above all an event of *problematization* which places in question existing attention to risk and its modes of identification, recognition and definition. This is not simply a cognitive issue at the level of the individual. Risk identification is socially organized by a wide variety of institutions which support prediction and related forms of intervention around the possibility of future events. These institutions which 'govern' our attention to the future include insurance companies (Ericson et al. 2004), credit rating agencies, security and intelligence services and regulatory inspectorates. Such institutions systematically invest in extensive data-collection systems and technologies of calculation, in early-warning systems and compensation mechanisms. However, while our capacity to sustain attention to, and communicate about, risk information is institutionally structured, there are always important specificities. Even where information is collected it may not be accurate; it may be held in local settings and not pooled; and there may be disincentives to collect and report the most relevant information, such as near misses. Organizations can be good at collecting relevant data but are often poor at acting upon it. And in the railways in the UK, data collection for risk management purposes was historically often incomplete and ad hoc (Hutter 2001).

In the case of Enron, it was well known to many, especially insiders, that the company and its reported growth were problematic and the collapse in retrospect was perhaps predictable, just as the fact of the September 11 attack on the US (if not the timing) is being reported in hindsight as predictable. But for the institutional actors at the time (financial analysts, accountants, FBI, CIA) it is necessary to understand the conditions under which such predictions and warnings could not be uttered, or if they were, could not be heard and processed. Institutional mechanisms which attenuate and suppress risk in this way suggest that organizational encounters with risk may be registered initially only at the level of privately articulated misgivings, characterized by ill-formed concepts and by limited capacities to clearly represent an event in terms of risk (Rothstein 2003). Dominant and accepted organizational routines may in fact be criminally negligent but get accepted as 'how things are done' (Beamish 2002). In these settings, the existing organization of risk intelligence is of limited use and may in fact be deeply implicated in the problem (Enron claimed to have a fully functioning enterprise-wide risk management system). Encounters with risk emerge just at the point where the question 'what is happening here?' can be asked, where existing techniques and local institutions of prediction, control and decision making begin to come into question. At this point possibilities for whistle-blowing, dissent and new modes of attention are critical, although such early-warning systems for encountering risk have considerable operational limitations.

Cues which seem to have been ignored in the 'incubation period' of disasters (Turner and Pidgeon 1997) are often easily identified after the event, but they will have looked very different to a decision maker at the time a decision needed to be made. Thus, the reflexive luxury of the observer looking back at critical events is not available to organizational participants who must make decisions and who need to decide now which piece of information should alert them to a potential risk event. As Douglas (1987: 76) puts it: 'Certain things always need to be forgotten for any cognitive system to work: there is no way of paying full attention to everything.' So, given the impossibility of 'hyper-attention' to risk by organizations and the likelihood of an 'atrophy of vigilance' (Freudenberg 2003: 115), there is a tendency to re-normalize in the face of potential deviance. Organizations which pride themselves on having cultures where everything can be challenged by participants must nevertheless find ways to organize and limit the production of dissent without compromising their capacity to detect and respond to critical events.

Many dramatic encounters with risk and their effects have been well documented; there is usually a wealth of knowledge as the result of official inquiries (by congress, parliaments, regulators, etc.) and litigation about disasters. These events tend to have substantive institutional consequences and the social amplification of risk framework (SARF) provides a model for understanding and investigating resulting changes to the organization of risk attention, particularly that of the 'regulatory regime' (Hood et al. 2001) which encompasses a class of risks. Other encounters may be more cumulative and long term in their effects. Their realization is insidious, creeping or latent, making the organization of attention even more problematic. Examples include apparent damage to the ozone layer, AIDS and asbestosis, while smoking and obesity are also becoming more prominent features on the agenda for health management organizations. In all these cases, institutional visibility and attention for the scale of the risk in question has unfolded over a longer period; the organizational encounter is not necessarily a sudden catastrophic occurrence but a cumulative process which may or may not reach a tipping point where orthodox thinking changes. Indeed, in many of these examples official recognition of the problem took time to materialize in part because the scientific evidence of the problem took many years to establish. Thus we should not restrict our analytical and empirical attention only to those apparent 'sudden' happenings at specific points in time (Beamish 2002). Indeed, there are good reasons to question the 'suddenness' of most adverse events.

Organizational encounters with risk are contingent on the existence of myriad systems, institutions and cultures for identifying and attending to unfolding events and for dealing with apparent deviance. Many railway inquiries in Britain have identified the so-called 'accident waiting to happen' which is typically the result of inadequate training and supervision, low worker morale, poor safety culture and inadequate investment in the infrastructure of the industry (Fennell 1988; Hidden

1989). The complexity of an organization means that mistakes or misconduct in one part of it may have serious repercussions elsewhere; anomalies may be systemic and relate to poor coordination and communication between different parts of a company. As the contribution of Kunreuther and Heal (Chapter 8 in this volume) shows, intra-organizational interdependencies can lead to systemic under-investment in risk management, thereby increasing organizational exposure as a whole.

Vaughan's contribution to this volume, and her earlier work on the *Challenger* disaster (Vaughan 1996), shows how anomalies, uncertainties and puzzles have distinctive organizational trajectories and are transformed into, or ignored as, risks according to specific organizational norms and routines. What she calls the 'normalization of deviance' characterizes the routine nature of organizational encounters with risk which unfold over long periods, a thesis which, like Turner's, explodes the myth of the sudden accident even where such accidents are most visible. Risks are 'built in' to the daily routines and operational culture of organizational life. As the collapse of Barings Bank in the UK and subsequent inquiries seem to show, the so-called rogue trader, Nick Leeson, operated in a 'notional normality' which in retrospect can be shown to be essentially deviant. Early-warning signals from the internal auditors about the lack of segregation of duties which gave Leeson the opportunity to manipulate transaction records could not be processed by the bank, whose senior management were responsible for the overall 'moral climate' in the organization. The organizational encounter with risk unfolded over a period of time in which senior management denial (Stein 2000) or ignorance, the overriding of formal controls and a culture of risk taking combined to destroy the organization. In a sense, the Barings Bank organization had all the information which might have alerted it to Leeson's unauthorized trading. Existing risk management systems were unable to organize sufficient attention to this information in the face of senior management preferences for optimistic, rather than pessimistic, interpretations of the apparent 'successes' of Barings Securities in the Far East.

Case studies of arrested risk incubation or near misses are harder to find, for understandable methodological reasons (absence of victims, lack of public inquiry, etc.) which makes Vaughan's work on air traffic control (Chapter 2 in this volume) all the more significant for the literature.

The extent to which the recognition of near misses and critical events is institutionalized within organizations is critical, especially where organizational participants have incentives to suppress bad news, hide errors and smooth over anomalies. Here one might contrast the incentives of doctors and medical organizations in relation to medical near misses with those of air traffic controllers described by Vaughan. Under one system, a mixture of denial and cover-up is possible, under the other near misses are hard-wired in the organization by a technology which defines, represents and makes visible the critical event, namely the loss of aircraft separation. Anomalies and near misses in such organizational contexts are co-defined by explicit and formal ideas about normal or tolerable levels of error, but are reportable only if systems of knowledge exist and are embedded in social systems where incentives to report are strong. Reporting of near misses may be mandatory, such as in Britain where the railway industry must report 'Signals Passed at Danger' (SPADs) regardless of whether or not the incident resulted in an accident. In turn, the UK Railway Inspectorate publishes statistics on SPADs as part of its annual reporting. In the context of different schemes for aviation incident monitoring, Pidgeon and O'Leary (2000) suggest that the balance of incentives to report or not is a complex one, with much depending on the trust between reporters and evaluators.

Faced with near misses, organizations vary in their social and technological capability to know or understand the nature or the extent of the risks to which they are potentially exposed as represented by the 'near miss'. Whether they are in a position to insure, diversify or otherwise systematically manage and address exposures depends on whether the 'near miss' can be captured in an organizational memory bank as an easily retrievable datum. Thus, whether organizations 'learn' from encounters with risk depends upon the capacity to institutionalize attention to near-miss events in the form of early-warning systems and upon the extent to which they embed an organizational memory. As Turner's notion of the 'incubation period' prior to disaster suggests, there is an accretion of often minor 'near miss' type events which get absorbed into the 'notional normality' of the organization, i.e. get forgotten, but which eventually accumulate to cause a disaster. Indeed, it may be that there are disincentives for the production of 'problematic' data in the first place, either for reasons of explicit 'cover-up' (Enron) or simply arising from a failure in organizational memory and classification practice: 'institutions systematically direct individual memory and channel our perceptions into forms compatible with the relations they authorize' (Douglas 1987: 92).

Technology

From the above discussion, it is clear that technology plays a crucial role in the organization of attention to risk. Technology includes hardware and software systems, which attempt to measure, calculate and represent risk for managerial processes of control. The development of financial risk management in recent years has been conditioned by advances in technology; financial markets themselves have always been constituted by technologies which make prices visible, knowable and decision-relevant (Preda 2004). In general, technologies may be as advanced as air traffic control systems or be more bureaucratic in form, such as accounting and internal control systems. They may function as the foundation for both compliance and deterrence-based management and regulatory systems (Reiss 1984), enabling critical events to be visible within risk regulation regimes. Vaughan's contribution (Chapter 2) shows how attention to risk is mediated by routine, daily information-processing systems, which are often residues of previous organizational and regulatory reforms.

MacKenzie's analysis (Chapter 7 in this volume) of option pricing models is one example of a tool for pricing which became institutionalized and routinized over time, providing a window on risk for market participants. In this case, the relevant organization is the options market itself, within which prices function as information to support exchange and in which such models support and normalize practices of risk taking. MacKenzie shows that technologies which mediate the knowledge of risk can also be sources of risk in so far as they generate normalities around themselves; it is well known that the collective use of risk management models, designed for the purpose of ameliorating the effects of market volatility in individual cases, can amplify volatility (Holzer and Millo 2004). This suggests that the problems in financial markets may arise less from so-called 'model fixation' and more from the cumulative effect of similar reactions in the marketplace, reactions which in the case of Metallgesellschaft AG led to a loss of market liquidity. The fact that a risk model was widely used as accepted 'best practice' meant that organizational responses were amplified by this performative aspect of them. In short, a risk management model can become a source of risk when everyone uses the same model. Reactions will be systematically replicated, thus exacerbating possible disaster. These models can also become risky if they are employed without a full understanding of their limitations.

This suggests another critical feature of the technological basis for organizational encounters with risk: how systems are connected. Despite media taste for clearly definable rogue acts or technological failure, encounters with risk always have elements of system interconnectedness. As Kunreuther and Heal (Chapter 8 in this volume) show, organizational sub-units may encounter risk precisely by virtue of this interconnectedness; investments in risk management systems may be influenced by the degree of possible risk contagion from other sub-units. The risks may be cumulative in their effects, the result of a chain of errors by a number of different parts of an organization with no institutionalized opportunity for override.

Technologies for risk representation are always embedded in social processes and the misinterpretation of technical warnings has figured in a number of major risk events. A simple example of the risks which may be posed by human misinterpretation of technological indicators is the Three Mile Island accident in 1979 when operatives at a nuclear power plant refused to believe indicators showing the reactor was close to meltdown and revealed a misplaced faith in the efficiency of safety back-up systems. This further underlines the ambivalence of tools for managing risk, which can become amplifications of risk and potential fatal remedies (Kasperson et al. 2003; Sieber 1981). New encounters with risk disturb the bargains between different conceptions and representations of risk, and between different values. Specific tools of visualization or calculation shape management attention to risk, such as the techniques of financial modelling described by MacKenzie. But visual representations can also prove inadequate in retrospect, as shown by the example of the simulated impact of an aircraft colliding with the World Trade Center in New York. The representation was both accurate from an engineering point of view (plane and building) and incomplete (the motives of the people flying the plane and the effect of the aircraft fuel on the building).

To conclude: organizational encounters with risk challenge highly institutionalized forms of attention and imagination, which often have a strong technological dimension. For example, when risks can be statistically well described and there are established tools and techniques, the management of risk takes the form of a routine, expert practice. Under these circumstances, risk management has an almost machine-like, cybernetic quality and organizational context appears irrelevant. Historically, the term 'risk analysis' is associated with this kind of pure engineering ideal, an ideal whose strength resides in its abstraction from organizational and behavioural issues and in its dependence on extensive data sets. However, despite the disciplinary strengths associated with such routine, mathematized encounters with risk, there is increasing recognition in practice, and in the academy, that the relationship between organizations and risk conforms to this normalized process only as a special and restricted case which cannot cover the risk management universe (Shubik 1991). Accordingly, there is widespread acceptance of the significance of the communicative and interpretive dimensions of risk handling. There are many examples of events which somehow escape existing mechanisms of predictability and provide a distinctive challenge to the way organizations think about and attend to the future. As existing processes of attention are disturbed by encounters with risk, organizations and their participants engage in 'sense making'.

Encountering risk: sense making

By emphasizing above that organizational encounters with risk are mediated by technologies of varying kinds we have already introduced the sense-making dimension of encountering. We do not mean to suggest that organizations encounter objective risks in some pure sense (the 'myth of the given') and then seek to make sense and interpret such events. Sense making rather is implicated deeply in the construction of the risk event itself; encountering as disturbance is co-extensive with sense making and with crises of sense making. For Weick (1995: 14), sense making as a concept is valuable 'because it highlights the invention that precedes interpretation'. Particularly in the face of critically disturbing events, meaning must be reconstructed and re-ordered.

Organizations and their human participants as producers of sense in the face of risk raise the question: 'For whom and to whom is sense making taking place?' Whether and how organizations cope with, and make sense of, risk encounters (accident, near miss, anomaly) will be mediated by sources of 'knowledge' and by practices which may heighten (amplify) or dampen (attenuate) organizational sensitivity and 'inventive' responsiveness to disturbing events. Accidents and crises provide the most extreme challenge to existing frames of interpretation; near misses, as we argued above, may be interpreted away by dominant normalities and anomalies may be suppressed by routines which are hard-wired into organizational memory. For example, formal internal control and enterprise risk management routines (COSO 2004) may have more to do with a certain kind of organizational legitimacy and responsibility framing than with enhancing organizational capacity to encounter risk inventively and intelligently (Power 2004a). Each risk encounter will be mediated by the legacy of organizational culture and its associated habits and always poses the problem of an alignment between human perception, conceptualization, assessment and management capabilities, and the risk 'event' itself. As Ghatak and Besley (Chapter 6 in this volume) argue, a shared sense of mission, a common culture, is itself the management of a certain kind of risk, i.e. the moral hazard that organizational agents engage in deviant, risk-amplifying behaviour. The alignment of motives is not simply pecuniary in form, but involves support for, and identification with, organizational missions, missions which provide a sense-making frame for organizational participants. It must of course be recognized that such cultures can be judged to be deviant (Beamish 2002).

Organizational actors engage in 'sense-making' work to transform new encounters with risk into acceptable managerial practices and to build new institutional facts as a basis for these practices. Sense making underlies the 'production' of institutional facts and is at the very heart of organizational encounters with risk. Such fact building is a function of many things. Clearly, scale should not be overlooked, partly because the perceived significance of an event (Bhopal, September 11, Enron) is usually measured in terms of human casualties (the category of death always being less ambiguous and hence more countable than that of injury). Scale of this kind will determine the nature and duration of media attention processes, which in turn can promote or deny specific explanations and facts in the public domain. However, one should be cautious about adopting too mechanical a view of the role of media in amplifying risks (Kasperson et al. 2003). Much will depend on how such media processes align with civic epistemologies as a cultural reservoir of collective sense making (see Jasanoff, Chapter 9 in this volume). Also significant will be the location of the risk, both spatially and socially. In the railways setting, the location of an accident was significant in determining the reporting and the organizational response. In general, accidents occurring on major commuter routes into capital cities and those involving multiple passenger fatalities receive the most attention by the media and by regulatory authorities (Hutter 1992). One might also speculate that had the Union Carbide disaster happened in North America or Europe, the media attention and organizational responses might have looked very different in coverage and resolution.

Another important sense-making element is what Vaughan (Chapter 2 in this volume) describes within the notion of a 'sociology of error' and is particularly salient in the context of so-called high-reliability organizations, such as the Federal Aviation Administration (FAA) and National Aeronautics and Space Administration (NASA). High-reliability organizations will engage in different sense-making activities and fact production from others. For example, some so-called high-reliability organizations may publicly commit, or seem to commit, to a zero tolerance of risk. However, they will of necessity have an appetite for some risk, even if it is not articulated publicly. The Securities and Exchange Commission (SEC), in the wake of Enron, seems to have adopted a tough zero tolerance operational style. However, a number of regulators are being explicit about their own risk-based approaches as a basis for signalling that failures are possible. For example, the publicly stated risk-based philosophy of the Financial Services Authority in the UK is an admission that no system of regulation is foolproof. For such organizations, the concept of risk is not just a feature of operational self-organization, it is part of organizational sense making; an explicitly risk-based operational discourse for regulatory organizations acts as a sense-making device for their mission as well as a signal to political masters. It begins to make politically and socially thinkable the possibility of adverse events, although such a strategy can be politically constrained when lives rather than livelihoods are at stake. So risk-based sense making may be more difficult in relation to health and safety events compared with those involving financial risk management.

While sense making and the restoration of meaning in the face of 'error' is a human necessity, organizational encounters with risk can result in the suspension of sense or in multiple competing senses or epistemologies (Jasanoff, Chapter 9 in this volume). There may be ambiguities and difficulties in discerning 'relevant knowledge' and in distinguishing 'good' from 'bad' explanations at the time of a major event. Facts and explanations may not be readily produced if the answer to the question 'what happened?' is difficult and contested. Manageability may be questioned and fear and anxiety become more readily apparent. In these settings, organizations need to produce new senses of risk manageability and security, although they may not always be able to. The need to allocate responsibility drives institutionally acceptable explanations (e.g. the auditors failed to do a good job) and solution sets (e.g. make auditors more independent). This is part of the well-known regulatory politics of 'doing something' (Hutter 1992), where the long-run suspension of sense is not an organizational option: 'Individuals and organizations sometimes act not because they understand risks, but because they feel they must act' (Short 1992: 7).

Sense making is closely related to the micro- and macro-politics of blame (Hood 2002), especially where internal reputations may be at stake. Pressures exist to 'clean up' dirty data (Marx 1984) and to hide known anomalies as defensive strategies in the face of possible blame. It follows that an important source of organizational sense making is the law itself. In situations of ambiguity and irresolvable conflict, organizations often resort to legal form and due process as a basis for closure (Sitkin and Bies 1994). Sense making may be channelled in legalistic ways by defensive organizational strategies in the face of legal liability, and ideal models of due process in apparent conformity with legitimate risk management standards can act as organizational templates and as a basis for restoring organizational order. Risk-based regulation can be used as a defensive template for not paying a great deal of regulatory attention to some risks or for rationalizing why more attention was not paid to something which later became a clear risk (Hutter, Chapter 3 in this volume). Enterprise risk management (ERM) is promoted as an ideal solution to organizational encounters with risk, seeming to address both risk and governance issues simultaneously (Power 2004b). At the political level, the Sarbanes-Oxley Act 2002 is a collective sense-making device, whose proposed changes also embody an 'explanation' of what went wrong with US corporate governance, namely inadequately controlled CEOs and CFOs. The law is therefore an important basis for framing risk so as to render it manageable (Ericson and Haggerty 1997).

The language and categories of error and mistake used in organizations are critical dimensions of sense making (Vaughan, Chapter 2 in this volume). Much technical risk management operates in a 'statistical climate' which may determine the path of organizational sensitivity to error, its definition and acceptability. In this way probability language and embedded probability values actually represent social behaviour and operationalize the boundaries 'between culpable and tolerable mistakes' (Pidgeon and O'Leary 2000: 26). However, the language of probabilistic risk assessment and discourses of control are used very imprecisely by managers and the idea of 'low-probability, high-impact events' may simply reflect efforts to make such events thinkable within management frameworks for dealing with routine non-catastrophic error. In reality, precise measurement is often less salient than the construction of meaning and forms of risk identification which depend on classification practices. Sense making depends on the kinds of language for mistakes and errors which are used by organizational agents in the field and how, if at all, these agents describe themselves in risk language terms. For accountants, much depends on whether an error is judged to be 'material' and the affective language of 'comfort' pervades the practice of audit (Pentland 1993). For air traffic controllers, errors are formally dictated by the rules of separation embodied in advanced technology and are dealt with on the spot rather than by historical exception reporting. In general, interpretative models and classificatory schema, implicit and explicit, are invoked and challenged in the encounter with risk.

Sense making involves processes of classification which support organized data gathering. Heimer et al. (Chapter 4 in this volume) show that processes of classification may emerge very slowly and that this hindered data collection in the context of AIDS. They also draw attention to legalization as a source of sense making in organizations and in risk management. 'Legal styles of thought' increasingly penetrate medical work and rule making is often defensive. Heimer et al. also discuss the importance of 'law from within' in the development of research and other protocols in the medical field as technologies of control. Sometimes these protocols are home grown, written in the shadow of the law as an interpretative and procedural paradigm, but also competing for legitimacy and jurisdiction with other logics of medical practice. For Heimer et al., scientific, medical and managerial protocols are intertwined as a dense assembly of overlapping forms of guidance which must all demonstrate 'legitimate complexity'. Encounters with risk are mediated by and challenge these webs of institutionalized protocol, webs which allocate issues and errors to legal solution systems.

Jasanoff (Chapter 9 in this volume) explains how some sense-making narratives are embedded in historically conditioned practices, for example those of nation states. But she also draws attention to the fragmented and often competing sites of risk explanation, and hence of fact production, around risk encounters. Public enquiries, local experiences, insider revelations, legal proceedings and press coverage constitute different expressions of civic epistemology, understood as collective forms of knowing with greater or lesser acceptability. Such civic epistemologies are not normally under the control of the organization in question and may amplify or attenuate organizational encounters with risk. Explanations may encode blaming or learning, may persist or may be short lived. In the case of Bhopal, many different forms of explanations, some not readily compatible, did endure (Jasanoff 1994; Chapter 9 in this volume). Such explanations are forms of retrospective sense making and reveal how and whether societies and organizations learn from encounters with risk and are able to develop institutional capacity for imagining and guarding against risk in an increasingly interconnected world.

Jasanoff also highlights the significance of preferences for forms of explanation which fit existing policy response possibilities. In the case of Enron and Worldcom, the Bush administration needed a short-run political explanation in terms of 'a few bad eggs', although the scope of the Sarbanes-Oxley Act suggests that the problem being addressed was perceived as more systemic. In other contexts, there are preferences for technical/mechanical-type explanations (the O-rings failed) rather than organizational failures (the situational pressures on NASA and its subcontractors). One of the contributions of the 'man-made disaster' literature already noted above has been to recover and emphasize the organizational preconditions of technological failure.

Different modes of explanation can be used simultaneously; in the case of Barings, official investigations formulated explanations of a more systemic nature, as well as pursuing Leeson, the individual rogue trader, in the courts. In major rail accidents specific individuals can be faulted, for example, for failing to check resignalling work before finishing a job of work, but it is increasingly the case that the systems which allowed this to occur are also recognized to be at fault (Hutter, Chapter 3 in this volume). In practice, explanatory emphases on systems or on individuals are intertwined: individual managers can be blamed for failing to oversee defective systems, as in the case of Barings or the King's Cross fire (Fennell 1988). Different explanations also have different cost implications: the reform response is more costly in one direction (defective track) than another (driver error). More costly still is the attribution of blame to a public sector/governmental failure to invest in the infrastructure of a public service (Hutter 1992).

As Jasanoff (Chapter 9 in this volume) notes, some explanatory tropes recur while others are ignored. For example, corporate greed, public irrationality, the co-optation of science, faulty communication and human error are among those favoured in the United States; other possible recurrent categories of civic epistemology might include rogue trader, act of God and sabotage. Despite all this, narratives are often divided on disasters and the inability to make sense can be very apparent. The aftermath of September 11 is the clearest example where, even by 2005, competing and overlapping explanations are still in play. *Who* does the sense making is critical and differences can emerge between explanations by organizational and political centres (not foreseeable; this was an act of war) and by the periphery ('it was waiting to happen'; America doesn't understand how it is perceived). Sense making and explanation will vary across different groups. Styles of explanation may vary across different issues (Hood et al. 2001) and patterns of blame may not be consistent across even similar risk events.

Even where institutional arrangements for the calculation of risk exist and are stable, there may be serious inequalities in the distribution of this knowledge. For example, earthquakes may be risks amenable to prediction by seismological experts, with low consequent demands for 'cultural' sense making, but will have more of the character of uncertainty for others, such as local communities faced with an immediate crisis. While an Enron might be regarded as the statistical price of the capitalist system, Enron pensioners are unlikely to see it this way. Different groups have differential capacities to make sense of what has happened. Inequalities and dispersion in provision, access and experiential understandings are significant aspects of sense making in organizational encounters with risk.

To summarize: organizational encounters with risk problematize the meaning and identity of organization itself, a process in which the possibility of rational management is placed in question, where promises of control and existing orders are broken down and challenged, where the distinction between experts and non-experts is no longer clear, and where the social permeability of organizations is increasingly apparent (Freudenberg 2003). Sense-making activity is not simply a window on a given organization, part of some process of communication; it is the organization's encounter with itself. And in this self-encounter, ambivalence is usually tolerated only temporarily before it demands the restoration of order via re-organizing.

Encountering risk: re-organizing

The third analytic theme of organizational encounters concerns the process of re-organizing, which is most manifest in the wake of crises and disasters. Reform trajectories are always contingent on forms of collective sense making and their institutional strength. Internally, new organizational structures, roles and management technologies are created. Externally, pressures exist to create or reform regulatory regimes and their programmes for risk prevention, reaction and resilience. In particular, new standards of practice get drafted and new categories, such as 'operational risk', play a catalytic role in these reform processes, creating new communities of interest in risk management and providing new mandates for regulatory organizations. Re-organization involves the enhancement or creation of 'organizing organizations', i.e. those which write rules and standards for others (Brunsson and Jacobsson 2000).

Many different kinds of organization may be involved in re-organizing and in the formalization and standardization of risk management practice blueprints. For example, the Committee of Sponsoring Organizations of the Treadway Commission (COSO), a body established to investigate fraudulent financial reporting in the 1980s, has published guidance on enterprise risk management which is likely to be a highly influential resource for organizations seeking to comply with the requirements of the Sarbanes-Oxley Act (COSO 2004). Trade associations and industry bodies also lead re-organization, for example Responsible Care, a US chemical industry initiative created in response to declining public opinion of the chemical industry following the Bhopal incident in the mid-1980s (Rees 1997) or the American Institute of Nuclear Power Operations (INPO), created in the wake of the Three Mile Island accident in 1979 (Rees 1994). More generally, the rise of the so-called 'regulatory state' has witnessed an explosion of agencies tasked with organizing other organizations. Examples in the UK include the Financial Services Authority, the Food Standards Agency and the Commission for Healthcare Audit and Inspection. But while some modes of re-organizing may take place at the level of professional associations or regulatory bodies (e.g. the Basel Committee on Banking Supervision), others are harder to pinpoint. The rise of the chief risk officer (CRO) (Power, Chapter 5 in this volume) has no specific institutional location or sponsorship, emerging from the practices of large financial and utility firms. Indeed, the rise of the CRO as a meta-regulatory agent inside organizations may be a specific example of a general re-organizing tendency to increase monitoring, inspection and oversight activity. From this point of view, more and better auditing and inspection is often the 'technological fix' demanded by public inquiries.

These different aspects of re-organizing activity raise the question of the proportionality of response, with scholars drawing attention to the prevalence of overcompensating, amplifying reactions (Kasperson et al. 2003). Organizations must increasingly be responsive not only to their own perceived reform needs but also to wider external constituencies. The emergence of reputation and ethical risk management as organizational repertoires reflects the changing relation between large organizations and their organizational environments. At its crudest, stakeholder perceptions of organizations are themselves a source of reputational risk which must be managed (Power 2003) and corporate social responsibility agendas can be articulated in terms of organizational self-interest. From this point of view, there may be some organizations which are more immune to public critique than others, e.g. emergency services, although public perceptions differentiate between rank-and-file actors (soldiers, firemen, nurses) and senior management. Perceived failures in the latter tend to have an amplifying effect on risk events (Kasperson et al. 2003). More generally, re-organizing actions may be counterproductive if done in haste, e.g. regulating dangerous dogs (Hood et al. 2001), and can be simply ignored if they are perceived as too expensive, as was the case with the recommendations following the Clapham railway crash in the UK (Hutter 2001).

The Sarbanes-Oxley Act in the United States seems to epitomize a style of hasty regulatory response involving ever more minute controls over directors and auditors. In re-organizing activity, reforming decisions often serve to confer meaning on confusing events and are constructed upon the residues of reactions to previous encounters with risk. Many of the safety regulations and innovations on the railways (Rolt 1986) and in financial markets reflect a history of cumulative reactions to accidents and disasters.

Sites of re-organizing may vary considerably, ranging from the specific organization to the organization field to the level of the state. Kunreuther and Heal (Chapter 8 in this volume) suggest that 'irrational' under-investment in risk management processes by organizations and individuals (e.g. earthquake protection) can be compensated by central 'regulatory state' activity. They highlight the interdependent nature of organizing security and the indeterminacy of investments in safety. They demonstrate formally that, as the chances of contamination from the under-investment of others (within the organization or outside of it) in safety measures go up, the incentives for specific groups/individuals to invest go down, a result suggesting that policy solutions in high mutual-contamination situations must be centralized and have a more traditional regulatory character.

Near misses are less powerful engines of change than actual accidents and disasters and may not generate sufficient organizational attention to trigger internal organizational reform processes, although this is not always the case (Hutter 2001: Chapter 11). Formal compliance failures, e.g. the lack of segregation of duties between front- and back-office operations at Barings and at Daiwa Bank, typically fail to stimulate any re-organizing activity and become dominated by other concerns. Only in retrospect do they come to have overriding significance. However, an emerging exception is likely to concern the reporting of 'material weaknesses' in corporate internal control systems as part of the Sarbanes-Oxley Act section 404 requirements. This section, widely regarded as an enormous compliance burden for SEC-registered companies, requires extensive certifications of the effectiveness of internal control systems by management and auditors. At the time of writing, there is much speculation about how and whether management and auditors will come clean about material weaknesses in systems of control and about how markets will react to these disclosures. In a nervous, litigious climate, one might anticipate the mandated reporting of such control near misses to lead to over-responsiveness and over-reporting by organizations. Much the same has been feared about the effects of money-laundering legislation, namely that organizational reactions become less risk responsive, the very opposite of what the legislation intends, in a downward precautionary spiral. Thus, while re-organization processes relevant to organizational encounters with risk have usually been reactions to adverse events, precautionary attitudes will drive 'anticipatory' responses.

The effort expended in responding to the Y2K threat, characterized by dramatic representations of possible computer system failures, galvanized management attention. Images of aircraft falling out of the sky and industrial, commercial and public computer systems crashing worldwide were no doubt exploited by systems specialists and consultants sensing a one-off opportunity to argue for critical investments. Y2K was symptomatic of increased public and managerial attention to, and fear of, so-called low-probability, high-impact events and there is some evidence of amplified precautionary reactions to the possibility of major systems failures (Macgregor 2003). It is argued that terrorism risks may be exaggerated in order to give meaning to political identities which might otherwise be merely managerial. More generally, a policy climate may be generated where worst-case scenarios increasingly have the ear of decision makers. The fundamental and perhaps irresolvable difficulty for organizations is to be 'optimally' responsive to risk alerts by utilizing some form of 'screening' to avoid both over- and under-investment in protective measures (Kasperson et al. 2003).

The standardization of internal process as an archetypical organizational response to risk relates to the role of legal styles of sense making discussed above. There may be legal risks to risk managers and other officials for the failure of specific management systems to deal with legal requirements on health and safety or race relations. In these settings, being able to demonstrate compliance becomes an organizational priority. 'Adversarial legalism' suggests an institutional context in which organizations increasingly define the risks they face, and appropriate organizational responses, in relation to imagined legal liabilities (Kagan 2000). Such 'legal risk management' may accentuate precautionary attitudes and lead to unintended side-effects. For example, victims demanding justice for corporate wrongdoing inadvertently decrease the level of cooperation which might be forthcoming in accident inquiries (Hutter 1992). In some jurisdictions, notably the United States and the medical domain, some commentators discern legal concerns taking precedence over ethical issues (Heimer et al., Chapter 4 in this volume). Classifying patients as having AIDS can enable medical treatment, but it may also preclude them from insurance regimes.

Where the reactive legalization of the organization, in which due process becomes an end rather than a means, increases risk aversity in the organization, risk management can create risks to the organizational capacity to innovate (Hunt 2003), especially where there is managerial amplification of law (Edelman et al. 2001). Modes of re-organizing can themselves lead directly to further encounters with risk as new forms of standardized 'best practice' close organizations around assemblies of codified risk management knowledge. If legalization processes determine the content of organizational memory, e.g. documentation for defensive purposes (Van Maanen and Pentland 1994), then organizational learning will follow a legalistic 'logic of practice'. This is the very antithesis of Besley and Ghatak's (Chapter 6 in this volume) proposal for overcoming agency problems by matching individual and corporate missions. Good motives get 'crowded out' (Frey and Jegen 2001) in the legalized or over-audited organization in which it becomes impossible to embed anything other than defensive incentives.

Efforts to re-organize risk management involve multiple actors, including government, professional bodies, insurers, businesses, hospitals, schools and so on. Re-organizing may involve contests over the direction of change, the legitimacy and expertise of the various participants, and negotiation over the rules (Heimer et al., Chapter 4 in this volume). Furthermore, re-organizing activities can be interdependent and motivations to react vary because of *inequalities* in exposures to risk, e.g. between nations and within organizations. Re-organizing may favour different groups in relatively privileged positions and the problem of free-riders on reform is a constant challenge. Efforts to organize constructive dissent and challenge are often visible. The ambivalent status of whistle blowing and mechanisms to support it within organizations illustrates the difficulties and paradoxes of re-organizing processes which seek to co-opt 'unorganized' sources of maverick risk intelligence. Making organizations 'smarter' in the form of critical feedback can also make them less legitimate. Indeed, if organizations are actually defined in terms of what their members choose to ignore (Weick 1998), how can re-organizing deal with these deeply established silences in their information systems? Much depends on the precise mechanisms by which risk events are internally and externally recognized, communicated and absorbed by different constituencies (Kasperson et al. 2003).

Overall, a chronic difficulty for re-organizing activity is that of being able to demonstrate clearly the benefits of risk management. Elaborate justificatory rhetorics are visible which make claims for such benefits and an important feature of re-organization is increased marketing effort in making value-based claims for risk management activity in terms of enhancing accountability, efficiency and profitability. In general, reform processes where benefits are difficult to demonstrate must attach themselves to widely held beliefs and values in the institutional environment, such as 'good governance'. From this point of view the 'risk society' is constantly being talked up as an 'opportunity society' (Power 2004a).

In conclusion: organizational encounters with risk are constituted by waves of re-organizing activity, embracing the reform of concepts and language as well as the mechanics of practice. New categories and vocabularies – e.g. 'operational risk', 'safety case' – are crucial dimensions of re-organizing activity. Re-organizing is not just a single response to an encounter with risk but an unfolding and continual process which is constitutive of the encounter itself and which usually embodies one or more implicit explanations of the failure. In this setting, risk management techniques themselves, such as risk maps and 'value at risk' metrics, have social histories of their own as part of an ongoing process of re-organizing in the face of risk encounters. Organizational responses are varied and are registered at different levels, from the local to the institutional, but will tend on balance to be conservative, reflecting the fact that the 'instituted community blocks personal curiosity, organizes public memory, and heroically imposes certainty on uncertainty' (Douglas 1987: 102). Responses are part of the process of reconstituting the possibility of meaningful organizational action. New risk management systems seek to respond to encounters with risk by re-normalizing them within existing decision-making practices. And, in keeping with the duality identified at the beginning of this chapter, the process is continuous because re-organizing is always a source of risk, as well as its solution.

Conclusion

In this introductory chapter we have tried to sketch an intellectual agenda which is suggested by the different contributions to this volume. Each chapter in this book deals with an aspect of how organizations experience the limits of their own capacity to organize in the face of uncertainty. In Chapter 2, Diane Vaughan analyses the manner in which two organizations, NASA and FAA, deal with anomalies, define error and thereby manage risk. In Chapter 3, Bridget Hutter argues that understandings of risk vary across different levels of an organization and that encounters with risk are by no means uniformly experienced and understood. In Chapter 4, Carol Heimer, Juleigh Coleman Petty and Rebecca Culyba explore different dimensions of the legalization of medical protocols and how local rule making can become drawn into broader organizational control frameworks. In Chapter 5, Michael Power analyses the rise of the chief risk officer as an organizational 'fix' and as a distinctive mode of responding to risk. In Chapter 6, Maitreesh Ghatak and Timothy Besley suggest that matching the mission of an organization to those of its employees can address some of the fundamental risks inherent in principal-agent relationships. In Chapter 7, Donald MacKenzie analyses two episodes of financial crisis which suggest that organizations can encounter risks generated by the widespread use of risk management models themselves. In Chapter 8, Howard Kunreuther and Geoffrey Heal also argue that intra-firm interdependencies can lead to suboptimal investments in risk management in the absence of central guidance. Finally, in Chapter 9, Sheila Jasanoff examines forms of collective learning and sense making at the level of the nation state in three specific cases.

Each of these chapters develops an aspect of organizational encounters with risk which we have described in terms of three critical moments: attention, sense making and re-organizing. These moments correspond roughly to the organizational level equivalent of stimulus, information processing and adaptation and have an institutionalized character. Put simply, encounters with risk challenge existing organizational modes of risk attention and sense making and can set in train a range of re-organizational activities.

This way of framing organizational encounters with risk is hardly novel and builds on existing studies in the sociology of organizations and risk (e.g. Short and Clarke 1992) and in regulation theory (e.g. Sitkin and Bies 1996; Morgan and Engwall 1999; Hood et al. 2001; Hutter 2001; Brunnson and Jacobsson 2000). Encounters with risk challenge, to varying degrees, existing ways of doing things and disturb the concept of the formal organization itself as a unitary actor. And, as we live increasingly in a world where ideas of risk and risk management are being operationalized across a wider range of practices, these ideas and models reflexively shape organizational and institutional responses to uncertainty. While there is no doubt much more work to be done of an empirical and theoretical nature to clarify 'encounters' with risk as a useful category, we believe that this collection of essays from authors in very different disciplines provides a useful starting point.

2 | Organizational rituals of risk and error

DIANE VAUGHAN

ORGANIZATIONAL encounters with risk and error are not restricted to the sensational cases that draw media coverage when mistakes, near misses and accidents become public. They are, instead, a routine and systematic part of daily organizational life that only occasionally become visible to outsiders.

Merton was the first to observe that any system of action can generate unexpected consequences that are in contradiction to its goals and objectives (1936, 1940, 1968). Recent research affirms his observation: unanticipated events that deviate from organizational expectations are so typical that they are 'routine non-conformity' – a regular by-product of the characteristics of the system itself (Vaughan 1999). The public learns about only the most egregious of these. Because routine non-conformity is a regular system consequence, complex organizations that use or produce risky technologies may have encounters with risk daily.

In this chapter, I compare daily encounters with risk for two organizations for which mistakes result in public failures and have high costs: the Federal Aviation Administration's National Air Transportation System (NATS) and the National Aeronautics and Space Administration's (NASA) Space Shuttle Program (SSP). My logic for comparing these two agencies is grounded in two related strands of research. Barry Turner investigated the causes of eighty-five different 'man-made disasters'. He found an alarming pattern: after a disaster, investigators typically found a history of early-warning signs that were misinterpreted or ignored. A problem that seemed well structured in retrospect was ill structured at the time decisions were being made (Turner 1978; Turner and Pidgeon 1997). Turner did not have micro-level decision-making data to explain how and why this could happen. Instead, he explained it skilfully by drawing on organization theories about information flows. However, no one had tested these theories with data about how people decide and why they make the choices they do. The second strand is Star and Gerson's (1987) study of anomalies in scientific work. Star and Gerson point out that every anomaly has a trajectory during which it is subject to processes of definition, negotiation and control that are similar to the response to anomalies in other types of work. They found that how anomalies are defined and negotiated depends upon the occupational context and the evaluation systems that have been developed to meet unexpected deviations in the work flow. Star and Gerson concluded that a mistake or an anomaly is never defined in isolation, but is always relative to the local and institutional context of work (1987: 148–50).

These two strands of research led me to the following conclusions. First, Turner's discovery of warnings of hazards over long incubation periods preceding accidents suggested the importance of research on daily encounters with risk. Second, Star and Gerson's work indicated that an appropriate focus was the trajectory of anomalies – how they are identified, measured and assessed for risk. I had a chance to investigate both these issues in my research on NASA's *Challenger* accident (Vaughan 1996). In the years preceding the accident, I found a history of early-warning signs – signals of potential danger – about the technology of the flawed solid rocket boosters that caused the disaster. These early-warning signs were misinterpreted as decisions were being made, contributing finally to the disastrous outcome. The seriousness of this became clear only in retrospect, after the tragedy. In contrast to the accidents Turner investigated, I had micro-level data on NASA decision making and also macro-level data on the NASA organization and its relations in its political/economic environment. These data made it possible for me to explain how and why signals of potential danger were misinterpreted. The answer was 'the normalization of deviance': a social psychological product of institutional and organizational forces. The consequence was that after engineering analysis, technical anomalies that deviated from design performance expectations were not interpreted as warning signs but became acceptable, routine and taken-for-granted aspects of shuttle performance to managers and engineers. The trajectory of anomalies, as they were identified and their risk measured and assessed, showed the importance of both the local organizational and institutional contexts of work.

Air traffic control was the next logical research site for subsequent study because I wanted to locate myself in an organization where people were successfully trained to recognize early-warning signs so that small mistakes did not become accidents. This research strategy contrasted with the retrospective analysis necessary in the *Challenger* analysis. The theoretical framework I use for the analysis of both cases is 'situated action', which examines the link between institutions, organizations and individual decisions and actions (Vaughan 1998; cf. Suchman 1987).

In the following pages, I examine the process of identification and definition of anomalies and the technologies of control in use at these two agencies. By technologies of control, I mean (1) rules and procedures that guide decisions about risk, (2) work practices and (3) surveillance technologies consisting of both procedures and hardware designed to identify anomalies that are potential signals of danger. I locate their encounters with risk within the institutional and organizational context of work. The comparison that follows is necessarily brief: I omit much of the institutional and organizational context, as well as much of the rich ethnographic and interview data on which these studies are based. The NASA analysis is from a completed project (Vaughan 1996). The air traffic control analysis is one part of a project, still in progress (Vaughan in progress). The research is based on ethnographic and interview data I collected during eleven months with air traffic controllers in four air traffic control facilities in the New England region during 2000–1. For both agencies, their technologies of control are so extensive that even concentrating on one of these organizations in an essay of this length necessarily would omit important aspects, so I will focus only on some of the more salient factors.

I begin by identifying how differences in the technologies of shuttles and aeroplanes affect the social organization of work and, therefore, encounters with risk. Then I examine the trajectory of anomalies in both organizations showing (1) the variation in the technologies of control employed by each agency as it attempts to identify, define and control risk and error, (2) the symbolic use and meaning of their technologies of control, as they come to function in both agencies as organizational rituals of risk and error, and (3) how these ritualistic practices have social psychological consequences with significant effects on how technical workers interpret signals of potential danger.

Launching shuttles and aeroplanes: the social organization of risk encounters

Both the Federal Aviation Administration's National Air Transportation System and NASA's National Space Transportation System (NSTS) do space work: launching vehicles into space, monitoring them while in flight and returning them to earth. Both have responsibility for high-risk technologies in which routine non-conformity may result in loss of life. Both organizations are government bureaucracies and large-scale technical systems in which rules, procedures and routines govern all facets of organizational life. Both are dependent upon Congress and the White House for funding; both are dealing with getting vehicles into space on a pre-established, schedule-driven timetable over which the people doing the hands-on work have little control.

During the periods of my research, both agencies were experiencing production pressure generated by the external environment. NASA was under pressure to launch a predefined number of shuttles every year in order to subsidize inadequate Congressional funding for the programme with funding from payloads; air traffic control was under pressure to reduce delays, a situation arising from congested skies due to deregulation of the airlines, a thriving economy that had more people able to fly, and inability to sufficiently increase the number of airports and/or runways of existing airports in order to accommodate the increased demand. Any accident, under these circumstances, has negative consequences in addition to the tragic and irrevocable loss of life for both agencies. For air traffic control, the threat of privatization hangs over all negative performance outcomes. For NASA, an accident or mistake could result in decreased funding or programme cutbacks. Because of the extensive harmful consequences of mistake, both agencies invest considerable resources into technologies of control: their apparatuses for encountering risk are well developed and central to everyday work, perhaps more so than many organizations where other types of risky work are done or where failures are less public or less costly.

Regulating risk tends to take two forms: a compliance strategy or a deterrent strategy of control (Reiss 1984; Hawkins 1984), although most organizations use some combination of the two. A compliance strategy is forward-looking and preventive. It aims for early identification and measurement of deviations from the expected, so an appropriate response can bring the technology back into compliance with the established parameters for system safety. A deterrent strategy is backward-looking, usually implemented after a mistake or accident, designed to prevent or reduce the probability of a similar event. Deterrent strategies are punitive, invoking sanctions that are directed towards the individuals or organizations responsible for an error or accident. A compliance strategy tends to be the strategy of choice when accidents are so costly that society (and the organization responsible) cannot afford them; the harmful consequences are so egregious that an after-the-fact deterrent strategy, on its own, simply will not do. For both the Space Shuttle Program and air traffic control, encounters with risk are a routine aspect of daily work that prioritize a compliance approach designed to prevent mistakes and accidents. Prevention is the goal: both use technologies of control designed to ferret out anomalies and correct them before small problems can turn into big ones.

Although both agencies do space work and have a lot in common, variation in the certainty of the two vehicles' technology translates into differences in the social organization of encounters with risk. NASA's Space Shuttle Program is still an experimental system, the shuttle itself an experimental technology. No two vehicles are ever exactly alike because technical changes are made to each vehicle after every flight. Air transportation, in contrast, is an operational system, the technology of aircraft highly standardized. As a consequence, time and division of labour are markedly different in encounters with risk at both places. The differences in certainty shape the time available for risk assessment, providing different windows of opportunity for identifying potential signals of danger and correcting mistakes. The pre-launch process for both organizations (controllers in towers, like engineers at NASA, also talk about 'launching' aeroplanes) reflects these differences. A shuttle flight has a long prelude. Planning, preparation and assessment of the readiness of a shuttle for flight begin 18–24 months ahead. The final countdown, launch and mission of a shuttle are a very small portion of the pre-launch process that has to be monitored for anomalies. Many anomalies are discovered and corrected during this long assessment period. Moreover, shuttles, like aeroplanes, are reusable, so the post-flight engineering analysis, repair of damage from a flight and technical adjustments to improve performance on the next shuttle flight are part of the pre-launch flight-readiness assessment, which can take months.

The launch and flight of an aeroplane does not have this long pre-lude, though it may seem that way to passengers. The comparatively leisurely process of risk assessment in the Shuttle Program is in stark contrast to the condensed window of opportunity in air traffic control. The turn-around time of a flight is short and any technical anomalies on the aircraft prior to takeoff are the responsibility of the airlines. Instead, the pre-launch process for an aircraft begins in an air traffic control tower when a computer-generated flight progress strip, identi-fying the aircraft, its equipment, its point of origin and the proposed route to destination, arrives at a controller's position, indicating the plane is coming into his or her domain of responsibility. Tower con-trollers monitor pre-flight plans, check planned routes, control all ground movement and takeoff. In the very short pre-launch phase – the gate – controllers are making decisions about aircraft with people on board, whereas in the shuttle's nearly two-year pre-launch phase, lives are not yet at risk.

Differences in division of labour at the two agencies are as opposite as the allotment of time for identifying and correcting anomalies. All decisions about anomalies and risk acceptability in the Shuttle Program are a collective effort. In the pre-launch phase, each component part of the shuttle is the responsibility of a project work group, to which NASA managers and engineers are permanently assigned. The experimental technology requires specialized skills, so engineers on the same work group have a division of labour dependent upon whether they are thermal engineers, structural engineers or some other speciality. However, the project members, in work groups assigned to technical components of the shuttle, collectively identify anomalies, assess risk and determine whether or not their component part is ready to fly. Post-flight analysis – assessing the performance of a few similar objects/ vehicles after each flight – is an important part of the task for shuttle engineers that has no equivalent in air traffic control.

In air traffic control, division of labour has individual controllers making risk assessments incrementally as flight progresses. The work is divided sequentially: the controller responsible for a plane at a given moment is the decision maker assessing risk. Responsibility is passed from controller to controller as the plane taxis along the ground and through sectors of airspace. Once an aeroplane starts moving, a con-troller's opportunity to identify anomalies, assess risk and take correc-tive action can be a split-second affair. Each controller may have control of a plane for anything from five to twenty minutes, depending upon the geographic size of the controller's air space, the flight plan, the speed and destination of the plane, the amount of traffic and the weather. Although in some circumstances that controller may have input from a supervisor or other controllers nearby, the typical case is one controller, aided by whatever technology is available in his or her facility, assessing risk, making decisions and communicating those decisions to pilots.

In both types of space work, more than one set of human eyes is monitoring a flight, but the number of human eyes monitoring a given flight, either directly or indirectly via some technology, is huge. For NASA, a shuttle launch is a relatively unique event: only one shuttle is in orbit at a time; in a 'good' year, eight shuttles may be launched. NASA personnel are monitoring progress and performance not only at the launch and landing sites but at numerous NASA facilities around the globe. Each vehicle is monitored by thousands of eyes. In contrast, launching aeroplanes is a routine event. At the busiest times of each day, major terminals are launching two planes a minute; typically, over 5,000 planes are in the air over the United States. Also in contrast with NASA, every controller has many more than one aeroplane to control at a time. The path of each plane is watched by a small number of people. Controllers 'own' sectors of airspace – a plane in a sector is controlled by that controller, but also by others in the room at a Centre (high altitude). The radar controllers' radar assistant watches all activity on the same scope and at a tower or a TRACON (Terminal Radar Approach Control, intermediate altitude). Airspace and architectural space differences make it possible for other controllers and supervisors in the room to see and hear what's happening for every controller, thus providing extra sets of eyes.

For NASA and air traffic control, the variation in certainty of their respective vehicles affects the time and division of labour for encounters with risk. These differences, in turn, lead to distinctive technologies of control.

The trajectory of anomalies: technologies of control and the determination of risk

Technologies of control can be thought of as manufactured sets of 'extra eyes': rules and procedures are designed to point human eyes and behaviour in designated directions; surveillance technologies are designed to supplement the human eye and cognitive capacity by revealing in detail what the human eye cannot see. Both have a significant impact on work practices, the third technology of control. I turn now to examine these three technologies of control as they affect the identification and trajectory of anomalies in these agencies.

Space transportation system

At the outset of the Space Shuttle Program, NASA acknowledged the uncertainty of shuttle technology. Its experimental character was reflected in a formal system of organizational and institutional rules and procedures that left wide discretion to engineers in work groups in all their attempts to identify, measure and assess risk. The formal rules set forth decision-making procedures that frame these expert technical decisions, setting standards for what happens to the information that the work groups produce. The assumption from the start of the programme was that this was a risky technical system because it was without precedent. Because the forces of nature experienced in flight could not be replicated in the laboratory and in field tests, the expectation was that always a shuttle would return from a mission showing physical damage and deviations from predicted performance. Part of the organizational context of risk assessment at NASA was the institutionalized belief that (1) a vehicle would never be risk-free and (2) anomalies were expected throughout the space shuttle vehicle after every mission. These cultural understandings were encoded in a written protocol governing all engineering decisions. Prior to the first shuttle launch in 1981, NASA created an overarching universalistic guideline for all risk assessments, entitled 'The Acceptable Risk Process' (Hammack and Raines 1981). This was the basis for all technical decision making at NASA, from daily decisions to the final formal decision process immediately prior to a launch, known as Flight Readiness Review.

The document stated that hazards that could not be eliminated or controlled would be subject to risk assessment determining the 'credibility and probability of the hazardous risk occurring' and required an engineering rationale for retaining the existing design or procedure. It explained that a hazard would be classified as an Acceptable Risk only after all risk avoidance measures were implemented and documented and after upper management, upon consideration, decided to accept risk on the basis of the documented engineering rationale. It concluded by acknowledging that after all feasible corrective actions had been taken, some residual risks would remain. Consequently, all risks needed to be monitored 'to insure that the aggregate risk (of the shuttle) remains acceptable' (Hammack and Raines 1981: 10). NASA had no coordinated or intensive in-house job training in risk assessment for engineers assigned to a project. Instead, the agency trusted in professional training and experience. Engineers were trained to work for corporations and government agencies that would assign them to specialized tasks, which they would learn on the job. In every position, they carried with them occupational rules: universalistic engineering principles and skills learned in schools and other jobs. At NASA, the identification of any anomaly was to be followed by an engineering investigation into its seriousness and risk acceptability that was to include the measurement of risk: how likely is it to recur and how risky is it?

Identification and measurement

The experimental character of the space shuttle made the entire process of identifying and assessing the seriousness of anomalies murky, but action had to be taken. Any problems would need to be addressed and corrected prior to the next launch. Because of the unprecedented character of the shuttle technology, engineers assigned to a project had no particularistic rules to guide their technical decisions. They had to create their own criteria for their component part's performance. These standards were developed inductively from experience, first determined by predictions from engineering principles, then continuously adjusted in response to experience in bench tests, lab tests and, finally, shuttle missions. This situation was not unique to NASA, but typical of engineering as an occupation. Wynne (1988) writes about the ad-hoc character of engineering rules, noting the absence of appropriate rules to guide fundamental engineering decisions. They tend to develop informally out of evolving engineering experience with a technology. Formal rules established prior to experience with a complex technical system are designed to apply to diverse circumstances, but are not sufficiently specific to guide decisions in specific situations.

They were, in short, learning incrementally, by mistake. Their long time line between launches allowed them in many cases to repair the technical cause of the problem and in others to find out whether it was tolerable in the shuttle: measure the amount of deviation from expected performance (in engineering-speak, calculate the margin of safety) to ascertain whether the anomaly was an acceptable risk. The latter determination was a matter of producing evidence that the damage might continue but would be contained, so that it did not threaten the safety of a mission. Consequently, the trajectory that Star and Gerson identified in scientific work was replicated in the technical work of NASA work groups: incidents that engineers first identified as anomalies that were potential signals of danger often, on the basis of post-flight investigations, were redefined as normal and acceptable in subsequent flights.

Wynne (1988) observed further that as engineers begin to develop experiential knowledge, much of what they understand is intuitive, based on tacit knowledge that is difficult to express. Yet, especially at NASA I found, engineers are challenged to convert their tacit knowledge into visible, discrete units that make communication and decision making possible. To do so, they have to rely on the methods of scientific positivism that they learned in engineering school in order to quantify, rank, classify, standardize performance and assess risk. For NASA engineers, a compliance strategy of control was one that had them identifying anomalies that had to be brought into compliance with continuously shifting rules that were created ad hoc, rather than rules that provided standardized measures that were constant and consistent. But guidelines for measurement were also murky. Because of the unprecedented technology, engineers had to create their own measurement devices, in the form of models and field or bench tests. Not only did they invent the rules as they went along, they also had to invent the technologies of control they used for surveillance of anomalies.

Research in science and technology studies shows that for complex technologies, experiments, tests and other attempts to measure outcomes are subject to 'interpretative flexibility' (Pinch and Bijker 1984). Engineers in the Solid Rocket Booster Project found that various tests of the same phenomenon produced differing and sometimes contradictory results. Even the results of a single test were open to more than one interpretation. Attempts to settle controversies by having additional tests run by outside research institutes or contractors not involved in the shuttle project often led to yet another set of findings, which Collins' (1985) research found to be common in attempts at replication of experiments. Consequently, controversies were part of the daily routine. Disagreements about what was risky and how risky it was were ongoing and continually negotiated in conversations and formal work group meetings. Further, as the engineers learned more about both the performance of the boosters and the measurement devices, they developed increasingly sophisticated tests and models, so data comparison at, say, time 1 and time 6 was impossible. For all these reasons, judgements were always made under conditions of imperfect knowledge (Marcus 1988).

As shuttle engineers performed these acts of identifying, measuring and determining risk, they were engaged in work that was more like a craft than a science. They were experimenting, tinkering, adjusting, inductively recreating the shuttle as they went along. They eliminated the anomalies that they could with targeted adjustments that fixed the problem. For those that remained, criteria for how risky an anomaly was and how much deviation could be safely tolerated were adjusted based on post-flight analysis after each shuttle mission. The retrospective nature of their interpretative work and standard setting was more a project in the invention of accuracy than developing standardized technical guidelines for assessing risk. For those doing the assessments, however, these shifting standards were not questionable actions. Indeed, within professional engineering culture, they were practising 'normal science' (Kuhn 1962).

The end point for the trajectory of an anomaly was a formal status of classification in which the nebulous became an organizational fact. Measurement of the amount of risk and probability of failure, however controversial, had to be converted into information that was conveyed to the rest of the system. Two NASA requirements reinforced the trajectory from anomaly to acceptable risk. Their unintended consequence was to aid in the conversion of uncertainty into certainty: the ongoing engineering controversies, negotiations, changing risk estimates and toleration levels for deviations were transformed into stable, formal, institutional facts that were binding. One procedure was a classification system called a Critical Items List that attempted to rank the relative risk of each shuttle component. The criticality categories were formal labels assigned to each part, identifying the 'failure consequences' should the component fail. These designations (Criticality 1, Criticality 2, Criticality 3) were conservative because their assignment was based on failure analysis under worst-case conditions.

A work group composed the entry for its component part of the shuttle, giving the engineering rationale explaining its decision for acceptable risk. Since all items were risky, the entries described the data and actions taken that the engineers believed precluded catastrophic failure and stated why, in spite of the risk, the design should be retained. As the document represented an official work group position, engineering differences of opinion had to be negotiated to get the document written and approved. Not everyone agreed about the level of risk or the engineering rationale and evidence included. But the document required a consensus, so one was always produced; decisions had to be made about which evidence or test had more weight. The documentary representation of reality was one of stable knowledge confirmed by scientific evidence. Producing these documents classified acceptable risks by sorting them into criticality categories that affected the definitions held by management and others in the Space Shuttle Program. Ambiguity was erased in the process.

The second NASA procedure that forced fact making in the process of defining risk was Flight Readiness Review (FRR). It is NASA's pre-launch decision-making structure that is the final, formal review in an intricate process of launch preparation and decision making involving thousands of people and engineering hours and taking 18–24 months. The goal is to collectively determine that the shuttle is ready to fly, and fly safely. FRR brings together all parts of NASA and relevant contractor organizations to assess engineering determinations of acceptable risk for each part and thus the aggregate risk of the shuttle. The review is a tiered process with four levels. To proceed with a launch, the decision to go must be based on consensus of all parties. It begins about two weeks before a launch at Level IV, with project work groups and their contractor counterparts bringing forward risk assessments and documented engineering evidence – based on the most recent data from tests and post-flight analysis – that their component is safe to fly. To prepare for this stage, the people assigned to the project must negotiate their differences and agree on the meaning of tests and other evidence about performance.

The entire FRR process is rigorously adversarial. As one engineer said: 'I've seen grown men cry.' The initial documentation and statement of risk acceptability are presented before knowledgeable others, who will challenge the work group's analysis. Hiding evidence, sweeping problems under the carpet is not possible, because every stage has a critical informed audience, some of whom have a vested interest in making a rival project look bad by finding problems that will hold up the process, giving their own project more time to work out their analysis. If the scrutiny produces unanswered questions, inconsistencies or inadequate evidence, the work group will be sent back to the drawing board to do more tests, analysis or whatever it takes to produce convincing evidence that the component is an acceptable risk. When the evidence withstands scrutiny and all challenges are met, project managers sign a document indicating the groups' decision that the component is safe to fly. As the engineering analysis for each component works its way through the four levels of the FRR hierarchy, the adversarial audience gets larger and the analysis gets tighter and tighter as more and more data are brought to bear affirming the original position, stabilizing and formalizing the definition of risk. At each level, senior management participants are required to sign a document stating their approval that the design is an acceptable risk and therefore safe to fly. These signed documents not only indicate consensus, they also affirm management's oversight responsibility in launch decisions. Officially and formally, responsibility for error, mistake and accident belongs to all participating parties.

After FRR, the final phase of the pre-launch preparation switches the responsibility for risk and error to a mission management team that supervises a standardized system in which computers and other hardware surveillance technologies dominate. Governed by two volumes of items that have to be checked one at a time, most decision criteria are quantified and precise, with predetermined criteria for stop or go (unless an unprecedented situation arises, as it did on the eve of the *Challenger* launch, when wind and cold produced eighteen-inch icicles and no one knew whether the hurtling icicles would damage the vehicle at lift-off). The final countdown is computer surveillance of each operating component that automatically stops the countdown by shutting down the system when an anomaly is detected. NASA engineers do not expect major glitches in this phase of the process: the purpose of FRR is flight readiness. As one engineer said: 'By the time it goes to the mission management team, the hardware is all cleaned and ready to go.'

To sum up: I have singled out for attention several technologies of control for the Space Shuttle Program that grew out of encounters with risk on an uncertain technology. Notably absent was any in-house training as a technology of control; in response to uncertain technology, the agency placed trust in professional engineering training and experience, allocating deference to professional expertise. Technologies of control in the form of rules and procedures were of three types: an overarching guideline, 'The Acceptable Risk Process', that created and reinforced an institutionalized belief system about risk that governed all NASA decisions about flight safety; a flexible schema of engineering rules, created bottom-up by engineers, that were the basis of specific engineering decisions evaluating the performance of the shuttle and resulting risk assessments; and top-down imposed, standardized rules and procedures, institutionalized across the NASA organization designed to coordinate decision making across the system. The work practices that were employed as a result had the technical experts doing the hands-on work and encountering risk on a daily basis, creating rules from experience with the technology in an ad-hoc fashion. These functioned as standards that were used to identify anomalies and convert anomalies to acceptable risks. These rules were consistent with the interpretation of evidence and determination of what was or was not a fact at the moment of their creation, but as new learning occurred with the shuttle technology, the facts changed. The rules were constantly adjusted.

Engineers also crafted their own hardware surveillance technologies: measuring devices, such as instruments, bench and lab tests. The results of measurement had interpretative flexibility that made controversy part of the daily routine. The NASA organization required consensus, however. Engineers' decision making was framed and shaped at crucial points by institutionalized beliefs and organizational rules for decision making and documentation of risk that were bureaucratic. These formal rules coordinated and regulated encounters with risk between shuttle project work groups and the rest of the organization. Because of the complexity of the shuttle as a technical system and the complexity of the NASA/contractor system, there were myriad daily documentation and coordination requirements. I focused on two because they play significant roles in the trajectory of converting anomalies to acceptable risks: the Critical Items List and FRR. These standardized rules and procedures are in contrast to the experiential and flexible rules of engineers. Although the strategy of having rules and procedures frame engineering decisions by defining what should happen to data and risk assessments after engineers have produced them would appear to have no effect on engineering data and determinations of risk, at NASA the formal rules and procedures had a significant effect on the technical decisions. They converted uncertainty to certainty, forcing contradictory evidence, ambiguous results and controversies into consensus and organizational facts. These processes were reinforced by structural conditions: structural secrecy within the organization, and the culture of production, which developed from political and economic relations in the environment. Neglected in this telling, they were equally influential in the normalization of deviance at NASA (see Vaughan 1996, Chapters 6–7).

Air traffic control

The certainty of aeroplane technology and the standardization of technologies of control in the air traffic system invest the tasks of air traffic controllers (ATCs) with a clarity unknown by the technical experts in shuttle work groups. The National Air Transportation System is part of a global system of regulation with both universalistic and particularistic rules that apply across national and cultural boundaries. However, particularistic rules dominate the system. English is the international language; the sky is divided into regions of air space that are 'owned' by specific air traffic facilities. Each defined air space has identifiable boundaries and each is crossed with named highways and intersections (e.g. Weir, Bronc) that indicate the routes of aeroplanes, like a city street map guides the path of vehicles. Commercial flights fly these standard routes at scheduled intervals that are known and predictable. Rules and procedures are designed both to control aeroplanes and coordinate the activities of controllers. How traffic is handled by controllers is set forth in the 'bible' of air traffic controllers, known as 7110.65. It is two inches thick and codifies all rules and procedures for communicating with pilots and controlling aircraft. In addition, a published volume entitled *Letters of Agreement* is specific to the needs of each facility. The *Letters of Agreement* contains all the procedures for coordinating activity with other controllers in other air traffic facilities within and adjacent to its airspace.

In contrast to the shuttle programme, in which engineers educate themselves in shuttle technology and invent many of their own rules, for ATCs these technologies of control all are imposed top-down. The goal is to produce an air traffic controller whose behaviour is as standardized and predictable as the system in which they are to work. Thus, education is a significant technology of control. The first line of defence against anomalies is controlling the decisions of the individual controller. Education aims directly at the decision-making process itself. The goal is to have controllers master the rules so well that they can make decisions without thinking (Vaughan 2002). An extremely important part of their job is the quick identification and correction of errors and mistakes in the movement, direction, speed, altitude or aeroplanes in motion, carrying people and cargo. The timing of decisions is so rapid that having to think or calculate everything is a threat to safety – a process that stands in contrast to the prolonged group processing of information and debate-style decision making in the Space Transport System (STS) programme. Therefore, the making of a controller is an intensive, arduous process. The training of controllers is in stages, its duration varying depending upon the type of facility to which each is assigned. The average training time across types of facilities is three years. Moreover, even after formal training is successfully completed and capped by the formal certification of a controller, retraining goes on continually, integrated into the work routine in all facilities, because the existing system keeps being refined to meet changing traffic demands and new types of aircraft.

Controllers are trained to achieve the FAA goal of 'the safe, orderly and efficient coordination of air traffic'. Unlike engineers, who come to the workplace already trained in engineering principles, ATCs bring no universalistic principles from professional training to the workplace. Their background work experiences and training are not in air traffic control, although there are some exceptions: some were pilots or military ATCs, but they still need to learn and be able to apply the technologies of control that are peculiar to the FAA system. Most controllers are either recruited off the street or from technical schools that specialize in aeronautics and give degrees for air traffic control specialists. Controller training requires mastery and integration of three layers of knowledge: institutional, organizational and tacit. The institutionalized rules of the national and international system are taught at the FAA training facility in Oklahoma City, where all candidates must spend time training. Firstly, they must pass a 'screen': tests on a computer-based instruction system that simulate skills believed to be important for ATCs. Following success, candidates take classes in which they learn airspace maps with thousands of bits of information, phraseology, technique and how to use the technology. They memorize and are tested daily. On simulators, they work traffic situations so realistic that the adrenaline is pumping. It is survival of the fittest and many controllers told me it was the most stressful experience of their lives.

Those who survive are assigned to a facility, where they acquire local knowledge: the facility's airspace, traffic patterns, types of aircraft, hardware technologies and *Letters of Agreement*. New controllers begin by memorizing maps and the rules for their airspace. Prior to working 'live' aeroplanes, they spend time on traffic problems on simulators, building up skill at handling complex situations and more and more traffic. The next phase is working traffic in an apprentice system. 'Developmentals' are assigned a primary and secondary trainer. After lengthy work assignments that allow them to observe experienced controllers at work, developmentals begin working traffic with a trainer who corrects them on the spot and takes over when necessary. This aspect of training is stressful for both the developmental and the trainer. Like NASA engineers, they learn by mistake, but working live traffic is a qualitatively different experience from the pre-launch or post-launch weighing of evidence and learning by mistake by lab tests and shuttle parts on the ground at NASA.

What controllers also begin to acquire during facility training is tacit knowledge: the essential subtleties of air traffic control – which types of aircraft can do what, or predicting competency of a pilot by the tone of voice, or sensing when the wind is changing, or how to coordinate with the varying skills and temperaments of colleagues. An extremely important skill they learn in training is 'room awareness': controllers are taught to pay attention not only to their own traffic but to what everybody else in the room is doing. At the same time they are talking to pilots, watching the scope or looking out the window, writing on flight progress strips and coordinating activities with other controllers through the computer or ground phone lines, they are acutely aware of what everyone else is saying, even to the private whispered joke of a co-worker on the other side of the room. No privacy is possible. All decisions immediately are public, and so are mistakes.

The outcome of the top-down imposition of technologies of control on controllers is that institutionalized rules, local knowledge from the facility and tacit knowledge become embodied: controllers can control traffic without thinking. Some bottom-up invention is possible in air traffic control: controllers identify airspace problems and help design realignments of the boundaries in the sky in order to improve the traffic flow; they also participate in the development of new technologies. However, particularistic rules and standardization govern every aspect of their decision making – what they do, what they say and how they say it. They do not have universal guidelines, like the acceptable risk process and FRR, as frames for wide discretion and bottom-up invention of technical standards for what is or is not an anomaly. Controllers' search for anomalies – the identification, measurement, risk assessment and correction of any deviations they spot – is done within detailed and narrow constraints. This layered system of institutional and organization rules and procedures leaves them a limited range of discretion. Although limited, however, their discretion is as critical to their work as it is at NASA, and so is the intuition that comes from experience and tacit knowledge.

Identification and measurement

Both shuttle project work groups and air traffic controllers are engaged in prediction and the search for deviation from expectations. However, identification of anomalies for an air traffic controller is far from the murky process of the Space Shuttle Program work groups. In a standardized system that is ingrained in controller cognition through extensive, intensive training, any deviations from expected behaviour instantly stand out. In air traffic control, aircraft behaviour either fits the standard pattern or it does not. Any deviation attracts the attention of controllers, who immediately act to bring the situation back into compliance with standards. They are trained to automatically spot and correct, for example, a pilot's deviation from assigned route; a routing error printed on the computer-generated flight progress strip; a pilot error in repeating a controller instruction ('climb and maintain heading one-two-zero' instead of 'one-three-zero'). These sensitivities are part of tacit knowledge, a result of formal training and experience, learning by mistake being a part of both.

Controllers' daily encounters with risk are equally reliant on hardware surveillance technology that aids in monitoring and identifying deviations – computer systems, radar, navigational devices, radios and radio frequencies. All are important aids to memory as well as tracking, communication and identification of anomalies. In contrast to shuttle work groups, whose hardware technologies for anomaly surveillance and assessment of risk are invented and changed as knowledge and shuttle technology changes, in air traffic control hardware surveillance technologies are standardized and slow to change because of the cost of replacing them throughout the system.[1]

Remarkably, within the rigid standards of this system and the plethora of hardware technologies at their disposal, much of the controllers' ability to identify and correct anomalies nonetheless rests upon experientially based human assessment and intuition. Controllers are even able to be prescient, taking preventive action before anomalies occur. Their tacit knowledge gives them almost a sixth sense about pilots, allowing them to predict and prevent a mistake waiting to happen. Their attention is attracted to differences between pilots' voices that are indicators of a need for what controllers call 'special handling'. Many pilots with foreign accents, controllers know from experience, may have mastered English well enough to be a qualified pilot but may misunderstand a directive or not have sufficient language to comprehend anything beyond the most routine instruction, so cannot handle an emergency in English. For foreign pilots, controllers speak more slowly, more clearly and break down instructions into separate parts. Controllers recognize the difference between the experienced pilot's command of phraseology and that of the infrequent flier or pilot in training, and pay extra attention accordingly. Controllers know the performance capability of the types of aircraft common in their airspace and recognize when one is behaving inappropriately for

---

[1] Some variation in technology-in-use exists between facilities, however. In the US, surveillance hardware will vary according to whether it is used by a tower, a TRACON or a Centre. Internationally, between National Air Transportation Systems, hardware technologies of control will vary due to different designers, manufacturers and ability and willingness of nation states to invest resources in their systems.

that type. Any signals of potential danger get passed on to the next controller ('Watch this guy, he's …').

In contrast to NASA, in air traffic control anomalies do not wait to be considered at leisure. The quick-fix ability of ATCs renders most anomalies momentary, so there is no protracted organizational trajectory in which every anomaly is routinely and systematically considered by a team of people, then formally and officially converted to some equivalent of the shuttle concept of acceptable risk. However, there is a trajectory of conversion from anomaly to error that has a formal classification as end point. Measurement with hardware surveillance technologies is central to the distinction. As in the Shuttle Program, scientific positivism and the assumption that science produces accuracy prevail. Controllers' primary responsibility is to avoid collision above all else. To that end, they must abide by the 'rules of separation'. These rules define the amount of space that must exist between aircraft in the air and on the runway. The spacing requirements vary by type of facility, its assigned airspace and type of aircraft, and are specified in 7110.65. For example, for high-altitude Centres the rules of separation require spacing of 1,000 ft above or below an aeroplane and five miles between aircraft. If the rules of separation are violated, the violation may be charged to the controller, so the anomaly is officially defined as an 'operational error' (OE). The anomaly is transformed into an OE when an investigation shows that the controller failed to act to avert the incident or acted erroneously or too late.

But there are other possible outcomes. The example of the high-altitude Centre, which uses radar to follow the route of aircraft flying at altitudes of 14,000 ft and above, shows the role hardware surveillance technology and interpretative flexibility play in the trajectory of an anomaly. In all facilities, radar is present, but it is exclusively relied on for controlling traffic at 3,500 ft and above. A radar scope contains not aeroplanes but representations of aeroplanes in the form of data blocks giving call signs, destination, type of equipment, speed and altitude. These data blocks are shown on controllers' radar scopes attached to targets that indicate the location of an aircraft in the sky. The blocks move as the aircraft move, allowing controllers to track the paths of the aircraft. Controllers can predict the future location and potential points of conflict of planes in their airspace by using the information in the data block, so are able to change headings or altitudes to avoid possible conflicts. Also, the computer can calculate the distance between two planes for them, based on the radar tracking system: figures appear printed on the scope.

Finally, the computer keypad offers a function key that allows them to put a six-mile diameter circle (formally known as a J-ring, or inform-ally to controllers, a 'sissy ring') around an aeroplane in a position of potential spacing conflict with other aircraft in a congested traffic situation. Two consequences follow, one human and one technolog-ical. Firstly, the six-mile diameter J-ring gives a visual boundary that increases the margin of safety one mile beyond that dictated in 7110.65 so controllers have ample time to give corrective headings. Secondly, the computer is always measuring the distance and altitude spacing between aircraft, based on the radar indication of a plane's location, whether the controller asks for it to be displayed or not. Consequently, when the rules of separation are violated (i.e. the separation between planes is 4.9 miles instead of 5 miles), a J-ring automatically appears around the two planes in conflict. The ring flashes off and on, also flashing the letters CA-CA, which indicates a Conflict Alert. This technological indicator of a Conflict Alert is a signal of potential danger that attracts controllers' attention so they can – and do – give pilots instructions that provide the necessary separation.

It is measurement that sorts these otherwise momentary anomalies into a formal organizational classification system and converts them into organizational fact. An official investigation follows every com-puter Conflict Alert. The flashing computerized warning on the scope of a Centre controller is matched by an alarm that is triggered on a computer (known to controllers as 'the snitch machine') located at the watch desk of the operations manager. The operations manager then calls the supervisor in charge to ask about the incident. The supervisor removes and replaces the controller (who has already fixed the con-flict), putting in a new controller to work traffic while the Conflict Alert is investigated. Having an OE is an emotional experience, from the moment of the Conflict Alert through the investigation, to the controller's decertification and reinstatement. For investigation, the controller writes a description of the incident, the supervisor retrieves a print-out of the two aircrafts' flight paths from the computer and also makes a duplicate tape of the recorded conversation between the con-troller and the pilots in his or her airspace at the time. The incident is investigated by a quality assurance officer and the operations manager; participants include the controller, a union representative to assure the process is fair for the controller, the supervisor and the controller's assistant if one was present because in that situation the responsibility is shared between the two controllers.

The radar track print-out is first examined to decide whether the five miles/1,000 ft rules of separation were violated. There are several possible outcomes and here we see where measurement of anomalies is typified by the same interpretative flexibility and the invention of accuracy as in the Space Shuttle Program. The computer may have made an error. By the time the computer sets off the Conflict Alert, one of the aeroplanes may have turned to a different heading that averts a conflict. Representations stand in relation to but are not identical to the object that they represent (Latour 1987). All radar representations are inaccurate because the radar is not in constant surveillance of all airspace but sweeps it at intervals. At the high-altitude centres, the sweep is at intervals of twelve seconds. The controller sees where the plane was twelve seconds ago, taking that into account when calculating the location of an aeroplane. Pilot responses to controller instructions are already under way before a controller sees them on the scope. The twelve-second interval has the deleterious effect of creating distrust among controllers for the Conflict Alert as a signal of potential danger. They report that often it seems like 'the boy who cried wolf'.

If, however, the investigating team finds the rules of separation were violated, the next step is to find out what happened, identify the cause and fix the problem so that it will not happen again. However, interpretative flexibility of the technology for measurement again confounds the outcome. Interpretative flexibility increases at towers and TRACONs. First, a computer Conflict Alert is not an OE when the controller gave the planes' pilots visual control of their descent or ascent and advised to watch for possible conflicts, a condition in which responsibility for separation shifts from the controller to the pilot. Second, it is not an OE when the rules of separation are violated but the two aircraft were on diverging headings, so collision was not possible. Finally, at all facilities, the investigators may attribute the error to the pilot, thus the incident is classified as a 'pilot deviation'. An example would be when the controller gives the pilot a heading or altitude change and the pilot verbally confirms the instruction but fails to make it or does not make it quickly enough, thus violating the rules of separation.

If the controller is charged with an OE, what has so far remained an informal conversion of anomaly to OE now becomes a formal, public, organizational fact. The controller, who was pulled off of his or her position at the time of the computerized Conflict Alert, is not allowed to return to working air traffic until he or she has completed some retraining, usually consisting of computer-based instruction designed to remedy the problem. Depending on the type of error, the controller may be retraining for a number of days. The outcome of the investigation becomes known through gossip channels. Word of the decision, who is to blame and the traffic situation that led to the OE spread informally and is discussed among other controllers in that facility, who are uniformly and obsessively interested in the details of OEs and accidents, trying to find out what went wrong and how it might have been avoided. The incident is formalized, written up and distributed to supervisors, who place it in the read-and-initial files on their desk. More formal attempts to learn from mistakes follow at high-altitude centres. Annually, all OEs for the year are reviewed in the facility by the operational error review board, comprising union members and quality control representatives, who examine what happened in each case and try to establish patterns. However, the degree to which it is public goes beyond the local. Every facility records its OEs and this count is tallied daily, monthly, quarterly and annually and conveyed to regional and national headquarters. Part of the national data system of the FAA, these totals are distributed to all facilities. Facilities are ranked by the number of OEs they have in a period.

Although the official response to OEs is designed primarily to learn from mistakes and correct the problem so that the same type of mistake is not repeated, it is a deterrent strategy of control that has no parallel in the shuttle system. Having an OE affects not only the status of the facility but also the status of the controller who made it. Controllers refer to having an OE as 'having a deal' because it is a big deal, organizationally and personally: three deals in a year, you're out of a job. Moreover, the controllers' crew also experiences it as punishment to the group because OEs are attributed to the crew as well as the controller. In some facilities, rewards, in the form of time off, are given to crews that have long records with no OEs; when one happens, they lose this 'good time'. Although almost all controllers have deals – they are impossible to avoid in some airspaces and some traffic situations – controllers experience it as punishment. The moment of the deal is emotionally traumatizing in its own right; being taken off of position, being the subject of an official inquiry and then being sent for remedial education is stigmatizing.

To sum up: encounters with risk in air traffic control leave little to guesswork. As one controller said: 'Structure and routine, structure and routine. If we have to improvise, we improvise from this base.' The division of labour in the system gives the responsibility for risk assessment to individual controllers with individually owned airspace, not a team. The certainty of the aeroplane technology controllers regulate has resulted in a high degree of standardization in the technologies of control employed in the air traffic control system. The primary focus is controlling the controller, which makes education and training significant as a technology of control. Institutional and organizational rules and procedures do not stand apart from decision making by technical experts, framing them, as in the Shuttle Program, but are the very essence of decision making, becoming cognitively embedded, as controllers integrate institutional, organizational and tacit knowledge (Vaughan 2002). Controllers quickly identify anomalies, which stand out from standardized, predictable patterns. Hardware surveillance technologies of control, also standardized across the system, are not only tools for communication and coordination but also aids in the identification and correction of anomalies.

The trajectory from anomaly to categorization and classification that Star and Gerson describe takes a different path in air traffic control from that in the Shuttle Program. Anomalies are converted by hardware technologies of control into pilot deviations or OEs, the latter adding a deterrent strategy of control to air traffic's primarily compliance system. Significant for our consideration of risk and error is that controllers are not trained to avoid collision per se; they are trained to avoid a violation of the rules of separation, a practice that builds in safety by timing their corrective practices sufficiently prior to a possible collision so that accidents are avoided. Despite the standardization of the system and tight constraints on controller decision making, preventing errors and identification of anomalies by controllers relies to a great extent on individual experience and intuition. In a system where more and more sophisticated hardware technology is being introduced to relieve congested traffic and reduce the reliance on humans, the experience and sensitivity of human interpretation and cognition is still essential. It is critical in air traffic control due to the occasional inadequacies of representation and measurement by hardware surveillance technologies. Ironically, however, exactitude and scientific principles govern the system, emphasizing standardization, technology and scientific measurement, while under-emphasizing the contribution of individual intuition and thought.

Organizational rituals of risk and error

This comparison joins other recent work that is designed to bridge the so-called Great Divide: recently, scholars studying the risk of complex technologies have been categorized as either followers of High Reliability Theory or Normal Accident Theory (see, for example, Sagan 1993; La Porte 1994). Following Perrow (1984), Normal Accident theorists study failures, emphasize structures and argue that complex systems will inevitably fail. They tend to study harmful incidents after the fact, concentrating on public failures with high costs (for an exception, see Sagan 1993 on near misses). High Reliability theorists, however, study safe systems, emphasize processes and argue for effective prevention. They study processes by linking them to successes. Rather than after-the-fact analysis, their research is done by locating themselves in an organization to interview and watch work practices and how risk is managed. The distinctions made between the two approaches have been very useful in pointing out the advantages and disadvantages of each. However, more recent work blurs the genres created by the dichotomy: for example, research on a risky industry (Carroll and Perin 1995; Bourrier 1999), research comparing organizations with failures to those without (Weick 1990, 1993; Roberts and Libuser 1993; La Porte 1994), studying the connection between structure, processes and cognition (Clarke 1992, 1993; Vaughan 1996, 1999, 2002), and variations in structure, process, performance and accidents across organizational settings (Schulman 1993; Marcus 1995).

In this analysis, I bridge the so-called Great Divide by arguing first that all formal and complex organizations are subject to routine non-conformity: all are systems that regularly produce incidents deviating from expectations (Vaughan 1999). Then, I examine two organizations, both of which have been defined as high-reliability organizations. Both NASA and the FAA's air traffic control system are organizations that routinely produce mistakes/deviations/anomalies that are not visible to the public (for NASA, failures on the rocket test range at a rate of 1 out of 25; OEs in air traffic control). I have treated anomalies as signals of potential danger, examining the organizational response. Defining technologies of control as (1) rules and procedures that guide decisions about risk, (2) work practices and (3) surveillance technologies consisting of both procedures and hardware designed to identify anomalies that are potential signals of danger, I examine how anomalies are analysed and transformed into formal organizational categories. In the comparison, I focus on the trajectory of anomalies in both agencies: how anomalies get identified, measured and classified as risks and errors at each workplace.

I found that both agencies are continuously engaged in 'clean-up work' (Vaughan 1999), applying technologies of control so that many deviations get corrected early, preventing small mistakes from turning into costly, harmful public failures. In response to differences in the uncertainty of aeroplane and shuttle technologies, the technologies of control for each agency differ because the tasks differ. So, for example, I found the agencies have very different kinds of rules and procedures, NASA allowing for more discretion in many circumstances and air traffic control much less. Variation in technological uncertainty also shaped fundamental differences in the time and division of labour for risk assessment and clean-up work.

What are we to conclude from this comparison? In spite of the different technologies of control in use, they had common consequences. Because they were repeated, regularly and routinely integrated into the daily work experience, the technologies of control developed ritualistic properties with symbolic meanings at both agencies. They created taken-for-granted cultural understandings that had an effect at the social psychological level, affecting the interpretation of signals of potential danger. As the technologies of control varied, so did their social psychological impact. The result was significant differences in technical experts' sensibilities about anomalies and risk at the two agencies.

At NASA, the cultural understanding that encompassed all risk assessment was that problems and anomalies were normal and tolerated (Vaughan 1996: Chapters 3–5). Owing to the uncertain, experimental nature of the shuttle, technical problems were expected to occur on every mission. Ironically, procedures, documentary requirements and rules designed to separate unacceptable risks from acceptable risks also had the consequence of declaring many anomalies 'acceptable' and therefore tolerable. The formal 'Acceptable Risk Process', the official category of 'Acceptable Risk' and bureaucratic language formalizing determinations of acceptable risks permeated everyday discussions of technical anomalies. Words like 'mistake', 'error' and 'accident' were not part of this language. 'Failure' and 'catastrophe' were, however; in fact, they were so much a part of standard engineering language that these words lost their attention-getting quality. Engineers routinely did analysis of the effects of possible failures, but the ability of these words themselves to serve as warning signs ('We're going to have a catastrophe if we do X') was mitigated by routine use on bureaucratic forms calling for engineers to describe the consequences of failure of every shuttle item (e.g. if a wing fell off, because the shuttle had no back-up for its wings, the failure outcome was 'catastrophe'.) Further, these acceptable risk procedures helped to create a culture where there was always a second chance. Thus, things going wrong were not signals of potential danger but a routine and taken-for-granted aspect of the daily routine.

The Space Shuttle Program's technologies of control desensitized technical experts to the possibility of error, mistake and failure. My research on the *Challenger* accident showed how these formal rules, categories and procedures, like FRR and the Critical Items List, had the effect of nullifying the sense of risk at the social psychological level, contributing to 'the normalization of deviance'. On the solid rocket booster, once the technical deviation was identified and labelled an acceptable risk (due to some engineering fix or engineering calculations predicting the damage incurred would be within worst-case limits), NASA engineers and managers continued to build on this original classification, so that the increased frequency and seriousness of the same anomaly was also acceptable. Only in retrospect, after the *Challenger*'s tragic demise, did participants who made the risk assessments for the solid rocket boosters redefine their actions as mistakes in judgement. At the time the decisions were made, however, accepting anomaly after anomaly in booster performance seemed normal and acceptable within the organizational and institutional context of work that existed.

In air traffic control, in contrast, the technology of aeroplanes is standardized and certain, the mechanical problem being the exception, not the rule. Technologies of control are similarly standardized. However, the cultural understanding is that error and mistake are not acceptable and will not be tolerated. The language of error and mistake permeates both formal categories and informal conversations: hear-back read-back error, violation of air space, pilot deviation, violation of rules of separation, accident. Anomalies that cannot be fixed result in a violation of the rules of separation and are classified as OEs. This formal designation is real in its effects because the procedures attached to a violation have social psychological consequence: the organizational response to these incidents leaves the responsible controller feeling stigmatized and punished. Individuals who have 'deals' are assigned remedial exercises and not allowed to work traffic. Even though the organizational response was designed to instruct and rehearse skills associated with the error to ensure that it did not happen again, the social psychological consequence was the experience of having failed to live up to professional standards for the controller.

Controllers learned not to fear accident but to fear mistakes that violated the rules of separation. Recall that controllers are not trained to avoid collision per se; they are trained to avoid a violation of the rules of separation, a practice that builds in safety by structuring their corrective practices while aeroplanes are still at a sufficient distance that collision can be avoided. The training process that produces controllers makes abiding by the rules of separation a priority. Moreover, the very language and surveillance technology in use assure a constant sensitivity to error and mistake. This message is continually reinforced. A technique started in 2002 uses a new technology that visually reconstructs real incidents of good controlling, OEs and accidents that include the pilot–controller conversations as an incident unfolds. All controllers are required to watch, which they do in small groups, then discuss how the controller handled the situation and possible alternatives.

As the monthly tally of OEs and runway incursions is circulated to all facilities, showing year-to-date figures and how they rank in number of errors, controllers are reminded of the status implications of errors for their facility. Another more detailed description circulated across facilities lists errors by facility with a sentence or two about the circumstances. One controller showed me the monthly list in the Read-and-Initial file. She said: 'Look at this. Isn't this ridiculous? I can't learn anything from this because they don't give enough detail about what happened. Why should I bother to read it?' She was correct about the insufficient detail, but the message that got through, whether controllers read it or not, was that errors matter in this business: do not make them.

Implications

I have focused on two compliance-oriented organizations and their preventive strategies. I have noted the differences in their technologies of control and the unintended consequences of those differences, as they generate vastly different cultural understandings about risk. These cultural understandings affect how individuals responsible for safety oversight perceive risk and response to early-warning signals that something may be amiss. A striking difference appears in the two agencies. The technologies of control that NASA employed created a culture in which anomalies were acceptable, flying with flaws was routine and within this context identifying serious anomalies and intervening was difficult because having anomalies was perceived as normal, not risky. NASA's technologies of control resulted in a culture in which the dangerous tendency to normalize technical anomalies was encouraged by the social organization of risk encounters. The technologies of control employed in the air traffic control system created a different cultural understanding about anomalies: they were not tolerated.

The significance of these findings adds a new dimension to the literature that shows how social context affects risk perceptions (see, for example, Heimer 1988; Snook 2000; Hutter Chapter 3 in this volume). First, the cases demonstrate how cultural understandings in organizations affect the interpretative work of employees charged with safety oversight. These cultural understandings are enduring, so that new employees are subject to the same influences. Second, these cultural understandings about risk are directly related to the technologies of control, which in turn are a response to the degree of certainty or uncertainty of the risky technology that the organization produces or uses (in these two examples, aircraft and space shuttles). Thus, the cultural understandings are unintended and unrecognized consequences of logical attempts to regulate risk. These cultural understandings can be beneficial or detrimental to the efforts of organizations to prevent accidents. While the analysis of the air traffic control system is an example of how these consequences can enhance the ability to intervene so that mistakes and accidents are less likely to happen, the NASA case shows the opposite effect. The 'dark side of organizations' explains how the very aspects of organizations that are necessary to accomplish the work can have unintended consequences that are detrimental to the original purpose (Vaughan 1999). Organizations that routinely have encounters with risk must be alert to and guard against negative unintended consequences.

In considering what we learn from this analysis that generalizes to other examples, we need to bear in mind that these two case studies undoubtedly have distinguishing characteristics. Although all organizations systematically produce incidents deviating from expectations, not all organizations try to proactively reduce risks, and not all try to measure and assess risk. How organizations respond to anomalies will depend on both the organizational and institutional contexts of work and important properties of the anomalies themselves: their 'seriousness, frequency, number and types of persons and activities involved, cumulative impact, and rectifiability' (Star and Gerson 1987: 150). Uncorrected anomalies at NASA and the FAA's National Air Traffic System can result in public failures with high costs. Thus, both agencies devote enormous resources – time, energy, personnel, money – to regulating risk. Both have compliance systems for regulating risk, but the compliance system of the FAA is alone in also having a deterrent strategy when mistakes result in OEs. Although their investigation and subsequent retraining of a controller charged with a violation was designed to bring the controller into compliance with professional standards, the social psychological consequence is one of punishment and stigma for the responsible individual. Both agencies systematically employ the principles of science to identify, measure and classify anomalies. These conditions will vary across organizations, so we cannot assume that all anomalies have trajectories or that all technologies of control have ritualistic properties with social psychological consequences.

A second consideration is that I dichotomized the risky technologies that these agencies regulate – aeroplanes and space shuttles – as either certain or uncertain. This conceptualization was developed inductively during the analysis, dictated by the characteristics of the organizations that I compared. It is a fruitful distinction for these cases. In other cases, however, the organization may not be assessing the risk of some technology. Under these circumstances, variation in the certainty/uncertainty of tasks alone is probably sufficient. For example, the technologies of control employed by hospitals diagnosing patients and caseworkers interpreting information about possible abuse of foster children would seem to have much in common with each other and with the NASA case when it comes to the problem of identifying and interpreting possible signals of potential danger. In such comparisons, other aspects of the social organization of risk assessment need to be taken into account: I found, for example, important differences in this comparison in the time available for interpreting information and the division of labour.

Third, there is the question of the origin of technologies of control. The FAA and NASA are public agencies, further distinguished by their status as monopolies. The technologies of control they employ cannot so readily be imported from other organizations. Instead, their technologies of control have been crafted specifically to suit the needs of their particular risky vehicles. In some organizations, however, the technologies of control may be imported from other organizations with similar tasks. We know little about the frequency of this importation process or what happens when one organization 'borrows' a technology of control from some other organization. Institutional theorists raise the question of how organizational fields come to look alike, arguing that organizations respond to normative, mimetic and coercive forces in their environments by changing structure and process in order to attain legitimacy (Powell and DiMaggio 1991). However, these adaptations may not be aligned with organizational goals of efficiency and effectiveness (Meyer and Rowan 1977). Joyce's (2000) analysis of hospital magnetic resonance imaging (MRI) technology is an example. Joyce found that MRI technology was adopted by hospitals often as a symbol of legitimacy rather than for its superior diagnostic properties and currently is used in numerous hospitals even in the absence of evaluation research that compares its effectiveness and hazards with other technologies of control (e.g. clinical diagnosis, ultrasound) used in the identification, measurement, risk assessment and formal categorization of anomalies. When technologies of control are imported, what kinds of re-organization ensue, how do they mesh or not mesh with existing strategies, and what might be the unanticipated consequences at the social psychological level for people with the responsibility for interpreting anomalies?

A fourth consideration is the rituals of risk and error invoked in the wake of accidents. Historically, the FAA and NASA have had similar post-accident rituals. Their mistakes are public and immediately known. When accidents happen, national accident investigation teams are brought in. Their charge is to gather evidence, identify the cause or causes and write an accident investigation report. Both the investigation and whatever changes are implemented as a consequence are also technologies for control. These post-accident investigations look for possible indications of technical or human failure. The search for the latter is oriented by human factors analysis, which targets individuals: was the controller tired, was the pilot poorly trained, was the manager incompetent, did the engineer or technician make a flawed decision or an incorrect manoeuvre, and if so, why? Unsurprisingly, then, investigations at both NASA and the air traffic control system have in common the tendency to pay insufficient attention to the effect of institutional or organizational factors on personnel. OE is a common finding in investigations of accidents and near misses (Perrow 1984; Sagan 1993), which Sagan referred to as the 'politics of blame'. Causes must be identified, and in order to move forward the organization must appear to have resolved the problem. The direct benefit of identifying the cause of an accident as OE is that the individual operator is the target of change. The responsible party can be transferred, demoted, retrained or fired, all of which obscure flaws in the organization that may have contributed to mistakes made by the individual who is making judgements about risk (Vaughan 1999). The dark side of this ritualistic practice is that organizational and institutional sources of risk and error are not systematically subject to either investigation or other technologies of control.

Here is how scholars can be helpful. All organizations that seek to identify anomalies and reduce the possible harmful outcomes of failure might benefit from research examining their technologies of control and evaluating the consequences – anticipated and unanticipated – for risk and error. Research can take several directions. First, we need more systematic data on signals of danger and their interpretation, as the situation is defined at the moment, not post-accident. Following Turner's (1978) identification of long incubation periods littered with early-warning signs that precede accidents, more micro-level research needs to examine the trajectory of anomalies, how they are identified, officially categorized and defined. The most appropriate method would be case studies where the trajectory of information and the process of definition negotiation can be analysed. Second, scholars must not study these matters in a vacuum but must examine also the social context: how might the behaviour of individuals and the choices they make be affected by the organization itself and its political and economic environment? Third, little research has examined the ritualistic properties of technologies of control and their possible unintended consequences. Scholars, organization administrators and other professions dealing with risky technologies have gone far in identifying and analysing technologies of control in use for both regulators and regulated. However, the organizational system, cultural understandings and their effects at the social psychological level are so far unacknowledged and thus unexplored.

Epilogue: After I wrote this essay, I found myself participating in a post-accident ritual of risk and error (Vaughan 2003, 2004). NASA's Space Shuttle *Columbia* disintegrated in the sky over Texas on 1 February 2003. Because I had authored *The Challenger Launch Decision*, I was viewed as an expert to be consulted about NASA and Space Shuttle accidents so was a regular source for media representatives looking for expertise. In April 2003, I was called to testify before the *Columbia* Accident Investigation Board, after which the board invited me to work with them in the investigation of *Columbia* and the writing of the board's report. I was surprised to discover that the board had read my book and had found many parallels between the social causes of *Columbia* and *Challenger*. Subsequently, the board rejected the human factors model typically used in accident investigations; instead, they focused upon social causes embedded in NASA's organizational system and its political and economic environment. The board broadened its search for relevant social science research on risk and accidents, which became very helpful to them in their investigation. As a consequence, the board's report (2003) is the first US accident investigation report to give equal weight to social causes and technical causes, locating the *Columbia* accident causes in NASA's political and economic history, organization and decision making. Each of these social factors is analysed in separate chapters, followed by Chapter 8, which I wrote. In 'History as Cause: *Columbia* and *Challenger*', I compare the two accidents to show the connection between the three social cause chapters and how the social causes of the first accident were reproduced in the second.

The flaws in NASA's organizational system that were responsible for *Challenger* had not been fixed. Because of the integration of social science research throughout, the board's report does *not* follow the ritualistic post-accident investigation practice of placing the blame on OE. Because elite decisions made in NASA's political economic environment were part of NASA's organizational system, the report extended the ladder of responsibility beyond errors made by middle managers to include powerful leaders whose political and budgetary decisions trickled down through the organization, changing the culture and structure and contributing to both accidents. At the time of writing this, Space Shuttle missions have been halted while NASA works on the technical and social causes that the report identified. How the board's recommendations are being implemented at NASA is yet to be determined.

3 | 'Ways of seeing': understandings of risk in organizational settings

BRIDGET M. HUTTER

M AKING sense of organizations is a persisting difficulty in risk management. There is a need to recognize the tensions between seeing organizations holistically and anthropomorphically and seeing them as a constellation of different groups and individuals. Dreams of unity and integration have to be balanced against realities of difference. While some risks will be common to everyone in an organization and understood in broadly similar ways, other risks may be differentially experienced and managed. Organizational scripts and strategies need to be disseminated and accepted by the many different hierarchical, professional and functional groups comprising the organization. Interests may vary and objectives may be differentially understood. This chapter will address these issues through consideration of commonalities and differences in the way risks are understood in organizational settings. It will draw upon case studies, with particular reference to the management of health and safety risks in a large national company in Britain. Attention will be paid to differences in the ways in which occupational health and safety are encountered, made sense of and coped with. We will consider the nature of the variations which exist between different groups within organizations and discuss the possible explanations for these variations. The chapter will also explore the implications of these debates for issues of responsibility and blame. How risk is apportioned within organizations is one area of debate, but perhaps more contentious is how external systems such as the law and public inquiries address issues of responsibility and apportion blame in the case of organizational risk management.

Mike Power and Diane Vaughan provided helpful comments on earlier versions of the chapter for which I am very grateful.

Ways of seeing organizations

There is a variety of ways of seeing organizations which pivot around the sociological dilemma of the relationship between structure and agency. One core issue is the extent to which organizations exist *sui generis* as independent entities which are greater than the sum of their parts. Conversely, what is the role of individuals in organizations? Are organizations best seen as collections of positions rather than a collection of people (Ermann and Lundman 2002: 6)? An extreme view on these issues is offered by James Coleman:

> The ... structure exists independently of the persons occupying positions within it, like a city whose buildings exist independently of the particular persons who occupy them ... In an organization that consists of positions in a structure of relations, the persons who occupy the positions are incidental to the structure. They take on the obligations and expectations, the goals and the resources, associated with their positions in the way they put on work clothes for their jobs. But the obligations and expectations, the goals and resources, exist apart from the individual occupants of the positions. (Coleman, quoted in Ermann and Lundman 2002: 7)

Such a view clearly underlines the serious limitations that may be placed upon individuals working in organizations who are subject to rules, expectations and broader influences around recruitment and promotion. Moreover, any individual can know only a small part of what is going on in an organization so thus has a restricted view. This raises a second core issue, namely the extent to which individuals in organizations have agency. An extreme view accords them very little agency, but a less entrenched position would see this as bounded and patterned according to structural variables. Doubtless reality has elements of both – recognizing the existence of an organization as something greater than the sum of its parts but also seeing the organization as reflecting the individuals and groups which work within it. The dilemmas surrounding this are crystallized in a third core issue, namely the intent which can be imputed to organizations. The neo-classical model derived from economics assumes that organizations are coherent, hierarchical and instrumental (Colebatch 1989: 76). The view of business is that it is wealth-maximizing and self-interested (Pearce and Tombs 1990; Sigler and Murphy 1988; Stone 1975). This model of organizational behaviour accords with the agency model found in some discussions of corporate crime: 'Agency logic ... is underlaid by market logic. This paradigm conceptualizes organizations and the individuals within them as rational, unitary, well-informed actors' (Lofquist et al. 1997: 4).

This rational view of organizational behaviour has been critiqued on a number of grounds. One argument is that organizations have multiple goals (Fisse and Braithwaite 1983; Selznick 1980; Wilthagen 1993). A second criticism is that there is variability between organizations so it cannot be accepted that they necessarily share common goals. The market comprises highly diverse organizations; it cannot be assumed that all firms are purely instrumental (Bardach and Kagan 1982; Braithwaite and Fisse 1985). Moreover, the rational model may also be critiqued on the grounds that there is variability within companies, so it cannot be assumed that everyone within an organization shares the same objective, or that organizations are able to translate clearly motivation into behaviour (Ayres and Braithwaite 1992; Lofquist et al. 1997). Such views underpin the structural model of corporations which ' ... conceptualizes organizations as complex, differentiated entities, with numerous, often competing goals, limited information, and imperfect communications' (Lofquist et al. 1997).

These difficulties in conceptualizing organizations are highlighted by legal debates where assigning responsibility and blame for corporate behaviour is laden with difficulties, especially in a legal system premised on individual culpable wrongdoing. Arguably the problems are exaggerated when corporations are anthropomorphized into rational thinking beings (Stone 1975; Wells 2001). This raises all sorts of questions about 'who' it is who acts 'officially' (Selznick 1980: 12). These questions are not fully resolved in British law. There are numerous examples of tensions between the punishment of individuals and corporate sanctioning. Likewise in the USA where the juristic person standard is held to be applicable to organizations and organizations are regarded as legal individuals liable for the acts and omissions of their employees (Lofquist 1997: 10ff.). However, attributing this status to organizations may be counterproductive to control objectives. For example, it has led organizational offending to be regarded differently from individual wrongdoing. Indeed, this partly fuels the debate about the criminality of risk events, for example the argument that corporations are less likely to be stigmatized as criminal than individuals (Baucus and Dworkin 1991; Richardson et al. 1983; Snider 1987; Yeager 1991).

One resolution of the difficulties associated with the attribution of responsibility is to denote particular senior personnel as responsible persons representing the organization. There are a number of problems with this which will be discussed later, but this 'solution' is the one which dominates in the risk management literature where risk primarily falls within the remit of 'management'. The emphasis is very much upon putting into place organization-wide systems for managing risks. A basic risk management text is illustrative of the approach. Taking the organization as the basic unit, Waring and Glendon (1998: 181–2) identify organizational risks in relation to the external environment of the organization and to the risks residing within organizations:

1. Outer context/organizational environment
   - Economies and markets
   - Public policy, regulation, standards
   - Social and political climate
   - Technology
   - History, operating territories and conditions.
2. Inner context
   Human factors
   - Perceptions, cognition and meanings of success
   - Organizational culture
   - Power relations, political processes, decision-making.

The distinction between the organization facing out to the external world and the organization looking in on itself is an interesting one. In its presentation to the external world the organization appears as a whole but internally it is differentiated into separate groups and subunits. In each case the interrelationships between the different factors are important. The ambition, maintain Waring and Glendon, is a holistic, integrated approach to risk management and this requires the third set of considerations which they outline as:

3. Formal coping arrangements
   - Risk management
   - Risk analysis and assessment
   - Management systems
   - Approaches to change.

These arrangements in theory should enable the organization both to exercise some control over the risks it encounters as a whole from the external world and over the challenge of coordinating its constituent parts to act as if they were one. It also requires appreciation of the fact that within companies there are likely to be cross-business effects of risk. There are varying areas of risk, such as business risk, market risk, operational risk and reputational risk, and there are likely to be multiple domains of compliance risk which may cut across each other and in so doing create more complex sources of risk (Jorian 2000; Meulbroek 2000) and thus an increased imperative to take a holistic view of the organization. Yet encountering risk in organizational settings requires us to consider the organization as a differentiated whole. This raises issues about ways of seeing within organizations and ways of seeing organizations with respect to issues of risk, responsibility and blame. It is these two important areas this chapter focuses on.

The issues will be discussed with reference to research I undertook in the late 1980s and early 1990s into corporate responses to occupational health and safety legislation in Britain. The aim of the research was to examine how the main railway company, British Railways (BR), managed compliance with health and safety legislation. It focused on the institutional and procedural changes that regulation may bring about within companies and the extent to which it may change understandings of risk across different sectors of the company. At the time of the research BR held a monopoly position over much of the overland railways network in Britain. It was a large nationalized industry which was being prepared for privatization. It was regionally, functionally and hierarchically organized and the sample upon which this research was based was drawn mainly from BR staff but also included regional and national union representatives.[1] The study considered their knowledge of risks, their views about how risky their industry was, understandings of the specific risks encountered in their everyday work and their management of these risks in terms of their compliance/non-compliance with the risk management systems incorporated in occupational health and safety regulations. Different interest groups were covered in the sample. These included staff from the four main functional departments of the railway and from different administrative (and thus geographical) regions. Different groupings of staff were also interviewed. These included company directors and senior managers, middle managers, supervisors who were the most junior of managers and were often recruited from the workforce, basic grade workers and

---

[1] The study involved 135 qualitative interviews. See Hutter 2001 for a full discussion of this research.

their representatives. In addition specialist health and safety staff from all departments, the sample regions and all grades were interviewed. This study therefore maps out the social dimensions of different groups and how they receive and interpret knowledge about regulation and risk and, in turn, how this shapes their perceptions of risk, responsibility and compliance.

This case is illustrative of the different ways of encountering and managing risks which may exist within an organization. It is an empirical question as to how generalizable these findings are to other types of risk and other organizations, although it can be said that the study's findings did resonate with studies of risk in other organizational settings (Hutter 2001: 297) so it is reasonable to suppose that the study reveals some characteristics shared with other organizations.

Ways of seeing within organizations

There is a large and burgeoning literature which details differential understandings of risk between varying cultures and between different groups in society (Krimsky and Golding 1992). Just as societies embrace a multiplex of different groups, so do organizational settings. Even fairly simple organizations may embrace a constellation of groups, differentiated according to social characteristics such as gender, class, ethnicity, education and organizational features such as location in the organizational hierarchy, professional allegiances, experience and so on. In each case ways of seeing may be patterned according to these characteristics and understandings of the organization and its attendant risks may be differentially comprehended.

Some understandings of risk, such as the viability of a business, may be common to everyone in an organization. Other understandings of risk may vary according to one's location in an organization, for example, manual workers may directly encounter risks with working with heavy machinery in ways which have indirect consequences for their fellow white-collar workers. It is likely that very few risks are experienced and understood similarly across all constitutive groups. More likely is that there is variance in ways of seeing, believing, managing and discovering which in turn has consequences for the identification of risks and for managing risks. It depends upon who or which groups see as to whether risks are identified and managed; there may be organizational barriers to seeing, for example a reluctance to move bad news upwards through the hierarchy, or practical obstacles to collating of relevant information such as accident statistics. Moreover, our understandings of risk tend to be situated so that how we see, what we see, how we interpret what we see and our ability to respond are all to some extent determined by our organizational locus. These themes are well illustrated by the BR case study. The research concentrated on the involuntary risks respondents were exposed to through work. Research previously has suggested that people are not very good at estimating risks (Heimer 1988: 494) and our ability to make sense of risk is limited. Thus the study focused on considering crude understandings rather than precise technical calculations, so deals with uncertainty rather than risk. One of the commonalities between groups within BR reflects this, namely the identification of accidents as one of the major indicators of risk. Accidents are tangible ex post facto manifestations of risk and therefore more accessible, readily understood and recalled than theoretical calculations or probability distributions of possible outcomes. Nevertheless, respondents' understandings of accidents were still broadly cast. They differentiated between major and minor accidents, the general consensus being that there were few major and numerous minor accidents. Major accidents were generally taken to mean those resulting in fatalities or serious injury to either members of the public or the workforce. Minor accidents were regarded as more 'routine' and 'everyday' and included such things as cuts, grazes and sprained ankles. These were categorizations that arose from respondents' experiences and understandings of occupational health and safety accidents and they broadly mirrored the distinctions in the regulations between major and minor accidents.

Beyond these broad-sweep commonalities, knowledge was patterned and the ability to answer more specific questions about occupational health and safety risks was structured largely according to position in the organizational hierarchy of the company. Those in the senior positions tended to know about the more serious accidents and those lower down in the organization had much more locally based knowledge, usually of minor accidents.

Understandings of the causes of accidents were departmentally related according to varying working environments. Mechanical and electrical engineering staff, for example, were the most likely to attribute blame to faulty or noisy equipment, something they may have been particularly aware of in their workshop environment. Signals and telecommunications department staff regarded working conditions, especially poor standards of housekeeping on or about the track, as a major contributory factor to accidents and typically they blamed the civil engineering department for this. Civil engineering staff were much more likely to blame a lack of supervision by supervisors for accidents. Variations according to grade of staff also reflected their different working environments. Safety representatives were, for instance, the most likely to blame management for accidents. A greater proportion of supervisors and workforce cited lack of supervision as the cause of accidents, both of these groups of course being the ones which experience the most continuous daily supervision at track and workshop levels.

It was striking that occupational health risks were rarely understood except by those at the top of the organization. Staff almost exclusively identified safety risks rather than health risks when asked whether there were any dangers associated with their work.[2] This response points to the importance of tangibility in risk perception. Risks where the harms are manifested at some future date are more difficult to comprehend than those where the harms are immediately effected. This is part of the reason why safety matters were more readily under-stood than health concerns:

... noise ... gradually you go deaf and you don't realize it. Though I must admit once again we are told that you should use such things as ear protection and I am afraid being a human being people tend to neglect these or they have left them in their locker and they are one end of the depot and somebody starts and revs engines and things. Well, over time as I say you go deaf, you don't notice it but other people do. (Safety representative)

One explanation of differential understandings of risk within one organization is the various ways in which different groups in the organization *encounter* risks. These differences very much reflect the contingencies of work. Workers' understandings of risk were directly informed by their everyday experiences in the workplace whereas managers experienced accidents indirectly through reading reports as part of their workload. In short, those in managerial positions had, as part of their job, access to data about the longer-term and more

---

[2] The literature suggests that there is an increasing awareness of risks to health (Nelkin and Brown 1984: xv). This is difficult to discern in this study as a long-itudinal study would be necessary to establish this more certainly.

insidious dangers to health and safety in the occupational environment. Thus they had a view of the bigger picture compared with the workforce whose knowledge was much more experiential and reliant on gossip. But managers were to some extent dependent upon the workforce for the information they received in these reports. Non-reporting of accidents was mentioned by all grades of staff from all departments. Minor rather than major accidents were the most likely to go unreported. Two main reasons were forwarded for not reporting accidents. The first was that people did not want to admit how silly they had been. The second and the main reason was that filling in the accident forms was too time consuming and they did not see the point in reporting, for example, a cut thumb:

R: There are many that are not reported.
I: Why might that be?
R: Sometimes I think mainly because the people concerned think they are partially or perhaps wholly to blame. I have always encouraged people over a good many years to report the accidents no matter whose fault and how it occurred, mainly in case there are after-effects of the accident later on, so there is a record of it, and since I have understood some years ago that records were compiled of accidents and more serious ones had to be reported to a higher authority, this part of it cannot be completed unless people at the ground level where these things occur initially report them ...
I: What sort of proportion of the total do you think are not reported?
R: Oh, at least fifty per cent. (Worker, interviewee 47)

Organizational/corporate understanding of accidents was patchy. Indeed, the availability of accident information within the company emerged as problematic. Information about accidents seemed to depend upon the sophistication of local grapevines. Not even senior managers received easily accessible accident information. The data they received often comprised lists of fatalities and injuries, typically on a regional or departmental basis rather than collated summaries accompanied by company-wide analyses. Decentralization seemed to be part of the problem since information collected regionally was not necessarily centrally collated in a form which could be used by the organization as a whole. Arguably a centralized and standardized properly designed system would have facilitated the reporting of accidents and the collation and effective analysis of data. The main purpose of centralized organizational data is to know better what the risks are. But there were also important symbolic aspects to data collection, for the fact that the data were being collected and used, and in some cases followed up by senior staff, indicated interest and concern from the 'top'. Moreover, as Rees (1988: 111) explains, statistics such as these influence powers of self-perception, for example notions of 'good' and 'bad' safety performance. In considering differential understandings of risk it is important to appreciate that risk perceptions were influenced not just by 'hard data' but also by the nature and quantity of information and how it is conveyed throughout the organization (Heimer 1992: 187). As we can see, the information flow may be restricted in both directions in the hierarchy, that is from top to bottom and bottom to top – and also horizontally, for example between departments and across regions.

The ways in which we make *sense* of risk are situationally generated. Workers' knowledge and understandings of occupational health and safety risks are pragmatically informed. This affects the levels of danger perceived and also what seemed dangerous (Douglas and Wildavsky 1982; Heimer 1988; Vaughan 1996). Wildavsky and Drake (1990) suggest that individuals perceive risks in a manner that supports their way of life and a central finding of this railways research was that understandings of occupational risks were inextricably related to respondents' social distance from the workplace. Thus occupational status has emerged as especially significant, in particular the differences found between various grades of staff. Senior managers took a broad overview of occupational health and safety issues and focused on systems and general trends. Further down the organization concerns tended to be more specific and focused and in some cases risks appear to make sense directly. For example, differential understandings of the magnitude of the risks faced on the railways very closely mirrored the risks presented in official accident statistics. So civil engineering staff, who spent much of their time working on or about the track, unequivocally regarded the industry as risky whereas mechanical and electrical engineering staff, who were seldom involved in track work, were much less inclined to regard the industry in this way. Yet these understandings could be processed in very different ways. For example, in some cases those in most danger refused to make sense of the risks confronting them and appeared to deny the risks they encountered. For instance, civil engineering staff, who were the most likely to suffer fatal accidents, were the most inclined to consider prevention as either not possible or difficult. Managers and especially supervisors were more inclined to the view than either safety representatives or the workforce that accidents could be prevented. Senior managers were divided on these issues. While the majority of them believed that more could be done to reduce accidents, there was a divergence of views about the inevitability of accidents. Some felt that accidents should not happen and nothing should be taken for granted, whereas others believed that a number of accidents are inevitable.

Familiarity emerges from the literature as an important factor in risk perception. Familiar risks are more easily accepted (Nelkin 1985: 16). Moreover, there is a documented tendency to underestimate the risks associated with familiar activities (ibid.: 83). This can lead to complacency or the view that 'it can't happen to me' (Cutter 1993):

I don't think it is risky. I mean, I have been on the railway twenty-seven years and I have never seen anybody hit by a train or injured. But at the same time I have seen near misses ... I have had a near miss. Usually when you haven't, usually in the first couple of years, you go on the railway and you are cautious and gentle and then you get blasé and you have a near miss. I have had a near miss and I don't know anybody who hasn't had a near miss and after that you change. (Supervisor, interviewee 15)

These findings corroborate other research which suggests that risks are viewed as more acceptable if they are familiar and have a low catastrophic potential (Slovic 1992: 124ff.). They also accord with the findings of Pollnac et al. (1995) who suggest that workers in high-risk industries may trivialize or deny the dangers associated with their work. Indeed, their denial may well become part of a subculture of denial. Writing with reference to oceanic fishermen, they say:

Constant exposure to the dangers of fishing probably habituates one to their presence and reinforces attitudes of denial, further reducing their salience ... Habituation appears to be part of the 'denial of danger syndrome', where denial of danger is reinforced by the reduction of salience caused by extended exposure. It is simply too costly in psychic energy to maintain a state of heightened concern for extended periods of time. Even in the most stressful conditions, such as combat, habituation occurs. (1995: 158)

This accords with a suggestion in some of the literature that a fatalistic approach to risk can develop alongside a view that accidents are inevitable and cannot be completely eradicated. Moreover, Slovic (1992) suggests that the social impact of accidents in familiar, well-known systems, such as rail accidents, is low.

Re-organizing

Fatalistic views have important implications for the possibilities and limitations attaching to re-organizational action to prevent accidents. Fatalistic views can quickly become a rationale for inaction. Indeed, some might regard fatalistic views as partially the result of organizational inaction. All staff reported broadly similar views about their encounters with risk. Minor accidents were generally regarded as having very little impact. Major accidents were felt to have a salutary effect but usually only in the short term. The majority view was that major accidents could change behaviour temporarily but would have no long-lasting effects:

Do I know what impact – I find that a difficult one to answer, more than most. It is rather like an accident on the motorway. I think everyone drives more slowly afterwards ... a driver who just either witnesses or sees an accident, you know, gives more care than he perhaps had done previously because it is on his mind and you get these sorts of things with level-crossing accidents. Rather like human nature, impact immediate and then tends to dawdle away with time and memory is erased. (Director)

It was only a minority of staff who considered that the impact could be long-lasting or even permanent. These exceptions, when the effect lasted longer than the short term, were when a worker had witnessed the death of a close colleague. This could result in a permanent change of behaviour, could lead to time off from work or could even cause a worker to leave the railways. Near misses were regarded by some as having a greater impact than news of fatalities. The behavioural impact ranged from a temporary change of behaviour and increased vigilance to promoting staff curiosity and causing a lot of questions to be asked:

I think it depends on what it is. If it is something that you are all probably doing wrong but it is a shortcut to achieving, you know saves time etc., and then somebody comes unstuck doing it. I think maybe people then sort of don't do it for a little while but it soon creeps back in, bad practices do creep back in. Otherwise in a lot of cases I do think that people do tend to think it is bad luck or somebody ... the idea of somebody being accident prone comes into it quite a lot. (Safety representative, interviewee 54)

The impact of accidents seemed to be structured by the exigencies of the job and important here were organizational goals and routines. Many spoke of an imperative to keep the trains running: some regarded this as a production pressure, others spoke of it in terms of a railway culture.

Nelkin and Brown (1984: 83) describe a variety of adaptations to workplace risks, ranging from carelessness to caution, denial to protest, and resignation to activism. Just over half – 55 per cent – of the BR workforce interviewed replied that there was nothing which they presently considered a risk to their health and safety. Those who identified risks to their health or safety were almost equally divided in their propensity to do anything about the problem in terms of complaining or simply raising the problem with someone else. Those who did not complain explained this either in terms of accepting risk as part of the job or because they saw no point – either because they felt that nothing would be done or because they believed that the management already knew about the problem.

There are a number of possible explanations for the apparent lack of re-organization at the individual level. For instance, social factors may be involved. Nelkin and Brown (1984) argue that responses reflect specific experiences at work such as personal economics and constraints, perceptions of occupational choice, trust in the system and identification with the goals of the organization. BR workers' inactivism may well be explained by their lack of occupational choice and poor pay, in other words they may have felt unable to be more choosy about their employment given their low skill levels and the general lack of work at the time of the research (Carson 1982). It may be therefore that attitudes to risk were shaped by the choices available (Nelkin and Brown 1984: 84ff.) so risks were normalized and accommodated because employees felt there was little that could be done to change things.

Another explanation was that understandings of risk were linked to a sense of autonomy and agency. Nelkin and Brown (1984: 4) argue that exposure to risks is related to social status, with production and maintenance workers being the most exposed. The effects of these social influences are reflected in adaptations to risk (Cutter 1993). But there was also a degree of trust in the system which was regarded to some extent at least as paternalistic. This said, respondents did come up with a variety of suggestions about how risks could be reduced, implying that they felt they did have some control over risks.

The stimuli for reorganizing following encounters with risk may be internal or external to the company. For example, much railway legislation has been prompted by accidents, as is evidenced in one of the more popular British railway books, Rolt's *Red for Danger*, which is subtitled *The Classic History of Railway Disasters*. Railway Inspectorate (RI) public inquiries into accidents very often lead to changes in corporate or national protocols for risk management (Hutter 1997). Indeed, this is the outcome of many public inquiries following major accidents and incidents (Hutter 1992). Once these organizational scripts and re-organizations are in place it is not necessarily the case that they are complied or co-operated with. The success of organizational scripts in counteracting non-compliance is dependent upon the implementation of organizational routines placing health and safety issues as paramount. This relies partly upon good enforcement systems, the support of senior personnel and employees' perceptions of company attitudes to health and safety. BR staff had a clear notion of a corporate view which was greater than the sum of its parts. Indeed, senior BR officials considered that BR as a corporate body had a concerned, caring and responsible attitude and a duty to protect the health and safety of its employees. Explanations of corporate compliance referred to compliance driven by moral imperatives and a dangerous working environment:

British Railways Board are very keen and very interested in a safe environment for all of staff for a variety of reasons, (a) the social implications because of the individual members and (b) at the end of the day – and this is probably the way the railway is actually looking at it – but if you have somebody injured or killed it is an awful lot of money to retrain or replace that person so at the end of the day it is in our interest to look after our men and staff. (Manager, interviewee 26)

I think that as a major employer of people, as an industry that has inherent risks in it and as an industry that views it ... as a fact of life we have got to be responsible employers. (Manager, interviewee 43)

Implicit in these quotations is the view that responsibility lies at the top of the organization. However, this may be variable according to the context of seeing; certainly in some contexts responsibility is apportioned to everyone. Moreover, issues of responsibility and blame are not, as we will now discuss, necessarily in a linear relationship with each other.

Responsibility and blame

External blaming

The way in which the organization/individual axis is perceived has implications for the taking of responsibility and apportioning of blame in organizational encounters with risk.

The example of the Barings Bank trader Nick Leeson illustrates the variety of ways in which risk attribution may be seen. Leeson's unauthorized trading while general manager of Barings Futures in Singapore led to the collapse of Barings, one of Britain's oldest merchant banks. The case raises questions not just about Leeson's own wrong-doing but also about the system which allowed him – even encouraged him – to behave in the way he did. Depending upon perspective, this is a case of white-collar crime (if Leeson is held to be at fault) or corporate crime (if Barings Bank is held to be at fault) or both. In the event Nick Leeson was held to be primarily and criminally at fault and he was imprisoned. But questions must be asked about the bank he worked for which in a number of ways may be seen to have encouraged and facilitated his actions. The question is why the bank was not also targeted as the culprit. Was it a matter of conspiracy or was Leeson made a scapegoat in the face of impotence to target the organization for which he worked? Other evidence suggests that the impotence of the legal system is at least a contributory factor. Certainly other non-criminal investigations held others to be responsible for the collapse of Barings. The accountancy profession (the Accountants' Joint Disciplinary Scheme), for example, excluded a former deputy chairman of Barings plc from membership of the Institute of Chartered Accountants in England and Wales, disciplined the finance director and took proceedings against the accountancy firm which audited Barings (http://www.castigator.org.uk/index.html?coopers_tr.html). In addition, the Securities and Futures Association brought disciplinary proceedings against a number of former members of Barings' senior management and the Secretary of State for Trade and Industry brought proceedings in the High Court to disqualify a number of former Barings directors.

The ways in which legal systems conceive issues of responsibility and blame in organizational settings highlight the uncertainties and implications surrounding how organizations are conceived. English law vacillates on the one hand between seeing organizations as anthropomorphic and capable of intentional acts, and on the other hand seeing certain individuals within the organization as representative of it and thus as responsible and blameworthy. There appear to have been some overall changes in perception over time. In the past there was a tendency to blame individuals – often quite junior members of staff – for risk events. Turner and Pidgeon observe that ' ... the responsibility for failures and disasters is often shifted from where it should lie – in the system or in management decisions – to the person committing the visible unsafe acts' (1997: 192). They relate this to the imperative to find a culprit, which they associate with 'myths of control'. But which culprit is identified has slowly changed and recently there has been a discernible pressure to target the corporation and to call the body corporate to account.

Wells (1996) traces the use of the term 'corporate manslaughter' back to the mid-1980s when she believes it first became a culturally recognized phrase. Since then there has been a growing campaign in Britain to attribute systemic blame to organizations for major risk events. Thus it has been increasingly recognized that individuals are situated in organizational settings which may contribute either passively or actively to risk events involving those individuals. There also seems to have been an increasing preparedness for public inquiries to attribute blame to organizations as well as to individuals working within those organizations. The Sheen Inquiry into the capsizing in 1987 of the ferry the *Herald of Free Enterprise* condemned the company P&O. Both the Fennell Report into the King's Cross Underground fire[3] and the Hidden Report into the Clapham Junction crash[4] identified systemic failures as contributory to these disasters. Hidden referred to the 'collective liability which lies on British Railways' (1989: 16.8). In the Hidden Report this largely centred on BR's recruitment and training procedures and the organization of

---

[3] Shortly after the evening rush hour had passed its peak on Wednesday 18 November 1987 a fire of catastrophic proportions in the King's Cross Underground station claimed the lives of 30 people and injured many more. A further person died in hospital, making the final death toll 31 (Fennell 1988: para 1).

[4] At 8.10 am on the morning of Monday 12 December 1988, a crowded commuter train ran head-on into the rear of another which was stationary in a cutting just south of Clapham Junction station. After that impact the first train veered to its right and struck a third oncoming train. As a result of the accident 35 people died and nearly 500 were injured, 69 of them seriously .... They were all travelling in the front two coaches of the first train (Hidden 1989: para 1).

the Signals and Telecommunications Department. The Fennel Inquiry criticized both London Regional Transport and London Transport[5] for not giving sufficient priority to passenger safety at stations; for not strictly monitoring safety; for faults in the management, supervision and training of staff; and also for poor communication within the company. Both reports criticized 'railway culture', in the case of London Transport for being too blinkered in accepting risks as 'inevitable' (1988: 1.12) and in the case of BR for its organization, training and recruitment (1989: 16.80). Both reports also criticized other organizations. For instance, the Hidden Report targeted the unions for resisting changes in working practices (ibid: 16.94) and the Fennell Report criticized the relationship between the Railway Inspectorate and London Transport for being 'too informal' (ibid: 1.25). Official reaction to two more recent rail accidents in Britain, namely the Southall and Ladbroke Grove accidents,[6] has also pointed to the underlying systemic failures which contributed to the fatal errors made by individuals. So, for example, the Health and Safety Executive's (HSE) First Interim Report into the Ladbroke Grove accident stated:

The immediate cause of the accident appears to be that the Thames Train passed a red signal (a 'signal at danger') some 700m before the collision point. The reasons why the train passed at the red light are likely to be complex. RI will be looking at the underlying causes as well as any more obvious ones. Our belief is that it is a systems failure and that any action or omission on the part of the driver was only one factor. (HSE 1999: para 5)

There have been increasing attempts to follow through incidents such as these with criminal prosecutions of both organizations and individuals. This is epitomized by the Southall case, which led the Crown Prosecution Service to charge one of the train companies involved with seven charges of manslaughter through gross negligence. The driver of the high-speed train was charged with manslaughter. The company was also charged with offences under the Health and Safety

---

[5] These organizations were responsible for the London Underground train system which is distinct from the overland rail network.

[6] Britain's overland railway system was privatized in the early–mid 1990s. These two accidents occurred post-privatization when the rail network moved from being run by one nationalized company (BR) to more than 100 separate units.

at Work etc. Act, 1974 (HSW Act). In July 2003 six senior managers[7] were charged with manslaughter due to gross negligence in connection with the Hatfield train crash of October 2000 in which four people died because of a train derailment.

But while the inquiry system can point to corporate failure, the courts have difficulty in sustaining convictions. This was highlighted by the Southall case. No convictions resulted from any of the corporate manslaughter charges because of the difficulty in identifying negligence by any individual within the company (the charges against the driver were dismissed because he was psychologically damaged by the accident). The judge in the case supported a change in the law to ease the prosecution of large companies for manslaughter. The company pleaded guilty to charges under the HSW Act so successful legal action was brought under regulatory legislation, but this was clearly viewed by the press, the families of those killed in the crash and the judge to be separate from the opprobrium which attached to more traditional criminal charges. The key issue, it seems, was the difficulty in attributing intent to the corporate body, in other words a failure of the anthropomorphized view of the company to match up with legal requirements.

The trend to invoke the criminal law in apportioning blame (and punishment) in the case of organizational risk encounters can have profound implications for system learning. In Britain it has effected a move from inquisitorial to accusatorial styles of accident investigation. The inquisitorial system is intended solely to determine the cause of the accident, not to apportion blame. But this system has encountered more and more problems as there has been increasing pressure to invoke the criminal law. It has led, for example, to defensive strategies which restrict the flow of information. Witnesses increasingly fearful of prosecution are refusing to give evidence to accident inquiries in case they incriminate themselves prior to a criminal trial (Hutter 1999). The Southall criminal prosecutions, for example, effectively held up the hearing of evidence in the inquisitorial forum by two years. The chair of the Southall Inquiry, Professor John Uff, commented upon the difficulties caused by the delay:

---

[7] These included managers from Railtrack, including the chief executive officer at the time of the accident, and managers from Balfour Beatty, the contractor's track maintenance firm employed at the time of the accident.

I cannot hide the fact that the inquiry has been unable to make the degree which everyone hoped for. I am acutely aware of the continuing anxiety of those who were bereaved or injured by the accident and their need to see the inquiry brought to a conclusion. It is unthinkable, to my mind, that we should still be in the same position in September next year, on the second anniversary of the accident. (Health and Safety Commission press release C56:98)[8]

There are clearly difficulties here as the public inquiry waits upon the criminal proceedings before commencing with the public hearing of evidence and thus potentially affects the institution of remedial action. So the accusatorial approach can pose serious problems for the flow of information. We need some mid point between the economics view that a high-blame strategy increases the incentives to minimize risk and the 'no-blame' arguments that provision of information is of maximum and overriding importance. Both extremes have their flaws and simplify the difficulties of risk management. And both may in their own ways militate against learning from risk encounters.[9]

Internal blaming

So far we have considered only the external attribution of responsibility and blame. In many respects we know very little about the attribution of responsibility and blame within organizational settings, what one author refers to as the micropolitics of blame in organizational settings (Horlick-Jones 1996). There are few studies which focus on the routine attribution of responsibility and blame within organizational settings,

---

[8] These trials may take place many years after the risk event. Following the Purley train crash in 1989 a train driver was convicted of manslaughter nine years later, in 1998, for going through a red signal.

[9] Another interesting aspect of the inquiry system in Britain is that it appears to distance the government from responsibility and blame. The declaration of a public inquiry underlines governmental concern about the accident and evidence that something is being done in response to it. It is a public acknowledgement of the accident's severity and a demonstration that it will be thoroughly investigated. But rarely does the investigatory net extend as far as government. The King's Cross (Fennell 1988) and Clapham Junction (Hidden 1989) inquiries, for example, attracted some controversy for not extending their investigations wide enough. Both of these inquiries considered the immediate circumstances of the accidents and to varying extents the railway companies involved. But neither inquiry considered the wider pressures on the railway industry, in particular government policy on the railways.

although a number of works do embrace discussion of these issues in the context of broader analyses. For instance, Jackall's study of corporate managers describes an organizational system in which power is concentrated at the top of a hierarchy and in which responsibility for decisions is decentralized 'as far down the organizational line as possible' (Jackall 1988: 17). Simultaneously details are pulled down and credit pulled up the organization, with the effects being to protect those at the top from guilty knowledge, increase the pressure to transmit only good news upwards and to blame the vulnerable: 'As a general rule, when blame is allocated, it is those who are or become politically vulnerable or expendable, who become "patsies", who get "set up" or "hung up to dry" and become blamable' (1988: 85). The view that those in powerful positions in organizational settings are successful in deflecting blame to other, often less powerful groups in risk encounters is more broadly documented (Sagan 1993).

Another view is that risk events are an inevitable part of routine organizational operations. In her analysis of the *Challenger* tragedy Vaughan writes: 'Mistakes are indigenous, systematic, normal by-products of the work process, and thus could happen in any organization, large or small, even one pursuing its tasks and goals under optimal conditions' (1997: 17; see also Perrow 1984). Echoing other studies Vaughan explains how the risks may increase the more complex the organization (Di Mento 1986; Hutter 2001). On the face of it this may appear to be a fatalistic view which absolves everyone from blame. But not so: Vaughan also notes that all too often the blame for risk events is deflected to less powerful groups which leads her to argue: 'Top administrators must take responsibility for mistakes, failure, safety by remaining alert to how their decisions in response to environmental contingencies affect people at the bottom of the hierarchy who do risky work' (1997: 17). She stresses the importance of top administrators keeping in touch with the risks in their workplace and also the need to recognize cultural diversity which may impact on sense making within organizations. There is undoubtedly scope for analyses of risk and blame within organizational settings akin to those offered by political scientists in their discussions of the risk games between elected politicians and the general public (Hood 2002).

Certainly the role of delegation as a blame-shifting device can be discussed, as can the use of defensive risk management strategies within the company. This is demonstrated by the BR study which offers some interesting findings about ways of seeing blame distribution within organizational settings. Respondents in this study were quite prepared to attribute blame for accidents: 91 per cent readily responded to questions about who to blame for risk events – 39 per cent blamed the victim (i.e. individuals) and 13 per cent directly blamed management. Many of the factors cited by staff did not directly attribute fault to any particular category of person. It was often a matter of interpretation as to who was held responsible. For example, housekeeping offences[10] were regarded by some as the fault of management, their argument being that management did not allow sufficient time to clear up once a job was completed. Others blamed maintenance staff for these problems, arguing that they did not bother to clear up the site. Non-compliance was also subject to variable interpretation. Some regarded it as the fault of those not complying, whereas others considered it to be a supervisory problem (that is, an enforcement problem), whereas another group blamed the rule makers for impractical rules. It is notable that these accounts blame either the victim or another group of employees within the company. It suggests that there was an abdication of self-blaming for accidents which were regarded as the result of another's actions (or lack of them).

All of this of course serves to highlight the diversified character of blaming. Blame is contestable and ambiguous. It is also dynamic, the dynamic being driven by who blames and who is blamed. This led some senior managers to blame more than one party for risk events. Senior managers certainly took this approach, the majority believing that accidents were the fault of both the victim and management, with a greater emphasis on the responsibilities of the latter. Management were attributed blame for a lack of enforcement, for not ensuring that good working/environmental conditions were maintained and sometimes for placing too much pressure on staff to complete work quickly. The workforce was considered to be at fault for carelessness and non-compliance whatever its cause:

---

[10] Housekeeping offences refer to a failure to tidy up and clear a site after work has finished trackside. Working on railways is restricted to tight time limits. After each work session all work implements and debris have to be removed so that the line is clear for trains to run safely, there are no obstacles for other workers who need to work trackside and no material is left behind which can be used to vandalize the railways.

... it is very easy to talk about categorizing accidents and whose fault it is, there are so many different factors – right tools provided, right materials, right advice, right management guidance. At the end of the day I think we probably glibly attempt to categorize and probably come up with missing the real reason behind it, which may be multi ... most work situations are fairly complicated. (Director)

A variety of reasons. Why do accidents occur, well that is a good question. I think ignorance, inability, lack of awareness and I think simply to quickly do something, to bodge something up or something or other where they were unaware maybe of the rules, that is some of the reasons. I would say that the majority of them occur because staff are unaware in some cases of the correct procedure ... some could well be attributed to bad management or bad supervision. It is not always the person who makes the mistake who is injured, it may be down the chain. It may be a circumstance, you see accidents, a lot of accidents actually occur through a set of circumstances but how those circumstances existed in the first place could be because of poor management, lack of attention to detail, lack of application of instructions and regulations or poor supervision of the shop floor. It may not be the person who is injured. (Safety officer)

Some discussion of defensive risk management emerged from the BR study to the extent that responsibility (and thus potentially blame) was perceived to be shifted towards particular groups within the organization. Employees, for example, perceived some aspects of protocolization with suspicion. There was a high degree of cynicism about the intentions of policy statements. The most frequently expressed view among all grades of staff was that one of the most important functions of the policy statements was to remove responsibility for the health and safety of the workforce from the managing board. Two points are important here. First, this view was expressed quite spontaneously by nearly 25 per cent of the sample, in response to an open question about their views. Second, the critics did not suggest that the board were aiming to enter into a partnership with their staff to promote health and safety but rather that they perceived the board to be 'buck passing' (a common phrase):

... basically it's (the rule book) the railway's insurance if anything goes wrong, to claim that we've got, that if we haven't abided by, that rule book then we haven't got a leg to stand on. (Worker, interviewee 23)

I think in the majority, well many, cases they (BR policies) are unworkable and they are done to protect the board against anything that the men might do . . . . It is the same as our rule book. The rule book is there so that when something goes wrong the blame can always be picked up at a very low level which unfortunately is something a lot of the men believe as well . . . (Manager, interviewee 74)

There is still a tendency for a 'them' and 'us' attitude. Whereas they are trying to take their responsibility and say 'it is your responsibility' and we are trying to say 'do, it's your responsibility' rather than looking at the thing as a whole and saying 'safety is everybody's responsibility'. (Safety representative, interviewee 123)

Multiple interpretations also surrounded the existence of separate safety departments and personnel. While each of the main four functional departments in BR had its own specialist safety department, there was debate about how far their remit should extend. In three departments there was a central and a regional safety organization but one department, the Signals and Telecommunications Department, was in the process of changing from a sophisticated training and safety organization which encompassed headquarters staff and out-based engineers to a new organization which involved no regional specialist health and safety staff. This was intentional and derived from the director's view:

I don't believe that with all levels in an organization you should have safety engineers because otherwise you can encourage line managers to abdicate that responsibility. If you do it that way you have got to make sure that you have got independent audits in place. This department is the only one that hasn't got safety engineers at regional level . . . but we consciously did that because of my very strong views that as long as 'x' (the technical and safety officer) is issuing very clear, simple and precise instructions to the appropriate levels of staff we are more likely to get it embedded in everyday line management.

The argument therefore was that too many specialist experts could easily be interpreted as holding primary responsibility for health and safety and thus run counter to the ambition that there be line management responsibilities for health and safety.

The role of specialist personnel and the attribution of responsibility are not well researched. Rees (1988: 112) describes the role of the safety department as that of 'nurturing and developing' management's sense of responsibility about health and safety. But other research suggests that the influence of safety departments and safety officers is highly contingent on a variety of factors. Beaumont et al. (1982) note the importance of ascertaining the safety officer's status within an organization; whether or not they are full-time; whether they are part of a specialist safety department; and who they report to. Whatever their position these specialist personnel are likely to be in an ambiguous position. Edelman et al. (1991) explain that they are at the call of many clients and the potential sources of conflict are multiple also. Structurally they are part of management but their remit requires them to act also on behalf of particular sections of the organization, in this case all employees. In turn this may reduce the effectiveness of these departments, if indeed they were ever intended to be effective. A cynic would argue that organizations may create 'symbolic structures' which '... appear attentive to law ... and at the same time, seek to minimize law's constraints on traditional managerial prerogative' (Edelman et al. 1991: 75). Alternatively, the existence of the specialist department may be seen as a blame-shifting device similar to the 'expertization blame boomerangs' Hood (2002) describes politicians using.

Examples such as these again reveal the tensions between the different ways of viewing the relationship between organizations, groups and individuals. A key issue which arises again and again is the fairness of holding individuals responsible for organizational failures and the fairness of holding individual misdemeanours to account without also holding corporate failures to account.

Conclusion

The understanding of risk, blame and responsibility in organizational settings is cross-cut by a number of tensions centring on difficulties in conceptualizing organizations. The external face of the organization contrasts with the internal reality and the legal view differs from organizational theory. Generally the organization's external face is holistic and its internal reality is one of differentiation and coordination. The practical task of risk management requires organizations to take account of different ways of seeing, to recognize the situated nature of understandings of risk and encounters with risk. This involves comprehending that the various groups comprising an organization may encounter risks differently. Risks may also be understood and explained differently, which in turn has implications for the ability to learn from risk events.

Taking responsibility for risk management must include taking responsibility for the recognition of difference. This may be difficult in settings where there is a blame culture which spreads responsibilities and blame unevenly and perhaps unfairly. Indeed, this may be related to the external world which seeks to apportion responsibility and blame and which appears unable to reconcile anthropomorphic views of organizations with commonplace and legal notions of intent.

Different views of organizations lead to various ways of seeing risk and different ways of apportioning responsibility and blame. Attempts to apportion individual blame for corporate failures are difficult where organizations are conceived of anthropomorphically. This leads to legal difficulties in identifying an individual who can be held responsible for organizational failure (Wells 2001). It may also come into conflict with normative views of who it is fair to blame. It may be, for example, that the blame-shifting and defensive risk management strategies employed within organizations may satisfy legal requirements (although that is in doubt) but prove counterproductive normatively as individuals are judged by their peers, and maybe by the wider population, to be scapegoats for more systemic failures.

4 | Risk and rules: the 'legalization' of medicine

CAROL A. HEIMER, JULEIGH COLEMAN
PETTY AND REBECCA J. CULYBA

Introduction: risk and the legalization of medicine

NOT a day goes by without a major news story about healthcare. Many of these stories are about the promise of scientific discoveries and technical innovations, the hardships that arise from inequalities in access to healthcare, the courage and fortitude of patients and their families, or the consequences of medical error. Even when their 'human interest' lies elsewhere, a surprising number of these stories contain a dual focus on risk and rules.

News stories about research often ask whether the research is too risky, what rules govern medical research, and whether these rules have been followed. When Ellen Roche, a healthy young participant in a Johns Hopkins medical research project on asthma, died in June 2001 from inhaling hexamethonium, questions were raised not only about the soundness of the science but about the ways projects and adverse events were reported and recorded (Glanz 2001). Likewise, when a young diabetic died in 2001, the spotlight fell on the consent process and whether he and his parents had been fully informed about the experimental nature of his treatment as the rules required.

Once drugs or procedures receive approval, attention shifts to other risks and rules. After Jésica Santillán received a heart and two lungs of the wrong blood type in February 2003, Duke University Hospital implemented a new rule requiring that three members of the transplant team verbally communicate the results of tests of the recipient's and donor's blood types (Altman 2003). When Baycol was withdrawn from

Prepared for the Workshop on Organizational Encounters with Risk, Centre for the Analysis of Risk and Regulation, London School of Economics, 3–4 May 2002. We thank conference participants, Lynn Gazley and Arthur Stinchcombe for helpful comments. Direct correspondence to Carol Heimer, Department of Sociology, Northwestern University, 1810 Chicago Ave., Evanston, IL 60208–1330, USA; email c-heimer@northwestern.edu.

the market in August 2001, the controversy over statins, used to treat high cholesterol, focused on the relationship between treatment guidelines and the regulatory processes (see, for example, Hilts 2001). One public interest research group has questioned the accuracy of information about statin-related deaths on the grounds that the Food and Drug Administration (FDA) has no protocol for collating information about deaths and adverse effects from distinct but similar drugs.

Even when effective treatments are available, patients face the risk that they will not get treatment because they are uninsured and cannot afford medical care, their medical facility does not offer the treatment, their insurer will not pay for it, or they are not told about the treatment. Disease classification and the matching of diagnosis with the categories of Health Maintenance Organization (HMO) or governmental payment schemes are important components of the story. In some instances, patients are unable to get care because the classification system has not kept pace with medical science. In the early days of the AIDS epidemic, women often were not tested and treated because the disease took a different form in them than it did in men and the definitions promulgated by the Centers for Disease Control did not include the symptoms most common in HIV-positive women.

Patients are not the only ones worried about coverage. In a national survey of 720 doctors, Dr Matthew Wynia found that a substantial proportion of doctors answering a mail survey felt they sometimes had to lie to get around rules that would prohibit or delay medically necessary treatment (28.5 per cent said it was sometimes 'necessary to game the system to provide high-quality care'; 39 per cent said they were not always honest with HMOs) (Wynia et al. 2000). An especially insidious set of rules prohibits caregivers from informing patients about particular treatments because they are costly, of uncertain benefit, or controversial. Although such rules often are introduced as cost-containment measures by managed care organizations, they have sometimes been introduced by governments, as occurred when the first Bush administration prohibited physicians from informing patients about abortion in clinics that received government funding.

Until recently, legal actors played only a very limited role in medicine. Professional associations have long sought the help of governmental bodies in limiting competition from rival professional groups (Starr 1982; Abbott 1988), and these disputes over jurisdiction continue into the present as controversies over which practitioners should be reimbursable by public and private insurance, eligible to practise in hospitals, and licensed by state boards overseeing the work of professionals. While licensure remains an important issue, the law, legal actors and legal styles of thought have now penetrated much more deeply into the medical world. The 1970s' malpractice crisis signalled an increased role for lawyers in medicine, as counsel for plaintiffs and defendants and as advisers on how to practise 'defensive medicine'.[1] Likewise the flurry of informed consent statutes passed in the 1970s (Faden and Beauchamp 1986; Meisel and Kabnick 1980) increased the role of legislators, lawyers and judges in decisions about how patients needed to be included in medical decision making. In all of these instances, the result has been a proliferation of rules; medicine has been 'legalized'.

In examining this increased concern with rules and legality in American medicine, we adopt a broad definition of 'law', recognizing that the 'legalization' of medicine is as much indigenous as imposed. An investigation of this indigenous legalization must think broadly about legal systems, including within its purview not only the actions and products of the formal legal system but the internal 'legislative' and 'judicial' processes that occur within the medical world. In this spirit, we discuss the rules generated by the medical community itself as a way of governing its own activities and managing risk. Although the legal system is surely an important source of the rules that govern social life, other sources of rules are also extremely important. In American medical care, for instance, rules are made by legislatures, but they are also made by government regulators (such as the Food and Drug Administration or the Surgeon General), professional associations (such as the American Medical Association, American College of Surgeons, American Academy of Pediatrics, and innumerable associations of specialists), insurers, private regulators that govern medical care (especially the Joint Commission on Accreditation of Healthcare Organizations), medical schools and research institutes, and healthcare organizations such as hospitals and managed care organizations themselves.[2] Our questions here are about how the rules have come about,

---

[1] Lieberman (1981) contends that the malpractice crisis was a fiction perpetrated by insurers to justify an increase in the number, size and cost of malpractice insurance policies.
[2] The Joint Commission on Accreditation of Healthcare Organizations (JCAHO) is a particularly interesting case because of the dramatic changes in focus it has

who is advantaged and disadvantaged by this increased legalism, and how risks are shifted from one party to another by the rules.

Let us be clear here: we are not suggesting that the new legalism of the medical world has any single cause. And among the important causes of this new legalism is surely the growth of medical knowledge, which makes codification and systematization of information crucial. Our contention, though, is that legalism is also partly a response to risk, in particular the risks faced by healthcare providers and organizations. With the heightened consumer activism and legal scrutiny of informed consent statutes, malpractice suits and the push for a patients' bill of rights, physicians and medical organizations have protected their turf by developing their own rules. Although the individual rules are important in themselves for establishing the standard of care in an area or establishing routines for informed consent, as a body these medical protocols also make a claim about self-regulation. For instance, they create a boundary between what is properly within the purview of the courts and what is not. Without clear protocols, courts are much more likely to question the appropriateness of medical practice. In establishing protocols, the medical profession asserts that these are technical matters best decided by trained medical practitioners. Courts and legal actors may investigate to verify that physicians have followed their own rules but, according to physicians, it is only those with medical training who should be making decisions about the rules for treatment. Once such a boundary has been established, we should not be surprised if medical rule making extends the range and enlarges the authority of physicians by formulating clinical practice guidelines about matters on the periphery as well as in the core of medicine.

But if we are not propounding a simple causal story here, neither are we suggesting that there is any simple effect. Rules may be created as part of a professional or organizational response to uncertainty, but because they are created by multiple groups, we should not expect to find them uniformly benefiting a single group. For instance, although clinical guidelines may serve the interests of physicians, governance

---

undergone over its history, sometimes functioning as a private regulatory body, at other times disavowing regulatory functions, and finally acquiring a semi-official role (Manley 2001). The Joint Commission in effect became an arm of the federal government when the Medicare rules stipulated that only healthcare organizations accredited by the Joint Commission were eligible for Medicare reimbursement.

rules, which often draw on clinical guidelines, attempt to restrict physician autonomy by making physicians answerable to managed care organizations or hospitals, and often, through them, to accrediting bodies and insurers. Governance rules thus manage the risks faced by healthcare organizations, not the risks faced by physicians.

Medical protocols as a legal system

Among the most important of these rules, at least in the United States, are clinical practice guidelines, rules for the conduct of research, and governance protocols – three sets of rules generated through the combined efforts of the groups listed above. The legal standing of these rules is not readily apparent and moves to increase legal scrutiny (e.g. to have university research overseen by the Food and Drug Administration) often follow accidental deaths, reports of drug reactions or revelations that researchers have exploited some vulnerable group. Although they overlap in any empirical setting, clinical practice guidelines, rules for the conduct of research and governance protocols have somewhat separate jurisdictions and purposes. They were responses to different pressures and were developed on different timetables. Clinical guidelines, whose roots can be traced as far back as the fourth century BC, were probably most strongly a response to the malpractice suits of the 1970s. Rules for the conduct of research, originating in the informal social control mechanisms of medical science (Halpern 2004), began to be formalized in the Nuremberg codes following the Second World War. And governance protocols are largely a product of the corporatization of both medical practice and medical research.

To put it simply, *clinical practice guidelines* are rules that translate the findings of medical science into recipes that tell medical caregivers how they should respond to the patient's medical condition – what medications to give in what dosages or when to do surgery given the patient's symptoms, medical history and personal characteristics. *Rules for the conduct of research* tell medical personnel how they are permitted to interact with patients and with each other, in this instance for the purpose of creating knowledge. They cover such topics as what kind of treatment must be given to members of a control group when new drugs are being tested or when and to whom the 'serious adverse events' of research subjects must be reported. *Governance protocols* lay out rules for how medical staff may interact with patients and with each other, as do clinical practice guidelines and rules for the conduct of research, but in this case their objective is to facilitate the practice of medicine, often within the framework of a larger medical enterprise. Among the most controversial of governance protocols are 'gag rules' of managed care organizations, which conceal other rules about coverage.[3] The distinctions among the three major types of rules are summarized in Table 4.1.

Each of these bodies of rules is the result of a long process of cooperation and contest, occurring on somewhat different timetables, between patients' rights advocates, professional associations, governmental bodies (regulators, granting agencies) and international health organizations, and other interested parties such as drug companies, insurers, HMOs and universities. As they produce these rules, such bodies necessarily make claims about best practices – which ways of doing things are the most thoroughly researched, have the most solid scientific backing or best pedigrees, or lead to the best results as medicine moves from a research phase to clinical use (roughly equivalent to the 'on the books' and 'in action' distinction common in socio-legal studies). The production of rules and the production of legitimacy thus go hand in hand.

In this chapter, we will be investigating medical protocols as a somewhat autonomous legal system. Within the medical world, medical protocols serve many of the functions of any other legal system (as described, for instance, by Lempert and Sanders 1986). Medical protocols make authoritative statements about what people may do, must do and must not do; they categorize actors and assign rights and obligations depending on which category people fall into; they arrange for punishment of those who break the rules. Although the system of medical rules is developed and implemented in dialogue with the formal legal system, it is important to recognize that medical professionals go to great lengths to cordon off the medical world and to govern it without undue intrusion from outsiders.

To some degree, then, three groups of professionals – medical professionals (largely physicians), legal actors and hospital administrators –

---

[3] Express gag clauses may forbid physicians from discussing treatment options not covered by the managed care organization, physicians' compensation schemes or other cost-containment schemes. Anti-disparagement clauses may also prohibit healthcare workers from criticizing the organization's policies to patients or the general public. In addition to these express gag rules, rules of conduct such as at-will or no-cause termination policies may function as implied gag clauses.

Table 4.1: *Purposes, creators and legal foundations of various types of medical protocols*

	Clinical practice guidelines	TYPES OF RULES *Rules for conduct of research*	Governance protocols
Purpose of rules	Recipe for how to respond to medical situation, given the patient's medical condition, history, age, gender	Rules for how researcher is to treat others involved in research project, including research subjects, fellow researchers and sponsors of research	Rules for how participants are to conduct themselves in medical caregiving organizations in order to reduce costs and protect profits, protect the organization's reputation with key publics such as patients or religious bodies sponsoring the organization
Creators of rules	Professional associations, professionals within medical organizations, for-profit writers of guidelines	Federal government, universities under whose auspices research is conducted, granting agencies and foundations whose monies support research	Medical organizations such as managed-care organizations, hospitals or clinics, with guidance from legal professionals

Legal foundation | Legal decisions, state-level law about medical practice and professions, federal rules about use of funds, laws protecting patients and giving rights to patient families | Federal statutes on research protections of human subjects, state-level statutes on informed consent, legal decisions, rules of international bodies such as WHO | Legal decisions; restricted by state law on informed consent and by some state-level statutes prohibiting some kinds of gag rules; federal regulation by ERISA compete for the right to shape the 'laws' that will govern medical practice (Heimer 1999). Just as lawyers develop and promote model codes, so physicians and other medical experts develop model medical protocols and attempt to convince others that one set of routines or protocols is superior to another. This contest over expertise and legitimacy takes place on several planes simultaneously. Medical experts compete with legal experts; professional bodies compete with one another as well as with commercial enterprises in the business of producing guidelines; hospital administrators and medical caregivers struggle over whether rules that improve the physical health of patients will also improve the fiscal health of the hospital; international regulatory bodies vie with national regulators.

Although we have distinguished between rules about what kind of care a patient should receive, rules about how research should be conducted and rules about the relationships among healthcare providers, healthcare organizations and patients, these rules have intertwined histories. Only in recent times, for instance, have these rules been elaborated in written form and adopted by a variety of domestic and international professional, legal and non-governmental organizations. Along with this codification has come a more pronounced split between healthcare providers, interested especially in clinical practice guidelines, medical researchers, interested especially in research rules, and medical administrators, interested especially in governance protocols. To be sure, the three sets of rules continue to be intertwined, with important common elements (e.g. informed consent is a key part of each), but they now have separate constituencies and address different kinds of risks. Because the rationalization represented in all three kinds of rules is fundamentally grounded in establishing a sound, defensible, 'scientific' basis for medical practice, we open our discussion of historical matters by focusing on changes in how research findings were reflected in rules about treatment as research became increasingly distinct from caregiving, and risks to research subjects were distinguished from those faced by patients.

Codification of medical knowledge in clinical practice guidelines

In reviewing the recent history of clinical practice guidelines, we focus particularly on the period when medical knowledge began to be codified in guidelines and when scientific findings began to be reviewed and compared in meta studies that summarized overall conclusions about best practices in particular fields. The Institute of Medicine's Committee on Clinical Practice Guidelines defines clinical practice guidelines (CPGs) as 'systematically developed statements to assist practitioner and patient decisions about appropriate health care for specific circumstances' (Institute of Medicine, Committee on Clinical Practice Guidelines, 1992, cited in Rosoff 2001: 308).[4] According to Dracup (1996) in an article on nursing, clinical practice guidelines are simply the most recent approach to standardization. In the 1960s, it was hospital policy and procedure manuals. In the 1970s, hospitals and nursing associations focused on developing standards of care. In the 1980s, the focus was on computers and algorithms (Dracup 1996: 41). All of these can be generally grouped under the heading of clinical protocols.

Recent history of clinical protocols and medical discourse

Controlling actions through written rules is an ancient idea, making the history of clinical protocols difficult to circumscribe (Berg 1997). As early as fourth century BC, Plato commented on the creation (by panels) of codified rules to govern clinicians' practice, even (in *The Statesman*) anticipating the role of law in ensuring compliance (Hurwitz 1999). Some of the earliest guidelines were practice parameters produced by speciality groups more than fifty years ago.[5] Contemporary clinical guidelines are concerned with ensuring 'appropriate' treatment and are linked to the shift to evidence-based medicine. Evidence-based medicine involves making decisions about individual patients using up-to-date scientific evidence (Rosoff 2001; Mulrow and Lohr 2001). It relies on outcomes research, the use of systematic methods and statistical techniques to study the effect of diagnostic and therapeutic techniques on patients (Rosoff 2001). Most

---

[4] See also Marshall et al. (2000). Clinical practice guidelines are one embodiment of evidence-based medicine and the two terms are often used interchangeably.

[5] The American Academy of Pediatrics produced its first set of practice parameters in 1938 (GAO 1991). Other speciality societies also produced guidelines before the recent guideline boom of the 1990s: the American College of Obstetrics and Gynecology in 1959, American College of Physicians in 1980, American Society of Anesthesiologists in 1986, American College of Emergency Physicians in 1987.

contemporary clinical practice guidelines are – or at least claim to be – evidence-based. In the past, standards were more likely to be based on physician experience, a practice some have characterized as 'eminence-based medicine' (Millenson 1999).

Although it has only recently gained legitimacy, evidence-based medicine is not an entirely new concept. Similar ideas were championed by such luminaries as Florence Nightingale and Ernest Amory Codman. Nightingale argued for what she called 'information-based medicine'. Her 1858 *Proposal for Improved Statistics of Surgical Operations* called for uniform reporting and comparison of the outcomes of all surgeries in Britain (Millenson 1999: 141). In the early twentieth century, Ernest Amory Codman's 'end result idea' called for measuring patient outcomes and standardizing care (Millenson 1999).[6]

Codman's 'end result idea' was influenced by Taylorism and the 1910 Flexnor Report on medical education. The reforms proposed by the influential Flexnor Report were supported by the American Medical Association, the Carnegie Foundation and the Rockefeller Foundation. Medical education was standardized and much more strongly grounded in science. The lack of standardization in education threatened the legitimacy of the medical profession in a way that the lack of standardization in medical practice apparently did not. Codman's attempt to standardize medical practice was not very successful.[7]

In the past fifty years, scientific research, and outcomes research in particular, has become more central to medical practice and policy. Numerous changes in the funding and organization of science and medicine have made possible an expansion in the volume of scientific research and in its applicability to medicine. Federal funds for research skyrocketed in the post-Second World War era, increasing from

---

[6] Codman was among the group of physicians that founded the American College of Surgeons (ACS) in 1912 (Millenson 1999). The American College of Surgeons was the major organization that set standards and surveyed hospitals (though never making the survey results public) until the Joint Commission (JCAHO) was established in the 1950s.

[7] Millenson (1999) argues that one factor working against systematic improvements in patient care is that the number of people dying from medical error paled in comparison with the ravages of disease and war in the early twentieth century. The First World War killed 10 million people. Following the war, thousands, even millions, of people were dying from diseases that doctors could do little to treat. Polio, for instance, killed 6,000 people in the United States and the 'Spanish flu' killed 30 million worldwide.

US$180,000 a year in 1945 to $46 million in 1950. By the 1990s, the annual medical research expenditure in the US had reached $50 billion (Mulrow and Lohr 2001). The second half of the twentieth century also saw the rise of epidemiology and clinical trials using human subjects. The proliferation of human subjects research (there were 250,000 clinical trials in the 1990s alone) has made medical research more directly applicable to medical care (Mulrow and Lohr 2001). Clinical practice guidelines are a crucial technology for translating medical research into medical practice.

Variability studies are an important source of standardization in the provision of healthcare. Studies of the variability in rates of tonsillectomies were published as early as 1934; others were published in the 1950s. But according to Millenson (1999), these variability studies did not receive widespread public attention until the 1970s. One of the biggest was the National Halothane Study of patient records, supported by the National Academies of Science, the US Public Health Service and medical professional societies (Millenson 1999). Although its objective was to determine whether halothane was more dangerous than other anaesthetics, the study found something quite startling: large variations in surgery mortality rates among regions and institutions. Although the government sponsors of the study were reluctant to attribute these differences to the quality of care, Stanford's Institutional Differences Study later evaluated the results of the Halothane Study and concluded that there was variation in the quality of care at different hospitals.

Among the pioneers in variability studies and outcomes research were John Wennberg and Alan Gittelsohn at Dartmouth Medical School, who completed a variability study of surgery rates in Vermont in 1968 (Matthews 1999). Wennberg's research was later picked up by a group of physicians and statisticians at Harvard who had begun applying decision analysis and statistical and economic theory to medical decision making in the early 1970s. Although Wennberg's variability research was somewhat influential in the medical field in the 1970s, his work was not on the public agenda until 1984. Following the publication of his research on variability in treatment practices in *Health Affairs* in 1984, the US Senate convened a hearing on variability in medical practice and invited Wennberg to speak (Millenson 1999). Meanwhile, researchers at Rand developed and popularized methods for measuring the quality and appropriateness of medical interventions. In their early research on carotid surgery to prevent strokes, they found that just over 30 per cent of surgeries were 'inappropriate' (Matthews 1999, Millenson 1999). Their work was cited in the Shattuck Lecture of 1988, in which Paul M. Ellwood, a policy-oriented physician, argued for additional outcomes research to 'move medicine forward as a sound applied biologic and social science' (Matthews 1999: 282). Since the late 1980s, outcomes research and guideline production have proliferated.

With the rise of clinical practice guidelines, notions about the problems of healthcare have shifted (or expanded). The quality of physicians' diagnostic and treatment decisions has been called into question and attention has been given to ensuring that physicians make rational, scientific decisions.

To recapitulate more analytically, although this history reflects a concern with the quality of physicians' diagnostic and treatment decisions, notions about the source of the problem and, therefore, the appropriate solutions have shifted. Just after the Second World War, most observers attributed the problems of medicine to external sources. In fact, one of the early protocols was developed to evaluate disability within the competing demands of the Social Security Administration and the Veterans Administration. Unlike later guidelines, it was developed to deal with complex external factors and did not imply that doctors' decision-making techniques were problematic (Berg 1997). Soon after the Second World War, the rise of scientific research led to a concern with the lack of uniformity in records and terminology. Uniformity, it was argued, would improve medical practice and the production of knowledge. Uniform records and nomenclature (especially the *Standard Nomenclature of Disease*) would 'fit medical practice more smoothly into the rapidly expanding postwar research enterprise' (Berg 1997: 21–22, citing Marks 1988). Still, within this discourse, 'scientific medicine' referred to the scientific base of medicine.

A shift occurred in the 1960s' and 1970s' work of Alvan Feinstein and Lawrence Weed, who depicted the practice of medicine as having the same structure as scientific research activity. They characterized clinical management as nearly identical to the form of the experiment: 'a doctor defines, separates, clarifies, records, and audits just as much as a scientist' (Berg 1997: 22). Crucially, they argued that the flaw of medicine was not external forces or inconsistent record keeping but the failure of clinicians to follow the scientific method. It was within this discourse that 'tools to "support" medical action [were] spoken of' (Berg 1997: 35). 'Now that the distinctive components of the scientific task of diagnosis are laid bare,' Berg continued, '... the protocol becomes the natural route to adequate performance of the science of medical practice' (1997: 35). The 'problem' of medicine was now internal rather than external, and quality of care could be improved with 'decision support techniques ... to aid the physician's floundering mind, not to amend the structure of medical action' (Berg 1997: 37). The problem of the 1980s and 1990s was thus to develop tools to help doctors make rational decisions.[8]

Production of clinical practice guidelines

An increasing number of groups have been developing practice guidelines since the 1980s. In 1990, twenty-six physician groups were involved in developing clinical practice guidelines and they had created 700 guidelines; by 1994, more than sixty organizations were producing guidelines and the number had grown to more than 1,600 (Sheetz 1997: 1348, citing Ayres 1994 and Walker et al. 1994). O'Brien et al. (2000: 1078) describe an 'explosion' of clinical practice guidelines. According to the AMA's (1996) *Directory of Practice Parameters*, 1,700 clinical practice guidelines have been created since 1970; more than three-quarters were developed after 1990 and almost half were developed between 1993 and 1995 (O'Brien et al. 2000: 1078). Along with this numerical increase has come a shift in form. Although they were once merely informative, clinical practice guidelines are now behaviour-modification tools aimed at shaping and correcting the activities of care providers and patients.

In the United States, a 'medical effectiveness coalition' of healthcare providers and payers supports clinical guidelines (Grogan et al. 1994). Three groups do the bulk of clinical guideline development: federal and state agencies, professional speciality groups and societies, and third-party payers (Merz 1993). Large research organizations also produce some guidelines. In the late 1980s, states, the primary regulators of hospitals and other healthcare settings, began developing guidelines for

---

[8] Berg (1997: 52) discusses three kinds of tools: computer-based decision tools, decision-analytic techniques and protocols. He uses protocol as a general term that includes algorithms, clinical practice guidelines, practice policies, etc.

cost-reduction and quality-assurance purposes (e.g. the 1988 Minnesota Clinical Comparison and Assessment Project) (Merz 1993: 307). More recently, malpractice insurers have begun producing guidelines. These 'fall somewhere between payer guidelines and professional societies' guidelines on the continuum of authoritativeness' (Mello 2001: 652).

As the largest payer of healthcare in the United States, the federal government has funded heavily the 'medical effectiveness movement', giving the Agency for Health Care Policy and Research $60 million in 1991 for outcome studies to develop guidelines. Congress established the Agency for Health Care Policy and Research (now the Agency for Healthcare Research and Quality or AHRQ) (PL 101–239) in 1989 to 'conduct and support research with respect to the outcomes, effectiveness, and appropriateness of health care services and procedures' (101 PL 239 §(a)(1)(A)). Until 1999, the Agency's mandate was to support the development of clinical practice guidelines. Congress established criteria for developing guidelines and instructed the Agency to begin by working on guidelines for procedures that affected substantial numbers of people or were especially costly (§1142 (a)(3)(b)(1)). In general, the Agency targets treatments that account for the bulk of Medicare expenditures and observers worry that 'costs, not quality of medical care, are driving the federal government's push for guideline development' (see, for example, Grogan et al. 1994: 8).

In its early years, the Agency rebutted critics by arguing that it produced 'guidelines' not 'standards' and noting that these less prescriptive guidelines could be used by others to produce more prescriptive standards (Hastings 1993). More recently, the AHRQ has completely dropped the language of guidelines in favour of even less prescriptive 'outcomes studies'. The AHRQ began moving away from guideline production in 1996 and now funds research – which, admittedly, may be used to produce guidelines. In 1997, the Agency established twelve evidence-based practice centres (EPCs), giving them the task of developing reports on clinical topics that are 'common, expensive, and/or significant for the Medicare and Medicaid populations' (Agency for Healthcare Research and Quality 2003). Potential users of these reports include 'clinicians, medical and professional associations, health system managers, researchers, group purchasers, program managers, consumer organizations, and policymakers' (Agency for Healthcare Research and Quality 2003). Importantly, then, two goals are acknowledged: these reports can be used to inform treatment or payment.

In addition to removing the Agency's mandate to support guideline development, the Healthcare Research and Quality Act of 1999 officially changed the Agency's name from the Agency for Health Care Policy and Research to the Agency for Healthcare Research and Quality. The dropping of the word 'policy' was not inconsequential, but was a response to concern that the federal government was mandating standards of care. Several controversies in the mid-1990s shed light on why the AHRQ moved away from funding the development of clinical practice guidelines. The AHRQ had funded some research that went against the interests of drug companies, speciality groups and patient advocacy groups. For example, in AHRQ-funded research, Dr Richard Deyo and colleagues reviewed published studies and reported that spinal fusion surgery might not be effective (Deyo et al. 1997). In response, the North American Spine Society created a lobbying group called the Center for Patient Advocacy and began a Congressional letter-writing campaign challenging the research. Dr Kanovitz, the leader of the Center, said his group called for the abolition of the AHRQ because its methodology was 'absurd'. According to Dr Deyo, this dispute led to a 25 per cent cut in the Agency's budget and an end to its clinical guidelines work (Kolata 1997; see Deyo et al. 1997 for a discussion of similar controversies).

Evidence-based medicine and guideline production have not been limited to American healthcare. The production of clinical practice guidelines has become an industry in most developed countries. Following a 1990 report by the US Institute of Medicine (IOM), many countries set up national bodies for clinical practice guidelines (Durieux et al. 2000: 969).[9] Alongside this growth came the development of clinical practice guideline appraisal instruments. In 1990, IOM developed eight 'desirable characteristics' of clinical practice guidelines. These have been accepted by AHRQ and have informed an appraisal instrument developed by AGREE (Appraisal of Guidelines Research and Evaluation), an international consortium of researchers (Graham et al. 2000).

Clinical rules and the collective authority of physicians

In addition to improving quality of care, clinical guidelines have been developed by medical speciality groups to 'defend against a variety of

---

[9] See Institute of Medicine, Committee to Advise the Public Health Service on Clinical Practice Guidelines (1990).

forces outside their speciality' including other speciality groups and third-party payers (Merz 1993: 308). Guidelines have also been produced, for instance, by the American College of Physicians and the AMA as risk management tools to reduce malpractice costs (Merz 1993). In 1986, the American Society of Anesthesiologists created guidelines targeted at practices that produce the most malpractice claims; malpractice claims subsequently decreased. Other speciality areas, e.g. ophthalmology, obstetrics and gynaecology, and cardiology, have followed suit (Merz 1993: 308). At least in theory, clinical practice guidelines might mitigate the 'crisis' of malpractice litigation in a variety of ways: they could reduce defensive medicine, lower the costs of achieving 'correct' outcomes in malpractice litigation, and decrease the incidence of 'incorrect' outcomes (Mello 2001). Healthcare payers and malpractice insurers often use clinical practice guidelines to counter 'defensive medicine', by which they mean overtreating patients to reduce exposure to liability. Some observers expected that clinical practice guidelines would reduce defensive medicine by reducing physician anxiety about being sued (Field and Lohr 1992).[10] However, some physicians are concerned that the spread of evidence-based medicine and clinical protocols may actually increase their exposure to risk (Rosoff 2001).

Clinical guidelines can potentially be used as both 'swords' and 'shields' in medical malpractice litigation, though legislatures in some cases specify that clinical guidelines can be used for only one of these purposes. Legislative protection against malpractice liability for physicians who give care conforming to standards dates back to the creation of professional standards review organizations (PSROs) in 1972 (PL 92–703) (Field and Lohr 1992). Physicians cannot be held liable if they have shown 'due care' and their care complies with the norms of the PSRO (129).[11] However, as of 1989 no physician had used this defence (Field and Lohr 1992 citing Gosfield 1989). More recently, legislatures in Maine, Minnesota, Kentucky and Florida have passed statutes about the use of clinical practice guidelines. Maine and Minnesota laws permit only defensive uses of guidelines; Florida allows use by both

---

[10] A 1990 US Congressional report on defensive medicine cited an AMA estimate that defensive medicine cost $11.7 billion in 1985 and a Health Care Finance Administration estimate that defensive medicine cost Medicare $2.5 billion in 1987 (Field and Lohr 1992).

[11] Although the names of these organizations have changed and their regulatory duties have become stricter, this particular provision has stayed the same.

defendants and plaintiffs (although Florida's programme is limited to Caesarian deliveries) (Rosoff 2001). Despite Maine's comprehensive guideline programme, between 1992 and 1999 only one physician used a guideline as a defence in Maine; the pre-litigation screening mandated by the Maine Medical Malpractice Demonstration Project may have eliminated other cases, of course (Rosoff 2001).

How courts will use treatment guidelines remains unclear. They might, for instance, treat a clinical guideline as the definitive standard of care or simply as evidence of a standard of care (Rosoff 2001). Scholarship on the potential effect of clinical practice guidelines is more voluminous than work on the actual impact of guidelines. According to a study by Hyams et al. (1996), clinical practice guidelines helped to establish the standard of care in less than 7 per cent of malpractice cases between 1980 and 1994. Plaintiffs used CPGs more often than defendants. However, clinical practice guidelines may have substantial pre-litigation effects. About half of malpractice attorneys were aware of CPGs, and some used them in deciding whether or not to take cases (Hyams et al. 1996). Thus, CPGs were useful screening devices for reducing a malpractice lawyer's risk in pursuing a case.

If the pressure from patients to participate in medical decision making emphasizes the non-technical aspects of those decisions, the responses of medical practitioners to medical malpractice suits have emphasized the technical aspects of medical decision making. If in early medical malpractice suits physicians stood essentially alone before the court, they now stand in the company of their peers. As the importance of the standard of care as a tool in malpractice defences (and, of course, therefore as a tool in plaintiff claims) became clear, physicians put more effort into creating comprehensive, well-articulated standards of care. Ironically, protecting physician discretion from lay intrusion has often meant limiting discretion through the formulation of rules by physician peers.

This is especially true of the more strictly medical protocols – clinical practice guidelines – because they are tools that shore up physicians' claims that medical decision making is a *technical* matter. That physicians as a group can show that they have something to say about such matters as when, how and by whom medications should be administered makes three distinct statements: (1) that physicians have a body of information and aggregated experience that provides an adequate empirical foundation for assertions about best practices, (2) that physicians have reviewed and systematized this knowledge, and (3) that statements about best practices do not rest on the expertise of a single practitioner but carry the weight of collective authority conferred through a process of critical peer review.

These then are statements about the adequacy of an empirical base, a systematic and scientific analysis, and authority conferred by peer review. The capacity to produce protocols is an important social accomplishment, the culmination of the process, described so well by Starr (1982, especially 54–9 and 79–144), of convincing relevant audiences that the profession of medicine is *legitimately complex*, rather than artificially complex. Starr (1982: 18) argues that the high status (and high income) of physicians has depended on establishing the cultural authority of medicine. In a democratic society, professionalism had to be 'reconstructed around the claim to technical competence, gained through standardized training and evaluation'; the status-based claims that produced at least the appearance of trust in more hierarchically ordered European societies did not work in America. Americans had to be convinced that medical knowledge was something more than common sense and that medical licensure was about assessing skill rather than just about protecting a professional monopoly. Developments in medical science and the construction of a medical curriculum on a foundation of basic training in science were crucial to the consolidation of medical authority that occurred between 1850 and 1930.

Clinical practice guidelines demonstrate the legitimate complexity of medicine in a particular area. They also implicitly challenge others' rights to participate. The existence of a protocol challenges others to display their data, explain their reasoning and offer evidence that their claims are supported by reputable others. Insofar as malpractice suits have encouraged the development of more protocols, they have increased the inequality between lay and professional by encouraging medical practitioners to shore up their claims that medical decision making requires *medical* expertise and is legitimately restricted to experts. If we have reached consensus about what makes a medical field legitimate and the existence of protocols is part of that, then professionals who can claim to be following a protocol are the winners in this contest.

This account illustrates how norms develop through a process of action and reaction in which the meta rules about how one recognizes 'technical' matters – and how one makes them even more authoritatively 'technical'– have important effects. Attempting to gain some measure of control over medical care, patients brought suits against physicians.

Because these disputes were settled in legal arenas, some standard had to be established to evaluate whether physicians had or had not acted reasonably. In effect, the standard of care in medicine has evolved as the medical equivalent of a 'reasonable man' standard in other tort cases.

Once the courts clarified that providing care in line with the 'standard of care' would often be defensible, physicians began working to ensure that the standard, on the one hand, was absolutely clear and, on the other, would not be challenged by a physician or scientist testifying for the plaintiff. Clarifying the legal rule also clarified the direction in which the medical rules had to evolve if medical practice was to be legally defensible and if medical professionals were to garner the support of the legal profession. The development of medical protocols has 'naturalized' (Douglas 1986) the classification of particular acts as strictly medical by cloaking the outward forms in the trappings of professionalism. It is an important social accomplishment to get some matters defined as strictly technical. When that classification is secure, disputes will be about whether a physician met the standard and whether the standard was appropriate, but not over who should define the standard. Once a classification as technical is firmly established, attention is directed *to* some questions and *away* from others. The terrain that is under attack is reduced and practitioners can concentrate on those few areas where defence is needed.

But why, one might reasonably ask, is legal defensibility so crucial in the practice of medicine? Do physicians in fact care whether what they are doing is legally acceptable? Zussman (1992) suggests that they do, and other accounts of medical practice agree. 'Is it legal?' is an easier question to answer than 'Is it moral?' and has implications for such practical matters as insurance rates and law suits. A physician may or may not be concerned about legal questions, but the organizations in which physicians work care deeply. A single malpractice suit, particularly when reinforced by an occasional threat of a suit, encourages talk about what should be written into the medical record and what should not, what language should be used, who should be present at meetings (e.g. as witnesses) and the like. All this is reinforced by the JCAHO, whose accreditation is important in the process of securing malpractice insurance.

What we see here is a mutually constitutive process in which 'the intersection of legality and other social structures ... provides legality with supplemental meanings and resources that do not derive from legal practices alone' (Ewick and Silbey 1998: 50). Arguments about the technical nature of medical decisions are stronger because they can reference legal decisions in which medical protocols play a prominent role. Likewise, the legal defence of protocol-based medical practice draws some of its force from claims that medical decision making has a strong technical component. It is also important for both sources of legitimacy that neither the law nor medical protocols are 'identifiably the product of any *particular* individual or group' (as Greenhouse 1989: 1640 says about the law).

Although malpractice suits have led to an elaboration of medical protocols that protect physician autonomy, these same protocols have had other effects. Firstly, the process of developing protocols has probably, by itself, improved medical practice by forcing physicians to systematize knowledge and defend claims about the appropriate use of particular procedures or medications. Although the general rule may be that legally defensible medicine is medical care that meets the published standard of care, courts have sometimes questioned the appropriateness of medical standards. In a few exceptional cases (e.g. *Helling* v. *Carey*, 83 Wash. 2d 514, 519 P. 2d 981 [1974]), they have found physicians at fault even when they provided care that met the current standard. In one important case, Gail Kalmowitz, who became blind from the oxygen therapy she received as a premature infant in 1952, sued even though she had received standard care.[12] Questions about the appropriateness of standards are particularly difficult in cutting-edge fields, such as neonatology (as in the Kalmowitz example), or in the treatment of newly discovered diseases, such as HIV/AIDS, where standards are evolving. These anomalous decisions that challenge the standard of care encourage patients and their families to take physicians to court when they think they could have done better and remind physicians of the difference between the generalization represented in a protocol and the needs of individual patients. But this in turn persuades physicians to revisit protocols and ask whether they remain scientifically defensible.

In sum, then, the defence of professional autonomy has evolved from certification of the arbitrary authority of 'credentialled' individual

---

[12] Kalmowitz had persuaded the jury, but accepted a settlement just before the verdict was announced (O'Connell 1979). Many premature infants were blinded during the 1940s and 1950s, but not until 1956 did physicians understand that oxygen therapy was the problem. Silverman (1980) argues that physicians could have reached the answer sooner had they been more careful scientists.

experts to the certified rules and guidelines that reflect a consensus about the current state of medical knowledge. A physician may still be seen to have fallen short, but that will now more often be falling short of standards developed by his or her peers rather than falling short of the judge or jury's notion of good practice.

Rules for the conduct of research on human beings

Rules for the conduct of research go far beyond the 'protocols' that are the instructions for carrying out specific studies (the technical recipes, so to speak). Instead, the standards for conducting valid, ethical, scientifically sound medical research focus on multiple components of the process (informed consent, participant selection, participant and researcher compensation, rules for withdrawal, cultural sensitivity) and come from multiple institutional sites (treatises of multinational bodies, professional organizations, institutional review boards, government committees, commercial enterprises, legal cases, patient advocacy).

Here we briefly examine the history of rules for the conduct of medical research using human subjects, looking at changes in thinking about risk. The relationship between science and medicine has been thoroughly transformed over the last couple of centuries. Although our focus is on medical experimentation, it is wise to remember that the historical relationship between science and medicine also properly includes non-experimental elements, including especially the scientization of medical training, the development of the germ theory of disease and aseptic surgical techniques, and epidemiology.

Among the important effects of the scientization of medicine has been some loss of autonomy for physicians, a topic dealt with above in our discussion of clinical guidelines. Physician competence has ceased to be simply a matter of experience (autonomous clinical judgement improving over time), but has come to depend on keeping abreast of the latest research and adhering to professional and institutional guidelines. Though clinicians may not be entirely sanguine about this decrease in autonomy, they are nevertheless obligated to attend to the findings of scientists, the scientifically grounded dictates of administrators, and the committees charged with formulating the consensus for their peers. But the relationship between clinical care and medical science goes well beyond this dependence of clinical guidelines on research. Because many new drugs and cutting-edge therapies are available only on an experimental basis, many physicians participate in research at least indirectly by informing their patients about opportunities to enrol in studies, a practice that can seem both exploitive (supplying the bodies on which medical experiments can be performed) and benevolent (securing precious drugs and medical attention for desperate patients). Given this layered symbiosis of clinical care and clinical research, rules about the conduct of research necessarily overlap with clinical guidelines.

At least until recently, the regulation of medical research has tended to be reactive rather than proactive. Bursts of regulatory activity have followed scientific atrocities both in the United States and abroad (Tuskegee, Nazi Germany). Following revelations of lapses, more than a dozen major research institutions in the United States had projects shut down by the National Institutes of Health (NIH) Office for Protection from Research Risks (OPRR) during a two-year period in the 1990s (Phillips, D. F. 2000). Whenever a serious medical error or ethical lapse comes to light, these touchstone historical cases are discussed alongside contemporary cases (see, for example, Altman 2003). In the international arena, there is lively debate about the legitimacy of conducting research in the developing world, particularly Africa, that would not pass ethical muster in richer countries (see, for example, Rothman 2000). Admittedly, the higher risks of disease in developing countries justify higher-risk research (under the venerable principle of lesser harm), but those higher background risks also tend to make a mockery of informed consent. Yet one would be hard pressed to claim that people without access to basic necessities or good healthcare were making completely uncoerced choices to participate in medical experiments. Researchers worry about whether history will judge them harshly for exploiting vulnerable populations or kindly for seeking cures that might save countless lives. Will they be vilified like the Tuskegee syphilis researchers or lauded as Pasteur was when he formulated the rabies vaccine? As we argue below, this shift from reactive regulation to proactive regulation has coincided with an expanded sense of who is at risk in medical experimentation.

A brief history of research rules

Clinical trials in the public health tradition occurred as early as the 1740s, when James Lind tested lemons as a treatment for scurvy.

However, the scientific revolution in medicine did not occur until the last quarter of the nineteenth century with the rise of the medical sciences (bacteriology, physiology, physiological chemistry, pharmacology) (Marks 1997). Indeed, Fred Banting's experimental use of insulin in the 1920s and the invention of the diphtheria anti-toxin were the most successful therapeutic innovations encountered by physicians from the 1880s to the 1930s (Marks 1997).

These new therapies were the product of both the laboratory and the market. As new serums and tonics became available to physicians, turn-of-the-century therapeutic reformers railed against the corrupting effect of drug company advertisements directed at laymen and physicians alike (Marks 1997; Hilts 2003). Reformers urged a more scientific approach, arguing that what practitioners needed to improve therapies was sound knowledge of a drug's uses and effects – not drug company advertising. Based on a belief that science could unite medical practitioners and researchers, the intellectual programme for 'rational therapeutics', inspired especially by Claude Bernard, began in the late 1860s with medical school professors in several European countries (Marks 1997). The invasion of medicine by science was slower in the United States with its fragmented medical educational system and loose licensing.

Reform entailed the production of a medical community amenable to scientific research. According to Marks (1997: 26): 'A rational therapeutics required not only a scientific assessment of the accomplishments and limitations of specific drugs, but practitioners capable of recognizing and acknowledging those limitations in their practice.' The AMA published its first set of standards for medical schools in 1905 and began inspections the next year. Physicians had to be trained – and sometimes pressured – to use research in their practice. Whether through licensure or education, professional physicians sought to use science to distinguish themselves from 'quacks'. Legal and professional standards for restricting drug promotion served to protect consumers from dangerous medications while making pharmaceutical claims a subject which only the scientifically trained physician could legitimately assess.

Linking medical research to the bedside involved a shift in the practice of research. By 1900, drugs were regularly tested on animals, but clinical scepticism made human research the ultimate test of a new drug (Marks 1997: 33–4). The use of human subjects raised both

practical and ethical dilemmas. The AMA Council on Pharmacy and
Chemistry had difficulty collecting clinical data and regulating the use
of drugs it deemed 'experimental' or 'provisional' (Marks 1997: 35).
The Council also met obstacles in its efforts to fund research. In 1911
the Council began giving research grants for pharmacological studies,
though the funding ultimately went to relatively small studies rather
than to studies that could independently assess manufacturers' claims
(Marks 1997: 36).

American anti-vivisectionists and other moral crusaders played an
important role in raising moral questions that were only gradually
addressed by professional societies and regulatory bodies. In the period
before the Second World War, the anti-vivisectionists spurred public
and professional debates over moral issues raised by experimentation
on humans (Lederer 1995). They criticized the Johns Hopkins and
Harvard dissection labs for exposing medical students to cruelty to
animals and the gore of dissection, worried that this training would
promote a callous attitude, whether the bodies on which physicians
worked were animal or human (Lederer 1995: 30). The replacement of
physicians by scientists, they suggested, would make humans vulnerable to non-therapeutic experimentation.[13] With these concerns in
mind, anti-vivisectionists advocated governmental restrictions on animal experimentation. The medical community had more than just a
practical reason for protecting their right to experiment on animals,
however. Animal dissection had become an emblem of therapeutic
reform and the laboratory became increasingly important as reformers
insisted that medical education and medical practice must be grounded
in science (Lederer 1995: 54). It wasn't clear, then, how to be simultaneously scientific and ethical.

Especially controversial were medical experiments involving
patients. Lederer (1995) describes several controversial instances of
physicians experimenting on patients without their consent prior to
1930. In *Schloendorff v. Society of New York Hospital*, a woman sued
after a surgical procedure was performed without her consent.[14]
Although the ruling did not make the hospital liable for the actions of

[13] Interestingly, it was George Bernard Shaw who coined the term 'human guinea
pig' in the early twentieth century, making clear the link between animal and
human experimentation (Bynum 1988).
[14] The Schloendorff rule, written in 1914 by Judge Cordozo, is recognized in almost
all jurisdictions. The decision is usually taken to mean that a competent adult has

its staff member, the possibility of legal action encouraged hospital administrators and pathologists to make physicians obtain written consent from families even for post-mortem operations on their relations (Lederer 1995: 16–17). The first research study to use written consent forms was the US Army Yellow Fever Commission's investigation in Cuba in 1898 to 1901 (Lederer 1995).[15] The consent form exaggerated the possibility of contracting the disease ('... it being entirely impossible for him to avoid the infection ...') and underplayed the danger that the disease posed (Lederer 1995: 21). The practice of paying subjects for their participation was established before the Civil War and had become routine by the 1920s and 1930s (Lederer 1995: 115). American soldiers received no financial compensation for their participation in the yellow fever study while other subjects, some of whom were Spanish immigrants, were offered $100 in gold, free healthcare and another $100 if they contracted yellow fever (Lederer 1995: 20). The yellow fever study raises issues about the use of deception and coercion in obtaining consent from patients. At a time when more soldiers died of disease than active combat, the military and the physicians who ran the study focused on the risk to society over the risk to the research subjects.

In the early twentieth century, researchers had little or no official guidance on many matters now regarded as core ethical issues. In fact, there was debate over whether to inform patients that they were participating in an experiment. So-called 'benevolent deception' in successful experiments was easily forgiven (Lederer 1995: 23). According to Lederer (1995), by the 1930s the public had confidence in the medical profession – a real change from the turn of the century – and for many people this obviated the need for formal regulation. Although the medical research community considered adopting a formal code of ethics for human subjects research, they ultimately rejected it in favour of strategies designed to limit the damage of physicians who seemed to transgress professional standards. 'Taking responsibility for the welfare of the subject, obtaining prior consent of the subject or guardian, and being willing to go first continued to

---

the right to refuse medical treatment even when that treatment is life-saving (Hancock 1994).

[15] The Yellow Fever Commission is sometimes referred to as the 'Reed Commission' after team leader Major Walter Reed, army pathologist and bacteriologist (McCarthy 2001; Topper 1997).

be essential to professional definitions of appropriate human experimentation' (Lederer 1995: 138); formal regulation seemed unnecessary. Only in 1946 did the AMA code of ethics add the obligation of the researcher to the subject. However, the AMA code of ethics did not include a formal guideline about voluntary consent of the subject, demand prior animal testing or define the distinction between therapeutic and non-therapeutic experiments until the 1940s (Lederer 1995).

The few professional regulations concerning the ethical conduct of research adopted by the AMA in the pre-Second World War era were oriented more towards protecting physicians. The events of the Second World War changed people's minds about the wisdom of formal regulation. The Nuremberg Code was created in 1947 by the US judges who tried Nazi physicians accused of atrocities (Woodward 1999: 1947; Annas and Grodin 1992). It served as a model for American scientists and ethicists. However, when the US Supreme Court had an opportunity to incorporate that code into a precedent-setting decision, it failed to do so (Morin 1998: 157, note 1). The Helsinki Declaration was created by the World Medical Association in 1964. Adherence to the latter is required by more than 500 medical journals in the 'Uniform Requirements for Manuscripts Submitted to Biomedical Journals' (Woodward 1999: 1947). Although there are differences between these codes, both insist that patient autonomy and patient rights should trump scientific and social goals.

Public attention was again turned towards the ethics of medical research in 1972 following a *New York Times* cover story about the Tuskegee Syphilis Study. Starting in 1932, the US Public Health Service ran the study, tracking but not treating 400 black men infected with syphilis. Although it was known in 1943 that syphilis could be treated with penicillin, the study continued until 1972 with the men being told only that they were being treated for 'bad blood' (Gould 2000). Although the study now seems patently unethical, it is important to remember that this was before the time of the randomized clinical trial and, indeed, statistical analyses were rare in clinical research through the 1940s (Marks 1998: 136). Public outcry about the study led to a Senate hearing, a federal investigation, a lawsuit, new rules about informed consent, the creation of the National Bioethics Institute and (in 1997) a Presidential apology (Reverby 2001).

In 1974 the US Congress passed the National Research Act.[16] The Act mandated formal protections for human subjects, including written consent and the creation of Institutional Review Boards (IRBs) composed of medical and lay persons. Some considerable time elapsed before these policies began to have any effect on research practice. In the intervening period, several controversial reports increased concern about the treatment research subjects, ultimately increasing pressure to implement the National Research Act. In the summer of 1975, the truth about experiments with psychoactive drugs (LSD) became public (Moreno 1999: 9). Several veterans sued the government for the suffering they endured. Subjects had volunteered for the study but they were not told they were taking a psychoactive drug and were not monitored during hallucinations (Moreno 1999: 9). One man's case went to the Supreme Court, which ruled that the Feres Doctrine barred him from suing because his injuries had been incurred during service in the armed forces.[17] In 1978, the Belmont Report was issued by the National

---

[16] The basic DHHS (Department of Health and Human Services) policy for the protection of human research subjects is contained in the Code of Federal Regulations, Title 45, Part 46 (45 CFR 46). It was revised 13 January 1981 and 18 June 1991. In 1991, the 'Common Rule' was adopted as the federal-wide policy for the protection of human subjects. Sixteen federal agencies are signatories to this policy: National Aeronautics and Space Administration (NASA), National Science Foundation (NSF), Environmental Protection Agency (EPA), Agency for International Development (AID), Social Security Administration (SSA), Central Intelligence Agency (CIA), Consumer Product Safety Commission, and the Departments of Agriculture, Commerce, Energy, Housing and Urban Development (HUD), Defense, Education, Veterans Affairs (VA), Transportation, and Health and Human Services (HHS).

There are three basic protections for human subjects in the DHHS regulations: institutional assurances, Institutional Review Board (IRB) review and informed consent. Institutional assurances are required for any institution engaged in federally funded research. Institutional assurance is documentation of institutional commitment to compliance with the Common Rule. It is a method of compliance oversight. The OHRP (Office for Human Research Protections) can recommend the suspension of assurance, which leads to the withdrawal of federal funds. IRBs are necessary because no one can be objective about their own work; researchers tend to overestimate the benefits and underestimate the risks. IRBs must follow the principles of the Belmont Report: beneficence, justice and respect for persons. The regulations require documented informed consent. The eight basic elements of informed consent are contained in 45 CFR 46.116 and the requirements for documentation are in 45 CFR 46.117.

[17] According to Moreno, from 1947 to 1973 the US military recruited an estimated 1,600 German scientists, including several tried at Nuremberg (1999: 15). It should be noted, too, that a general mistrust of governmental institutions

Commission for the Protection of Human Subjects of Biomedical and Behavioral Research. Hospital and university Institutional Review Boards (IRBs) subsequently began the task of approving or rejecting protocols involving human subjects (Lederer, 1995: 140).

These declarations and documents provide a framework for IRBs and researchers in their assessment of rules for the conduct of clinical research.[18] These standards are now being challenged, though, because the meaning and cultural support for these requirements vary from one social context to another. It is far from clear that Western notions of what is ethical can be transported unrevised to non-Western societies (Levine 1991; Loue et al. 1996).

Researchers have long observed limits in their experiments on humans (Lederer 1995; Halpern 2004). However, the formal regulation of research has proceeded by fits and starts, and often it has been more about reducing the risks experienced by researchers, drug manufacturers and consumers rather than those of research subjects. It is important to remember that the failure to codify ethical obligations may not stem from a lack of commitment to ethical behaviour. In fact, Dr Beecher, whose 1966 article exposed the extent of unethical research in the United States, was opposed to formal, codified rules for the conduct of research. He argued that an 'intelligent, informed, conscientious, compassionate and responsible investigator offered the best protection for human research subjects' (Harkness et al. 2001: 366). The case of Nazi experiments during the Second World War also reveals the insufficiency of formal rules. While many scholars trace the origins of the debate over human experimentation to the 1947 Nuremberg Code, German regulation of human experimentation preceded the Code. As of 1931 Germany already regulated experimentation in considerable detail (Morin 1998). Thus, rules by themselves cannot be expected to eliminate the risk to research subjects.

Contemporary debates about medical research

In their haste to create a system, regulators devised a labyrinthine network of regulatory bodies and an arcane and sometimes

emerged after Nixon's resignation and the news stories about CIA activities during the 1950s and 1960s (1999: 9).
[18] Emanuel et al. provide a very useful table of the guidelines on ethics of biomedical research with human subjects (2000: 2702).

inconsistent patchwork of rules. But complex systems also invite abuse when tangles of rules are too difficult to administer or follow. By the late 1990s, both the Helsinki Declaration and the International Guidelines of the Council for International Organizations of Medical Sciences (CIOMS) were under review. In the United States, the National Bioethics Advisory Commission (NBAC), first appointed by Clinton in 1995, is in charge of reviewing federal guidelines regarding human subject experimentation. The Office for Human Research Protections (OHRP, formerly the Office for Protection from Research Risks, or OPRR) reviews and revises guidelines, for instance in 1998 updating the 1981 federal regulations governing expedited review of research (Woodward 1999: 1947).

Much of the debate has focused on inconsistent definitions and interpretations of risk and disagreements about how to solicit and document consent. However, review panels have also noted problems in the practical operation of IRBs. Although regulators envisaged a system involving solo investigators working with government grants at single institutions with a distinct cohort of research subjects, in fact these types of studies constitute a minority of today's research projects. Most are privately funded and involve multi-site trials with large numbers of subjects (Phillips, D. F. 2000: 730). American IRBs are not well structured to review these kinds of projects. As Everett Hughes (1958) famously observed, professionals make routine business of other people's troubles, and the troubles of IRBs have now become the work of new occupations and professional associations. Bodies such as Public Responsibility in Medicine and Research (PRIM&R) and its membership organization Applied Research Ethics National Association (ARENA) agree that IRBs are in trouble and that practical solutions are needed (Phillips, D. F. 2000). Among the proposed solutions are a programme for certifying IRB professionals (including office administrators and chairpersons)[19] and the appointment of data-monitoring committees (DMCs) to relieve IRBs of some of the burden of monitoring. These data-monitoring committees would review interim study data, review study protocols and designs, and make recommendations for continuation, modification or

[19] Information about ARENA's training programmes, workshops and conferences are available at http://www.primr.org/about/overview.html (last viewed on 4 August 2004).

termination. To cover the high cost of performing these reviews, some institutions now charge fees for IRB review.

Part of the problem is the (re)blurring of the line between clinical practice and medical research. Medical research is expanding and information-processing technologies have the potential of turning every patient into a research subject. But blurring has occurred for other reasons as well: patients, desperate for a cure, have little incentive to adhere to a rigid distinction between treatment and research (see, for example, Epstein 1996). They have every reason to seek any 'care' that seems likely to help and to abandon therapies and studies that seem to be failing. Under these circumstances, Miller et al. (1998) argue, the emphasis should be on professional integrity and ethical ways to integrate research and treatment rather than on increased regulatory oversight.

Governance protocols: using clinical practice guidelines for medical management

Healthcare has changed radically in the past few decades. In the past fifty years, American healthcare has become increasingly concentrated and specialized (Scott et al. 2000). Physicians are more likely to practise as members of a healthcare organization than as private practitioners, and these healthcare organizations have increasingly merged into larger administrative systems (Scott et al. 2000: 57). The number of medical speciality groups has increased.

With this concentration has come an expansion in the number and complexity of the rule systems that apply to the provision of healthcare. Speciality groups produce their own sets of clinical guidelines, increasing the overall number. At the same time, specialization may have increased the need for clinical guidelines. Physicians report that clinical guidelines are most useful when they are dealing with health issues outside their speciality (Tanenbaum 1994). Moreover, these more numerous rules are now used for administrative as well as clinical purposes. Although in the not-so-distant past the suggestion that 'there was a deliberate linking of care objectives with cost goals would have been greeted [by physicians] with healthy skepticism at best, but more likely flat denial', now 'health care policy, medical practice and cost of care are no longer considered distinct entities ... [and] clinical practice guidelines are the linchpin that connects them' (O'Brien et al. 2000: 1088 and 1078).

Unlike clinical guidelines and rules about the conduct of research (the first two categories we discuss), governance protocols seem not to be a category of rules recognized as such in the medical world. This may be partly because they have a shorter history and it is also surely because they have not yet received much legal scrutiny. Moreover, the professionals most concerned with these kinds of rules, i.e. hospital administrators, have usually not been thought of as 'real medical people' and so have been accorded less legitimacy than the physicians and scientists who could treat patients, develop cures and evaluate treatment effectiveness. Medicine has come to be big business and, as Starr (1982) predicted, American health professionals have ended up being regulated by corporations more than by the government. Governance protocols are a key part of this corporate regulatory apparatus, though both governmental bodies and private organizations (especially managed-care organizations) have a role in their production.

Although managed-care regulations became especially influential in medical practice in the early 1990s, health-maintenance organizations and rules for rationing care date back to the 1970s. In 1973, Congress passed the Health Maintenance Organization Act, awarding HMOs $145 million in grants and $219 million in loans (Paese and Paese 1999). Although managed-care organizations may take a number of forms, all share the goal of containing the cost of providing health-care.[20] They control costs through the use of a wide variety of governance protocols, including utilization review, gag clauses, referral controls, formularies, capitation and various financial incentives (Allred and Tottenham 1996; Paese and Paese 1999). Utilization review involves reviewing a treatment or diagnosis prior to authorizing reimbursement. With capitation schemes, physicians are paid a pre-defined amount per patient for whatever services they provide. Formularies allow healthcare organizations to monitor and control drug prescriptions, curbing physician discretion. 'Gag clauses' are contractual agreements between physicians and managed-care organizations that, for instance, prohibit physicians from discussing with

---

[20] Battaglia (1997) offers this list of types of managed-care organizations: health-maintenance organizations, preferred provider organizations, physician-hospital organizations, integrated delivery systems, managed-services organizations and combined provider organizations.

patients certain treatment alternatives (not covered by the plan) or from criticizing or discussing some aspects of the managed-care organization (Picinic 1997). Managed-care organizations may also set annual or lifetime limits on treatment (e.g. limiting the number of treatments, days of treatment or expenditure on treatment).

Of all cost-containment methods, utilization review has had the most direct impact on patient care. Utilization review is often closely linked with treatment protocols, making it the cost-containment mechanism with the most potential to influence treatment decisions and clinical standards. Physicians are particularly concerned with this technique of rationing care because it threatens physician autonomy in medical decision making. In utilization review a third party judges medical necessity and the appropriate level of care. Often, healthcare payers translate treatment guidelines into utilization review criteria. Utilization review has rapidly become a key managerial tool, with 10 per cent of insurance plans incorporating some form of utilization management in 1980 and 95 per cent in 1990 (Schlesinger et al. 1996: 256).

In the United States, rather than regulating the entire medical system directly, the federal government imposes regulations indirectly in its capacity as a major payer. Rules are imposed first on Medicare and Medicaid and then diffused throughout the system when hospitals and other healthcare organizations adopt those rules for other parts of their operation in order to reduce complexity. The original Medicare/ Medicaid legislation called for hospital reviews of physician-provided services, essentially allowing physicians to regulate themselves. By 1970, the costs of Medicare/Medicaid had increased to twice the expected budget and the legislature made more direct attempts at control (Campion 1984). As a response to legislators' concerns about the over-utilization of medical care, the AMA proposed the use of peer reviews; these had been used as a teaching tool by the medical profession for about fifty years. Congress created professional standards review organizations, but unlike peer review, PSROs emphasized cost surveillance (Campion 1984). The AMA opposed PSROs and the emphasis on 'norms' of treatment, fearing that the latter would lead to 'cookbook' medicine (Campion 1984: 328). The AMA House of Delegates 'seethed over the PSRO issue' and in his 1973 address, AMA president-elect Malcolm Todd charged that 'PSRO poses greater threat to the private practice of medicine than anything ever developed by the Congress of the United States' (Campion 1984: 330).

Despite resistance to PSROs, physicians were given a great deal of discretion in administering care compared with what was to come. PSROs paid most attention to the 'appropriateness' of hospital admissions and the length of stay (Campion 1984). Standards were relatively loose – applying only to the kinds of medical procedures that were reimbursable and guidelines for how hospitals should monitor activity (Ruggie 1992). This changed in 1983 with the Medicare Prospective Payment System based on Diagnostic Related Groups (DRGs). Based on more than 400 categories of illnesses or diseases, each DRG is associated with a particular level of payment. Although this shift was motivated by a desire to reduce federal regulation, Ruggie (1992) argues that it has in fact increased federal control of medical practice.

We have noted above that the rules for the conduct of research and clinical practice guidelines have tended to merge as new data-collection and information-processing techniques turn 'patients' into 'research subjects'. Scientists use medical care as an opportunity for research. Likewise, governance protocols overlap with clinical practice guidelines as hospital administrators turn tools designed to improve medical practice into administrative tools for controlling costs. Yet, to employ Bosk's (1979) distinctions, clinical practice guidelines concern matters of technique and matters of medical judgement, while governance protocols are more concerned with normative and quasi-normative matters – with the relations between caregivers and their patients and between caregivers and their employers. In the best of circumstances, governance protocols appear to be about quasi-normative matters – rules of procedure that are neutral with respect to medical outcomes, more or less like the preferences of particular surgeons about how incisions should be sutured. But for some patients some of the time, these matters will be consequential. A prohibited expensive test might be just the one that is needed, and a managed-care organization's gag rule prohibiting the physician from informing patients about such tests could then have grave consequences. It is here that quasi-normative shades into normative. And it is here that legal intervention has occurred to restore the information balance between healthcare providers and patients that legislators hoped to establish with informed-consent statutes.[21]

---

[21] The evidence on the importance of gag rules is mixed. Explicit gag rules do not seem to be common, except in US federal government rules prohibiting

To see this point about risk distribution, it is useful to supply a bit of context, firstly about legal rules on negligence, then about medical care. Disputes over who is responsible when an untoward event occurs frequently appear in courts of law, and legislators have attempted to redress imbalances in the distribution of risk. These rules, some statutory, some common law, range from *caveat emptor*, in which buyers rather than sellers bear risks, to strict liability, in which manufacturers rather than consumers bear the risks of defective products. In employment relations, risk-distributing rules have changed over the years from the fellow-servant rule (in which employees received no compensation if accidents were caused by their co-workers) and the contributory negligence rule (in which employers' obligations were reduced, often to nothing, if employees could be held to have contributed to the accident), to workers' compensation rules (in which the costs of workplace accidents are more often covered, albeit stingily, by special-purpose funds). It should be no surprise, then, that rules created in the medical world also attempt to redistribute risk – in this case, away from medical care organizations and physicians. It matters who writes the rules and whether governmental bodies, which may have somewhat more interest in fairness, set limits on how organizational rules, such as governance rules in healthcare organizations, can redistribute risks.

Within the medical world, governmental intervention has taken several forms. Rules about informed consent (now often embodied in statutes), medical neglect (which can be used both by and against patients and their families) and compensation (e.g. by Medicaid and Medicare) all place important limits on private governance protocols.

discussion of abortion in any government-funded programmes (both nationally and internationally) and in US FDA restrictions on distribution of information on off-label uses of licensed drugs. In 1997 the US GAO reviewed the contracts of 529 HMOs and found no clauses specifically restricting physicians from discussing medical options with their patients, though many of the contracts did contain non-disparagement clauses (GAO 1997). Nevertheless, physicians themselves seem to be feeling pressured. Reporting on a 1998 national survey of physicians, Wynia et al. find that over the past year '31 percent reported having sometimes not offered their patients useful services because of perceived coverage restrictions' and within that group, '35 percent reported doing so more often in the most recent year than they did five years ago' (2003: 190). Although many states have passed anti-gag legislation, consumer groups and medical professional associations (such as the American College of Physicians – American Society of Internal Medicine) continue to believe that the issue can be settled only with the passage of a national patients' bill of rights.

Note, though, that many of these limits have not yet been tested in court cases, and until that happens the governance rules of managed-care organizations may continue to operate despite their apparent violation of other rules intended to protect patients. AIDS patients, for instance, might not learn about certain tests because they are not covered by the insurer. They may become uninsured altogether when HMO rules exclude coverage of people with particular conditions, although HIPAA rules (on privacy of medical information) are supposed to prevent this from occuring. And once an AIDS patient becomes disabled, he or she may no longer be accepted as a patient in hospitals and HMOs that no longer accept Medicaid or Medicare.

Any study of the legalization of medicine must look at the discrepancy between 'law on the books' and 'law in action', the law as it is actually implemented and experienced. 'No longer accepting Medicaid patients' is not written into any law, but lower reimbursement levels are. Scholars also have uncovered systematic biases that tend to favour the 'haves' over the 'have nots' and 'repeat players' over 'one shotters' (Galanter 1974, 1999). Moreover, such biases are also manifested in legal consciousness and the kinds of expectations that citizens have about what the legal system can and should do for them, in legal institutions, and in the legal endowments passed on from one generation to the next in constitutions, laws and the everyday practices of the legal system (Ewick and Silbey 1998; Merry 1990; Lempert and Sanders 1986, especially Chapter 13). Somewhat less attention has been given to whether and how a 'tilt' favouring elites, repeat players and the like enters into the production of law. Governance protocols are a good illustration of how biases, which in this case reduce risks to organizations, enter into 'law under construction'.

Comparative rule and guideline making

It would be foolish to assume that rules for the conduct of research and governance protocols work the same way as clinical practice guidelines. Table 4.1 compared the three types of protocols, showing the differences in their purposes, creators and legal foundations. While clinical practice guidelines have been written largely by and for the professionals who practise in medical organizations, other kinds of protocols are less clearly instruments of professional domination.

Rules for the conduct of research, for instance, typically have not originated with the researchers themselves. Nevertheless most researchers now seem to agree that some regulation is needed. Rules about the conduct of research protect researchers from two kinds of harm: (1) the harm that might be produced by overzealous drug companies which might be willing to sacrifice patient welfare or accept shoddy research in their eagerness to get new products to the market, and (2) the harm from less scrupulous researchers willing to cut corners in order to claim priority in scientific discoveries. Recognizing that researchers are lumped together in public consciousness, researchers may accept regulation as a way of reinforcing the commitment of individuals to protecting their collective reputation. In this, rules for the conduct of research may function much like the regulation of nuclear power companies described by Rees (1994). With rules for the conduct of research, the core question is not so much who gets to decide as how to supply public evidence of a sound ethical foundation. Without convincing evidence that researchers are behaving ethically, the whole research enterprise is in jeopardy.

Governance protocols do not tend to be written by medical professionals for the benefit of medical professionals but instead by and on behalf of medical corporations such as insurance companies and managed-care organizations. They are grounded in medical science but written with an eye to managerial objectives. Here Starr's words seem especially prophetic. In resisting governmental regulation, Starr concluded in 1982, physicians have instead ended up with regulation by corporations. Rather than strengthening professional autonomy, governance protocols tend to subordinate physicians and other medical staff to the authority of the medical organization, limiting physicians' rights to prescribe treatments and even to inform patients fully about other options. When faced with corporate regulation, physicians sometimes find themselves allied with patients and seeking the aid of the state. With governance protocols, as with clinical practice guidelines, the struggle is about who gets to decide. Large organizations that employ and pay medical workers are formidable opponents. Although it retains considerable force, an argument that medical professionals know what is best for their patients is harder to sustain in the face of the organizational claim to be looking out for the interests of the group (e.g. in cost control) when those conflict with the best interests of individual patients.

The core (tentative) lesson to be drawn seems to be this: the appropriate strategy for protecting professional autonomy depends on whom one is protecting it from. Protecting professionals from the incursions of lay people such as patients is a very different matter from protecting the legitimacy that garners research dollars. Protecting front-line medical workers from the authority of organizational superiors is a different matter still. All three of these are regulatory problems, matters of contesting and collaborating authorities. In all three instances, at least one player is following a legalistic strategy of rule creation. But we should be careful not to let such labels as 'medical protocol' or 'standard operating procedure' blind us to crucial diversity in how rules have come about, how they are justified, how and by whom they are used.

Conclusion

In this brief look at the historical development of clinical guidelines, rules about the conduct of research and governance rules, we have seen that rules became more elaborate as people began to worry not just about the risks faced by individual patients or research subjects but about those faced by practitioners and the organizations in which they work. When we consider the legalization of medicine as a response to the risks of medical treatment and research, we find a generally legalistic response – an increase in rule production – coupled with considerable variability.

The relationships and activities governed by clinical guidelines are somewhat different from those regulated by governance protocols or rules about the conduct of research. Clinical guidelines focus on people as patients, professionals as caregivers and organizations as coordinators of caregiving. Rules about the conduct of research focus on the person as research subject, the professional as researcher and the organization as an entity that supplies research infrastructure and support. Governance protocols focus on the person as a client, the professional as service provider to the client and an 'employee' of the organization, and the organization as an entity that orchestrates care, arranges contracts, collects bills and distributes any profits.

In all of these instances, rules are crafted with an eye to protecting an essentially vulnerable lay participant. But the purity of this impulse varies somewhat from one type of rule to the other. It may be hard to imagine that the codification of knowledge in clinical guidelines can be regarded as anything other than virtuous. Clinical guidelines protect patients by increasing the likelihood that their caregivers will be able to understand the relations among bodily systems, assimilate new information, track exceptions to general rules and anticipate adverse effects such as drug interactions. But even here the impulse to protect *patients* is joined by an impulse to protect *caregivers*. When dissatisfied patients question the competence of their caregivers, caregivers may turn to guidelines for protection. True, guidelines cannot cover all contingencies and courts very occasionally rule that the standard of care was inappropriate, but they nevertheless offer a measure of reassurance and reduce the risks faced by physicians and other medical professionals. As healthcare has become more organizationally based, concerns about the risks faced by healthcare organizations have been added to concerns with risks to patients and caregivers. When dissatisfied patients sue caregivers, the employing organizations suffer as well, either in the loss of income from patients and their insurers or because organizations are included as parties to the suit. Facing these risks in aggregated form, organizations are especially likely to seek routinized ways to manage them.

Whereas clinical guidelines arguably augment the work of clinicians by helping them do a better job in what they were already fully intending to do, rules for the conduct of research instead are aimed at a conflict of interest between researchers and their human subjects. Although in the long run the interests of research subjects and patients are aligned with those of the research community, in the short run researchers may benefit by exploiting their subjects. Rules for the conduct of research help realign the interests of individual researchers, now obligated to follow the rules, with those of their subjects, who now cannot be subjected to inappropriate risks.

But research guidelines and reviews do more than this: they also protect researchers. While clinical guidelines protect clinicians from a danger emanating from their patients, rules about the conduct of research also protect researchers and research organizations whose reputations can be tainted by the unscrupulous behaviour of even a small proportion of researchers. The good name of particular institutions and of research as an enterprise must be protected, given the dependence of research on the willingness of subjects to participate in medical experiments and granting agencies and pharmaceuticals to support the research. Moreover, in the era of institutional review boards and government oversight, any hint of non-compliance can shut down the research of an entire institution. Rules – especially clear and detailed rules – then become an important component of organizational risk management.

Clinical guidelines are important in shaping the dyadic relationship between clinician and patient. Rules about the conduct of research are important in regulating the relationship of researcher to research subject. They also regulate relationships among researchers, protecting the ethical reputation of medical research, a crucial collective good. In contrast to clinical and research rules, governance rules are less focused on the professional/patient (or research subject) relationship and more concerned with people's relationships with healthcare and insurance organizations. Healthcare organizations especially face risks associated with rising costs. In attempting to control costs, then, they adopt rules about what caregivers cannot do, can do and are obligated to do. Interestingly, clinical guidelines have a downside for healthcare organizations. In establishing a definitive standard of care, these guidelines may act as a shield protecting physicians who have met that standard. But they may also legitimate patient claims that healthcare organizations should be obliged to offer care described in the guideline, whatever the economic constraints faced by the organization.

Medical care and research are no longer just the concern of individual patients, research subjects, scientists or caregivers. In the move from the office of the family doctor or investigator to the managed-care organization or university research office, medicine and research have also become much more 'legalized'. Whatever else they do, rules help organizations manage risks.

5 Organizational responses to risk: the rise of the chief risk officer

MICHAEL POWER

I N 1993 James Lam became chief risk officer (CRO) at the firm of GE Capital. It is widely accepted that Lam was the first to hold a formal role with that title, taking his lead from parallels between the position of the chief information officer and the management of organizational risk more generally (Lam 2000; Hanley 2002). The following decade saw a conspicuous growth of discussion about the role (e.g. Conference Board of Canada 2001: 2) and a number of large companies have established a CRO post or its functional equivalent. These positions signify an organizational commitment to a broad conception of risk management in which the CRO assumes responsibility for the oversight of a wide range of risk management and internal assurance activities, operating in a much broader framework than the purchase of insurance (Dickinson 2001; Lam 2003).

Understanding the CRO as an emergent occupational category within the management and regulation of risk requires that 'analyses of regulation and the sociology of professions can no longer continue to co-exist in ignorance of one another ...' (Dezalay 1995: 6). CROs are both a potential new occupational class and internal regulatory agents or 'merchants of norms' in the competitive field of corporate governance, a field in which internal auditors, insurance specialists, credit controllers and others vie for precedence. As regulation is designed to be more 'responsive' in orientation (Ayres and Braithwaite 1992), the self-governing activities of organizations become an important internal resource for regulatory and management systems alike. Specifically, the corporate internal control and risk management system has become a

Earlier versions of this essay were presented as the third of the 2002 P. D. Leake Lectures, Oxford Business School, and at the Universities of Alberta, Canada and Uppsala, Sweden. I am grateful to Michael Barzelay, Bridget Hutter and Carlos Ramirez for helpful comments.

core focus of regulatory systems (Power 2000), making the CRO a potentially significant, if unwitting, regulatory agent. However, as in the cases of compliance (Weait 1993) and environmental (Rehbinder 1991) officers, a fundamental tension exists for CROs between this public meta-regulatory role and their private function as agents of management (Parker 2002).

This chapter addresses a number of questions about CROs. Who are these senior risk managers and what background and knowledge base do they have? Are CROs a functional response to real risks or a passing management fad? What is the status and function of the role in relation to other corporate control activities and is this a proto-profession, which poses a challenge to traditional functions, such as the finance director?

This argument is structured as follows. The next section describes the rise of the category 'chief risk officer' in the late 1990s, drawing on industry surveys and an eclectic practitioner literature. This is followed by a consideration of the generic significance of organizational control agents. The CRO is one of the latest in a long line of corporate 'officers' created in response to specific problems. The sections that follow offer a more critical analysis of the rise of the CRO. First, the argument addresses the complex position of CROs as potential blamees who are constructing a new moral economy of the organization. Second, the emergence of CROs is discussed from the point of view of a profes-sionalization project, drawing on the work of Andrew Abbott. Overall, the chapter suggests that CROs provide a distinctive form of structur-ing for organizational encounters with risk. This 're-managerialization' of risk (Beck 1992) via CROs is not without risks of its own.

The rise of the CRO: definitions and trends

The rise of the CRO has its roots in a general climate of concern with corporate governance and internal control issues in the 1990s. Specifically, the emergence of enterprise-wide risk management (ERM) and its variants as an organizational change programme and potentially new 'logic of organizing' (Powell 2001: 54) places CROs at the centre of a new concept of organizational control (Power 2004b). A survey of large companies by Miccolis et al. (2001) reported that 15 per cent had a 'complete system for looking at risk across the organiza-tion' and 43 per cent expected to develop one. Additionally, there was a discernible move to a single coordinating executive for the risk management process, namely the CRO.[1]

Specific internal histories have a bearing on the emergence of new organizational roles. Losses on mortgage-backed securities suffered at Merrill Lynch in March 1987 resulted in the creation of one of the first dedicated risk management units in a financial organization. A founding member of this unit was Mark Lawrence, later of ANZ and a contributor to the operational risk debate (Power 2005). However, this early initiative was primarily a defensive need to ensure that 'this must never happen again'. In 1987, very few organizations had an explicit risk management strategy, the role lacked credibility and a collectivized organizational memory of risk events did not exist. In this early setting the risk management function was more or less that of transaction clearance with right of veto, and there were no pressures to institutionalize a new organizational role (Wood 2002). Indeed, over time the unit at Merrill lost power.

A more recent example concerns Amex Financial Advisors, which in August 2001 created the position of CRO (Steve Lobo) as a reaction to huge investment losses. Although the stimulus for organizational change was similar to that of Merrill in 1987, by 2001 the concept of a risk management head had evolved from defensive administrative 'cop' to, at least in aspiration, a partner/adviser in risk taking (Wood 2002). Indeed, in the early 1990s the change in the status of risk management in financial organizations was increasingly driven by concern about the adequacy of risk-related returns on capital and a perceived need to manage and avoid sudden losses at point of origin. This shifted the risk management model out of its back-office cage into a more strategic function. The creation of a dedicated unit headed by a senior role was also a response to regulation, especially Basel 2. However, the rise of the CRO is not confined to the financial sector: Sulzer Medica (Swiss) created the CRO role (Gabor-Paul Ondo) in 2001 following legal losses and Delta Airlines promoted Chris Duncan to CRO with a brief to increase 'visibility of risk' across the company (Hanley 2002).

An early UK survey of risk officers by Ward (2001) sought to compare the aspirations with the realities of the senior risk management role by looking at thirty senior practitioners whose job title

---

[1] See also *Risk Management Reports* 28, no. 9 (2001): 3–5.

included the word 'risk'. The survey was based on membership data supplied by the Association of Insurance and Risk Managers (AIRMIC) and so the results are somewhat biased towards individuals with an insurance background. In contrast to the high-level ideal, Ward notes the dominance of reporting to the finance director, of an insurance cost-reduction rationale for CROs rather than any general enterprise risk management development role, and of a focus on pure (hazard) risks rather than speculative or strategic risks. As far as the operational role of these risk managers is concerned, the survey suggests variability and jurisdictional overlaps with internal auditing. Territorial tensions were also evident in organizational attempts to separate risk manage-ment monitoring functions from risk design/policy issues, except in those cases where the internal audit controlled the overall risk manage-ment agenda. All this suggests considerable organization-specific path dependency in the emerging role of risk officers and related implemen-tation of new risk management mandates.

Another survey by the Conference Board of Canada (2001) was also limited in scope (twenty-one responses from eighty identified CROs) but the direction of the results is instructive. There had been a dramatic rise of articles mentioning the CRO term since 1995, suggesting at least that the category was becoming institutionalized in advance of opera-tional reality. Predictably the role is most evident in energy, utilities and financial services organizations since the mid-1990s, organizations where imperatives to manage complex risks and to respond to loss experiences have focused management attention. These organizations tend to report the CRO as a recent position, established as part of an ERM programme, involving the internal promotion of individuals with strong accounting and audit skills, and also higher-order quantitative skills, particularly in the financial sector. Half of the survey respond-ents claimed to report to the chief executive officer (CEO) directly, but the rest did not or reported to the chief financial officer (CFO). Indeed, relations with the CFO, a role which has also undergone considerable change and adaptation in recent years, is one of the key territorial issues for the emergent CRO and respondents to the survey reported the existence of jurisdictional issues.

As far as the operating function of CROs is concerned, the survey suggests that they tend to have responsibilities for the design of risk management frameworks, the implementation of ERM, the commu-nication of policy and the oversight of processes (see also COSO 2003).

The survey also detects a 'particular emphasis on operational risk' and risk identification, together with a broad view of stakeholders. This suggests that the impetus for the CRO role may have more to do with organizational encounters with problematic, recalcitrant and difficult-to-identify risk areas than mainstream areas such as market and credit risk in financial institutions. Accordingly, common tools include but are broader than RAROC (risk-adjusted rate of return on capital) and VAR (value-at-risk) metrics and embrace qualitative mapping and profiling practices. The Conference Board survey draws the conclusion that the dominance of 'qualitative' assessment reflects the 'relatively immature state of assessment mechanisms for integrated risk management in general'. This is a view which is widely held and reflects deep assumptions about the superiority of quantitative techniques in a 'hierarchy of calculation' (Power 2005).

An insurance industry survey by Tillinghast Towers Perrin (2002) cites the joint growth of the CRO role and broad risk management programmes. The report suggests that the CRO is an internal 'ambassador for ERM' in the most advanced companies, although the reality of integration is patchy. These insurance CROs report most frequently to the CFO and chair the risk committee. Furthermore, internal appointments are most common from the actuarial department in insurance companies, as contrasted with non-insurance companies where internal audit departments are a prominent supplier of CROs. There is an interesting 'Canada effect' where reported frequencies are higher and commitment to a broad conception of ERM seems clearer. This is consistent with the profile and prominence given to ERM by the Institute of Internal Auditors in Canada and by the Conference Board itself.

The category of CRO is evident in an electronic newsletter *Erisk* in the late 1990s and early 2000s with its series entitled 'CRO profiles'.[2] These essays and interviews focus primarily on the CRO in the financial services area. The series reveals that many CROs have a background in credit risk, an area undergoing redefinition within a broader ERM framework, e.g. Hogan at Fleet Boston, Truslow at Wachovia Corp, Lawrence at ANZ. However, while CROs have become much broader than buyers of insurance, there is considerable role variability. In 1999 the Bank of Montreal reported a CRO as an executive vice president

---

[2] See www.erisk.com for more details.

reporting directly to the CEO and chairing the risk management group committee. In Sun Life Financial the hazard and financial risk management divisions were merged in 2001 and the CEO remained the effective CRO.[3] At BP there is no CRO role as such and in a culture in which engineers manage physical risk, and the chief economist handles country risk, the CEO is the effective 'head' of risk. These examples suggest that the realization of the CRO role depends on specific organizational histories and resource legacies.

The category of CRO has become firmly established and institutionalized, despite the existence of other labels for risk-handling functions. A conference of the Risk and Insurance Managers Society (RIMS) in 2001 talked of 'the CRO's expanding influence'[4] and CROs, and related risk committees, are becoming part of the architecture of good organizational governance. As a project of classification, the creation of the CRO title has been spectacularly successful and officerships are a distinctive kind of organizational and regulatory innovation in the face of uncertainty. Before considering CROs in more detail, this phenomenon deserves attention.

Encountering risk and the construction of organizational categories

Chief risk officers are a recent manifestation of a longstanding feature of organizational and occupational design: functionally dedicated 'officers' with some degree of regulatory role inside organizations. These positions provide internal organizational representations of externally encountered norms and rules. They are part of the way that organizations manage uncertainties in their environments, specifically those created by legislative, regulatory and market pressures. For example, health and safety officers have a long history as compliance agents (Hutter 1988); environmental risk officers are more recent in origin (Rehbinder 1991). In the case of chief information officers (CIOs), their emergence can be traced to the rise of data security issues as part of operational risk management and the repositioning of information technology as a strategic issue (e.g. GAO 2001).

---

[3] See *Risk Management Reports* 28, no. 8 (2001) 8.
[4] See also *Risk Management Reports* 28, no. 6 (2001).

Following the Financial Services Act 1986 in the United Kingdom, the role of compliance officer was institutionalized. According to Weait's (1993) empirical study, the development of the compliance officer as a 'distinct organizational actor' was characterized by the problem of establishing internal authority while preaching the integrationist ideal that compliance is the responsibility of all organizational members. Weait argues that compliance officers were charged with articulating the business case for compliance, with 'turning law into profit'. They needed to mobilize internal actors with 'win-win' rhetoric, a change programme that was fraught with difficulties. In a different setting, Willman et al. (2002) observe similar barriers to the integration of control and business objectives. In the context of a securities firm, managers of traders, like other internal regulatory agents, need to negotiate and maintain personal authority in order to promote changes in management and control practices.

Another instructive example from an earlier period concerns the safety officer role (Beaumont et al. 1982). These officers reported concerns about status in the management hierarchy and about occupational identity given the diversity of functions charged to the role. Once created, organizational control positions can become dumping grounds for issues and for problems regarded as a residual nuisance in other functional areas. The creation of officers is part of an organizational politics of 'doing something' which, despite claims to the contrary, can de-responsibilize other parts of the organization (the 'organizational fix' problem). The emergence of safety officers also suggests that the varied nature of their competence, in terms of formal qualifications, did not seem to be a constraint on the growth of the role. The perceived effectiveness and importance of safety officers was often idiosyncratic and conditioned by local, firm-specific experiences; there was no 'obvious, single route to becoming the safety officer'. Indeed, the riskiness of the industry in some general sense was a weaker predictor of the power of the role than organization-specific factors. Like compliance officers, safety officers reported the problem of balancing their role as independent internal agents and advisers with their role as an arm of management.

Dobbin et al. (2001) track the rise and fall of the chief operating officer (COO), arguing that the role emerges as part of the spread of diversified companies, with the explicit aim of allowing the CEO to concentrate on strategy and long-term planning. The diffusion of the position slows down as the CFO appears as a CEO 'sidekick' to support a new organizational focus on 'core operational competence'. The study shows how corporate control roles exist essentially relationally and their dynamics can be understood only in a broader setting of changing management structures and models. This is an important finding which is relevant in the CRO context.

The history of organizational control agents suggests a specific kind of organizational response path to problems and disturbances. Creating a dedicated officership category is part of problem definition and its subsequent management. The external legitimacy of such roles will increase in so far as the category is embedded in legal or other forms of external regulation. The quasi-legal aura of the term 'officer' is an essential and not an accidental feature of this process: the category suggests a potential remedy that is likely to increase the internal 'legalization' of the organization. Indeed, the relation between the rise and fall of these roles and a certain legalization of organizational life is critical (Sitkin and Bies 1994). The creation of new control agents reformats the 'moral economy' of an organization with a new set of corporate norms. This is visible in the cases of race relations officers and ethics officers who are created to manage legal exposures and reputational risks. It is equally true of the CFO who is the gatekeeper for a certain kind of financial rationality in organizations.

To summarize: the rise of the CRO must be understood in the context of organizational strategies for dealing with uncertainties in the environment. As a well-tried form of administrative innovation, officerships signal organizational seriousness about issues. However, the history of such innovations also suggests that CROs are a potential fad, which may be short-lived. Internal officers become quickly embroiled in a complex organizational politics in which their effectiveness and legitimacy is constantly in question, and the role may be a dumping ground for high-blame problems. In short, they are risky positions.

CROs: functionality or blame shifting?

Economic explanations of the rise of the CRO role suggest that it is a rational organizational response to increased risk in the environment of organizations and to the cross-functional nature of these potential threats. Volatility in financial markets, anti-corporate activism, adversarial legal environments (the so-called compensation culture) (Sitkin and Bies 1994) and growing awareness of ignorance in the face of high-impact operational risks all support the creation of a dedicated risk function with a broad remit. In addition, increased market completeness in new areas, e.g. intangibles, with more contracting possibilities drives a need for greater monitoring of returns on newly visible and vulnerable assets. The credit downturn in the early 1990s, together with the mid-1990s' financial scandals, demanded a rational organizational response to capital maintenance. Indeed, Wood (2002) argues that the CRO role was created to fine-tune the calculation of economic capital for organizational control purposes. Put simply, it can be argued that CROs have come into being because of the way the world is (cf. Shiller, 2003), a view supported by the internal history of CROs (Lam 2003).

Another explanation is more *institutional* in form, namely that CROs have become part of being a legitimate organization, part of good governance together with audit committees and internal auditors, irrespective of any demonstrable economic effectiveness. From this point of view, surveys of the CRO role do not just record the facts but are part of this institutionalization process, furthering isomorphic tendencies to copy the role. For example, the Conference Board of Canada states that the CRO position is 'on the rise in many organizations', but it has also created a Council of Chief Risk Officers as a discussion forum to create a CRO community in Canada. Surveys by associational bodies must therefore be understood as strategic texts which promote new organizational forms and practices. They are instruments by which the CRO role becomes normalized. However, institutional and economic explanations are not mutually exclusive, especially for a practice which unfolds over time (Dobbin et al. 2001). Adoption of the CRO role may initially depend on a variety of specific factors, such as whether CEOs see risk as a discrete area, industry scandals and regulatory changes. But the explanatory purchase of such variables, including economic ones, diminishes as the level of industry adoption increases (Tolbert and Zucker 1983).

Another possible explanatory path locates the CRO, and officerships more generally, within 'blame-shifting' strategies (Hood 2002). Douglas (1999) argues that where organizations are 'simple, linear and loose', the management of risk is co-extensive with the running of the entity and the CEO is the de facto CRO. Any other risk officer or control agent is a 'lowly technical support function' or 'sidekick' (Dobbin et al. 2001). In these settings, the CRO role is 'nice but trivial', nice in the sense that the CEO is the ultimate bearer of blame. In contrast, complex, tight organizations generate 'normal accidents' (Perrow 1984) and routine errors, which are suited to the creation of a specialist CRO role. But while such a role may be necessary, the CRO gets blamed when things go wrong. At its simplest, the CRO is a potentially high-risk position with a crude precautionary performance criterion, e.g. 'bad things must never happen'. In such settings, CROs must work hard to create representations of their own effectiveness and performance; they are pressure points in the border territory between risk controlling and risk taking (Douglas 1999).

As with compliance and health and safety officers, performance and effectiveness issues are repeatedly visible in professional discourses around the CRO role (Butterworth 2000, Falkenstein 2001, Fishkin 2001). As a counter-blame strategy, it is persistently argued that the CRO is not an 'owner' of risk: the CRO supports and enhances the management of risk but detailed risk management remains the responsibility of line management. AIRMIC, an insurance managers' trade association, defines the role as 'coordinator and advisor' and in other contexts CROs are described as strategists, analysts and catalysts for change, developers of best practice, designers and communicators, but *not* implementers. So there is some ambivalence about the CRO, where 'risk managers [are] not ... managers of risk at all' (Ward 2001), and this leads to problems in securing an institutional definition of the CRO.[5] For example,

... the problem has been determining just what this new creature should look like. That is, what is the right role, the right responsibilities and the right competencies for a CRO? At first look, it seems the CRO should be a master technician, someone who commands the technical expertise of every sub-discipline of risk management in their organization, from credit, to market to operational risk. But it turns out this is not the case. In the first place, that model of universal expertise exists in very few, if any, individuals. Second, the sheer accumulation of analytic detail ... is not really what the organization needs .... What is required is someone who can coordinate the company's risk management efforts .... It is more of a synthetic rather than an analytic

[5] See *Risk Management Reports* 28, no. 7 (2001): 1–3.

task ... a leader, facilitator and integrator. In this role, the CRO serves as a coordinator, more than a manager, of risks. (Lee 2000: 3)

This conception of CROs makes sense as a blame-shifting strategy in which they play a role in defining and formally allocating internal responsibilities for risk (COSO 2003: Chapter 12). In practice this can mean reminding and educating traders about risk. Tools such as value at risk and risk-adjusted rate of return are part of this moral economy of risk responsibility allocation.

To the extent that CROs allocate responsibilities and require risk 'sign-off' in different parts of the organization, they allocate blame themselves. Being subject to a broader set of expectations that cannot be controlled, they are also in a potentially 'blamable' position. Indeed, the performativity of CROs is shrouded in the problem of counter-factuality, so they must work hard to establish a legitimate form of performativity in the organization, something most easily achieved as guardians of process. As Weait (1993) argues in the case of compliance officers: 'Departments able to render themselves in some sense *critical* to the firm's success will achieve authority.' But what is critical is not absolute; criticality and relevance (Power 1997) must be constructed by CROs in a political pitch, in which they represent themselves as 'modernizers' and as moral guardians of legitimate values of good corporate governance.

The job of the CRO is to 'organize' the way in which an organization processes risk. In an important sense, this is the re-institutionalization of certainty from uncertainty and the fashioning of risk management into a new moral technology. CROs preside over organizational 'clean-up' work (Vaughan 2004) to produce organizational facts about risk, and to reproduce the manageability of risk. CROs also preside over an internal organizational community, which is made increasingly aware of, and responsible for, risk and its management. The allocation of responsibility and related accountabilities is a fundamental part of the CRO role involving the 'reformatting' (Callon 1998) of the internal economy of the organization and the risk responsibility map. Indeed, risk maps are both tools for use in specific decision contexts and symbolic representations of an ideal organizational domain, one infused with risk attentiveness.

The CRO is also part of a larger risk management 'industry' in which risk management is marketed as a valuable product. The claimed business focus and 'win-win rhetoric' of CROs as they present their roles is part of a translation process to represent cost as value. Wood (2002) suggests that this business focus became a necessity as the policing role was subject to veto and overrule by business units. Like other internal agents, CROs must create an 'immaculate image' and must represent risk management as an integrative and 'productive function' (Weait 1993). This presentation of the management of risk is part of a more generally observable phenomenon in which policing and regulatory activities are being reinvented with value propositions, turning them into new products.[6] In making risk management into a business, with potentially high stakes, professional competition for senior organizational roles is also evident.

CRO: an emerging profession?

The rise of the CRO represents a new occupational form for internal organizational agents competing in markets for prestige and status. The ambivalence of the CRO role described above exists because, as Abbott (1988: 126) suggests, aspiring super-ordinate groups will seek to offload 'dangerously routine' activities. Such a strategy is clear from the promotional statements of CROs. Some organizations separate a head of risk as a (high-status) troubleshooting, advisory role from the (low-status) independent internal audit and checking function. Needless to say, internal auditors normally contest this representation of what they do and Abbott's (1988) thesis about the 'system' of professions can be usefully projected on to the organizational level. Organizations can be understood as discrete subsystems of expertise, with their own internal hierarchies and jurisdictional struggles. Given the fluid and diverse nature of the bodies of knowledge involved in the management of risk, an important role exists for 'the ability to define old problems in new ways' (Abbott 1988: 30). Enterprise-wide risk management is a clear example of a rearrangement and repositioning of existing tasks and routines under a new umbrella, an umbrella which gives the CRO in principle a central role.

Abbott argues that it is important for the status of internal actors that they are connected to prestige transactions and projects. However, they should be loosely coupled to the results in such a way that successful

---

[6] I owe this point to John Braithwaite.

performance is defined in terms of process. CROs work hard to maintain the value proposition for risk management, to make it prestigious, and metrics such as value at risk which provide links between control activities and value statements are important persuasive resources for them. As Abbott (1988: 103) suggests, 'expert action without any formalization' is perceived as craft knowledge and as lacking legitimacy. From this point of view, hierarchies of quantification are important (Power 2005) since the existence of high-level metrics such as VAR and RAROC are important to the legitimacy of all risk management agents, even if not actually used. Vaughan (2005) argues that NASA engineers work in craft-like fashion rather than in terms of hard science, and the same is true for CROs as they report their own work. But the symbolic backing of science is an essential feature of the organizational effectiveness of these agents. For Abbott the critical difference is between a certain kind of 'descriptivist' expertise and elite mathematical inference as the basis for practitioner status; CROs in banks are normally capable of elite mathematical inference and promote this as an ideal, but in fact spend most of their time in descriptivist, mapping and communication mode. In general, organizational agents will talk up the complexity of what they do, thereby acting as sources of internal risk amplification (Freudenberg 2003).

The CRO is a hybrid embodying different forms of expertise and control styles (Hood 1996). The ambiguity of the CRO identified above allows the role to expand its domain of influence and internal jurisdiction. The potentially strategic role of the CRO also has important implications for other control agents. Specifically, there is competition in the ability to have a particular organizational model accepted internally. While the rise of the chief finance officer corresponds to the finance conception of the organization (Fligstein 1990), the CRO role represents a risk management concept of the organization (Power 2004b). This means that the CRO/CFO interface is a potentially important fault line in organizations. COSO (2003: Chapter 12) represents the CRO as one internal control agent among many and implicitly reproduces the existing jurisdiction and organizational model of the CFO (COSO 2003: 96). This leaves the CEO as the ultimate risk owner, and the CRO and the internal auditor as 'sidekicks'. In contrast, other conceptions of risk management place the CRO at the very centre of the process. We cannot be sure how these different representations do or do not correspond to practice, but they remind us that the CRO role cannot be considered in isolation from others. It must also be borne in mind that the chief financial officer and internal auditor roles are undergoing constant change and are themselves hybrids.

The control of professional language which, according to Abbott, makes work appear 'more coherent and effective than it really is' is another critical factor. In particular, new categories of management attention, like operational and reputational risk, allow CROs to 'seize residual areas' (Abbott 1988: 235) in the name of risk management. Risk management thereby becomes a critical organizational storyline (Hajer 1997) or conversation (Black 2002) through which existing practices can be re-expressed and validated, and by which the CRO begins to control organizational discourse. However, the capacity of CROs to realize their role as legitimate agents in organizations should not be empirically overestimated and, as noted above, all control agents are beset by an expectations gap between what they do and what is demanded of them. The front line of jurisdictional competition is with other control agents, like internal auditors, and with business lines which may not perceive the risk management role as functional for what they want to do. Constant work is required to maintain the legitimacy and functionality of the role. It has also been argued that intra-organizational conflict is inevitable, particularly between risk-taking and risk-managing functions, and that it is functional to institutionalize this conflict in separate roles which bargain with each other (Wood 2002). The suggested organization control model is that of collibration (Dunsire 1993) with the CRO as the pessimistic conscience of the corporation and a necessary counterweight to over-optimistic CEOs.

Professionalization projects are performative: 'To say a profession exists is to make it one' (Abbott 1988: 81). Numerous references to the risk management 'professional' in practitioner conferences and texts have this performative quality. A number of associations (GARP, AIRMIC) exist with aspirations to represent risk management practitioners. Some have examination and certification systems, but there are no barriers to operating in the risk management area. Some conflicts and territorial issues are evident, e.g. the emergence of a new spin-off association, the Professional Risk Managers International Association (PRMIA) in 2001. However, in terms of numbers, the Institute of Internal Auditors (IIA) is bigger than GARP, AIRMIC and the Society for Risk Analysis (SRA) put together and has been a leading contributor, especially in Canada, to the development of the new risk management thinking.[7] But this numerical strength is not a necessary condition for capturing an elite CRO market, especially where links to higher education systems remain undeveloped. While the CRO label is increasingly visible, CROs as a group are not, despite the efforts of the Conference Board of Canada and similar bodies. Like all internal agents, the first tendency of CROs is to identify with their local organizations rather than deriving any status or identity from wider associations. Indeed, the fact that most CRO appointments seem to be internal promotions from within existing functions suggests the preponderance of local dynamics. Equally, very different types of people are included in the function (Dietz and Rycroft 1987). The CRO in a high-safety environment, such as the nuclear industry, is likely to be very different from a CRO in a bank. This militates against the creation of a trans-industry occupational grouping.

The rise of CROs to date remains an idiosyncratic story with weak institutionalization beyond the category itself. This could change dramatically if the CRO function is specifically inscribed in regulatory projects which depend on risk management.[8] Basel 2 is a possible platform for the role in the banking sector and history shows that the banking sector tends to lead generic developments in control, reporting and governance ideas. In the end the fortunes of CROs as a profession will be heavily dependent on the managerial and regulatory projects of classification within which the role is inscribed.

Conclusion: CROs and the integrationist dream

This chapter has explored some of the general features of the emerging role of the CRO. In contrast to accounts of the CRO as an efficient and effective response to an increasingly risky environment, the argument has focused on two other explanatory emphases: blame shifting and professionalization. The CRO is a standard type of organizational innovation and dedicated officerships have many precedents. CROs are a new mode of structuring risk expertise and symbolize high-level

---

[7] See *Risk Management Reports* 27, no. 12 (2000): 5.

[8] The history of management accountants, their professionalization and the publication of key textbooks is also instructive (see Loft 1988; Ahrens and Chapman 2000).

organizational commitment to rational risk management. As risk management and good corporate governance come to be increasingly co-defined, the CRO role can also be expected to grow in institutional significance, even to challenge that of the chief financial officer. However, experience also suggests that the CRO and enterprise risk management are the latest in a line of managerial fads which will mutate in due course; what remains constant is the organizational effort to transform encounters with risk into routine, formalizable processes – literally to organize uncertainty.

Like all internal control agents, CROs face a number of generic and recurrent difficulties. First, the effectiveness of organizational control agents is persistently difficult to demonstrate, largely because it depends on unprovable counterfactuals, i.e. what would have happened without the intervention of the agent. In these circumstances, effectiveness will be constructed in a network of organizational allies who, in some sense, 'buy' the storyline of effectiveness. Since the belief in the effectiveness of internal control agents may, by virtue of influencing behaviours, actually bring it about, working hard to create these beliefs is essential to *being* effective. However, the functionality of CROs, like all internal control agents, can always be doubted and they may simply be part of an organizational 'clean-up' process. From this point of view, VAR and other metrics are part of the fantasy of safety (Clarke 1999) and risk management is simply a bureaucratic defence against anxiety.

Second, like all organizational control roles, the CRO is a hybrid, emerging as a re-assembly or spin-off from existing expertise. The CRO is represented by practitioners as a multidisciplinary coordinator in contrast to an isolated risk specialist.[9] CROs may have an organizationally idiosyncratic history, but the role is becoming institutionalized well beyond any originating economic rationale to become part of 'standard managerial corpus' (Dobbin et al. 2001). However, like all organizational control agents CROs walk a tightrope between being a 'captured' insider and a disenfranchised outsider, between appropriation by operational units and marginalization by them. They are responsible for selling new 'regulatory' ideas internally, ideas which may threaten existing patterns of work. In this respect the position is an essentially unstable one in terms of role conflicts that are hidden by

---

[9] See *Risk Management Reports* 27, no. 12 (2000): 4–5.

official blueprints. So while the CRO role is becoming institutionalized at a policy level, in specific organizational settings it must be understood as part of an internal economy of expertise which may be highly competitive. Reported interviews with, and essays about, CROs are littered with integrationist and partnership talk, but also acknowledge they must work hard to assemble and communicate risk management knowledge in potentially adversarial environments.

Third, the relation between the CRO and the CFO will be a critical axis of development and each role will evolve in relation to the other. While it may be argued that the CFO was the key agent in late twentieth-century firms, the CRO may assume this status in the twenty-first century, promoting a risk-based concept of control. This shifting relationship takes place against the background of a changing corporate governance landscape of audit committees, risk committees, risk disclosure and risk sign-off. Who will provide the dominant organizational memory, the accountant and his or her data commitments within management and financial accounting systems, or the risk officer with new forms of accounting for near misses, contingencies and value at risk?

Fourth, formal representations of the emerging CRO role suppress the risks of the risk officer role. The creation of CROs may cause others to relax their risk management efforts, leading to higher risk overall, despite their role in delegating responsibility. In addition, CROs may contribute to the increasing legalization of organizations (Sitkin and Bies 1994) and to a risk-averse culture of 'timid' corporations (Hunt 2003). These issues require further investigation, but much depends on the precise nature of the moral order that CROs do or do not create. CROs are 'merchants of norms' (Dezalay 1995) who elaborate a local 'responsibility order' where degrees of risk sign-off build an organizational responsibility architecture. But can the CRO live up to theoretical expectations as an agent of 'reflexive governance' or 'meta-regulation' (Parker 2002: Chapter 9) in which public regulatory objectives and internal control are aligned? In an environment of increasingly de-centred and 'enforced self-regulation', more dimensions of social responsibility may be handed over to organizational risk management systems, suggesting that the CRO, fad or otherwise, will become a de facto manager of social risk.

6 Incentives, risk and accountability in organizations

TIMOTHY BESLEY AND MAITREESH GHATAK

THIS chapter discusses incentives and risk management in organizations and how economists have thought about these issues. Risk is not merely the possibility of 'bad things happening', such as damage, loss and accidents. Any deviation from expected outcomes constitutes risk, whether it is positive or negative. Clearly no organization can hope to achieve its objectives without putting its resources at risk to some degree. An excessive focus on risk minimization leads to forgone opportunities. The issue is striking the right balance between the risk that an organization is exposed to and achieving its objectives (e.g. shareholder value if it is a for-profit firm). A direct implication of this is that risk management and fulfilling the objectives of the firm are interrelated and cannot be studied in isolation from one another (see, for example, Poynter 2004).

An organization can mitigate risk by buying insurance, diversifying its portfolio and maintaining sufficient solvency. However, it is impossible to eliminate all risk. If this was possible so that the earnings of the organization were invariant irrespective of its performance, this would also eliminate the drive to perform well. Therefore inevitably the problem of risk comes back to understanding how actors in an organization make key decisions that affect risk exposure. Variability of returns needs to be interpreted by managers and investors to determine whether their strategies are working. Here, therefore, we will focus on aspects of risk that can be altered by decisions made within the organization even though the outcomes of such decisions may in part be influenced by events outside of the organization.

Risk management in organizations whether public or private requires that incentives of those who work within an organization be appropriately aligned. The traditional economic approach to risk management stresses how explicit financial incentive schemes can play a role in making sure that members of an organization seek common goals. This is the cornerstone of the principal–agent approach to

149

organization design. The key idea in such approaches is the importance of the fact that many actions taken in organizations are not observable. In this chapter, we review and assess this approach to risk management and its limitations. We then explore approaches that go beyond the standard principal–agent framework.

The standard economic approach to risk management has in mind a profit-maximizing firm with agents who are primarily motivated by financial concerns. The narrowness of this perspective in focusing only on money as a motivator has been questioned in the management and organizational behaviour literature (see, for example, Herzberg 1987; Kerr 1995; Kohn 1993) and more recently in economics literature (see Frey 1997). For organizations that pursue non-pecuniary goals – such as government bureaucracies, public service providers and non-profits – the limitations of focusing only on financial incentive schemes is widely agreed upon (see Dixit 2002).

Starting with the same premise that the exclusive focus on financial incentives is misguided, we offer a different perspective that we characterize as the 'three Ms' approach – missions, motivation and matching. We view individuals as being motivated not just by money but also by missions. However, only when matched with the right organization, and within the organization the right task and project, is this intrinsic motivation fully realized. Therefore, matching mitigates some of the potential principal–agent problems at the entry level by reducing the need to use explicit financial incentives or supervision. This approach is able to meld the classical economic approach with non-economic approaches to organizations. It has rich implications for changing accountability structures and regulatory regimes.[1]

We begin by laying out the classical principal–agent model as well as discussing some more sophisticated variants of it. We then consider the three Ms approach, following this with a discussion about how it can be applied to offer new perspectives on various aspects of risk management in organizations.

---

[1] While our analysis is relevant to issues of risk management in an organization, the basic notion that organizations have individuals within them that make decisions that are not observable to their principals is of much wider applicability. It arises even when these decisions do not necessarily expose the organization to any significant amount of risk that needs to be managed.

The classical principal–agent model

The economic view of an organization is that it is a network of principal–agent relationships. The shareholder–CEO relationship, the CEO–divisional manager relationship, the divisional manager–employee relationship are all examples of principal–agent relationships. An individual who is a principal in one relationship can be an agent in another relationship. The resulting network of relationships characterizes the accountability structure of an organization, i.e. the chain of command and control.

In the classical principal–agent model there are two parties, a principal and an agent. Each principal has some authority over the agent, in that he or she can determine what tasks the agent has to perform and shape his or her compensation package. However, the principal's power over the agent is limited by the presence of alternative employers who could hire the agent. In other words, the overall payoff of the agent must be at least as high as what he or she could earn under a different principal (less the cost of moving and finding another job).

The agent works for the principal and undertakes some task that the principal cannot undertake, either because it requires some special expertise or because the principal has a limited amount of time. The task could be in the nature of things that the agent has to do, such as working 'hard' or choosing the 'best' project. Alternatively, it could be in the nature of reporting to the principal some piece of information that the principal needs to make some decisions, such as the true cost or true value of a project, bad news or good news. These actions affect the payoff of the principal and so the principal has a direct stake in inducing the agent to take actions that are most desirable from his or her point of view. However, the agent is likely to have better information than the principal as to what actions he or she undertakes or what information he or she possesses. That is, there is likely to be asymmetric information between the principal and the agent, with the agent having an informational advantage. Given this, the agent is likely to undertake the action that is most convenient from his or her private point of view. Similarly, he or she is likely to report information that is most favourable from his or her private point of view. These may not coincide with what is most desirable from the principal's point of view. In the literature the former possibility is described as the problem of 'hidden

action' or 'moral hazard' and the latter as 'hidden information' or
'adverse selection'. For the most part, our focus in this chapter will be
on the former type of problem.[2]

The principal–agent model assumes that the principal and the agent
have objectives that are not fully aligned and that the actions undertaken by the agent cannot be perfectly monitored by the principal. If
both these features are present, then the principal–agent problem has
bite, i.e. there is an 'agency problem'. For example, the principal may
care about the profits of the organization (e.g. if he or she is the owner)
whereas the agent may care only about his or her remuneration and
how hard or easy the alternatives are from his or her private point of
view (e.g. if he or she is the manager). Similarly, the principal may have
only a 'noisy' measure of what the agent actually does or whether his or
her reports are truthful or not. This 'noise' arises from the difficulty of
perfectly monitoring or supervising the agent. Typically this is because
the outcome of the relevant task is uncertain since it depends on both
exogenous factors and the action of the agent.[3] For example, sales
could be low because of some general factors affecting most firms in
the industry, some specific factors affecting the firm that are beyond a
manager's control, such as delays by a supplier, or because the manager
was not putting in enough effort. If the principal has access to a good
monitoring or supervision technology, he or she can either directly
observe the agent's action or can infer it from the outcome by filtering
out the effect of exogenous risk. In this case there is no agency problem
and the agent can be induced to take the desired actions from the
principal's point of view by making it part of the job description.
Alternatively, if the agent is completely loyal to the principal, then
too there is no agency problem – the agent can be trusted to take the
desired actions from the principal's point of view. The combination of
these two elements raises the possibility that the agent could be

---

[2] The terms 'moral hazard' and 'adverse selection' originated in the insurance
industry. Purchasers of insurance are viewed as having a struggle with their
conscience as to whether to do the right thing when it's tempting to do otherwise
(e.g. not take enough precaution to prevent a loss). Similarly, those who select
(i.e. choose) to buy insurance are the ones who are most likely to have an accident
and are therefore 'adverse' or undesirable from an insurance firm's point of view.

[3] It is possible that the outcome of the agent's action is not subject to any uncertainty, but the measurement of it is noisy from the principal's point of view, say,
because the supervisors can make mistakes.

undertaking actions that are not in the best interests of the principal, and yet there is no way the principal can directly catch him or her.

In the presence of moral hazard, the principal has to use indirect means to induce the agent to take the desired actions from the principal's point of view. In other words, the agent must be given incentives to perform.

Foundations of agency problems

Is it possible to design incentives such that the outcome is the same as when there are no differences in objectives between the principal and the agent, or when the principal can perfectly monitor the agent? In other words, can contractual methods achieve the 'first-best' situation, i.e. as if there is either no asymmetry of information or perfect alignment of objectives of the principal and the agent? The answer, as one would expect, is typically no. There are costs associated with providing incentives. The source of the problem lies in the difficulty of making the agent's objective closely aligned to that of the principal via an incentive scheme. The obvious way to do this is through rewards and punishments. However, if the agent is risk averse or there is a 'limited liability' constraint that limits how much the agent can be punished or fined in the event of the performance measure being unsatisfactory, there will be a loss of efficiency due to the agency problem. Let us consider these in turn.

Suppose the agent is neutral towards risk. Technically, this means that if he or she faces an uncertain income stream, he or she cares only about the mean or expected income and not the potential variability of income around this mean. In this case, the principal can design incentives that will achieve the first-best, i.e. it will be as if the principal could perfectly monitor the agent. The trick is to make the agent what economists call a 'full residual claimant'. For example, suppose the outcome can be either satisfactory or unsatisfactory. If the agent works hard, it will be satisfactory with probability 0.75 and unsatisfactory with probability 0.25. If the agent does not work hard, the probabilities are 50:50. Working hard is considered a more costly option to the agent, since he or she can presumably store his or her time and energy and devote them to more pleasurable pursuits. Because of exogenous uncertainty, just by observing unsatisfactory performance the principal cannot conclude that the agent did not work hard. The principal can, however, tell the agent that he or she will be paid a salary only if the outcome is satisfactory. Faced with this reward scheme the agent is very likely to work hard.[4] Examples of such incentive schemes are piece rates and fixed-price contracts.

The trouble with the above incentive scheme is that it puts too much risk on the agent. Even if he or she works hard, due to exogenous uncertainty performance is sometimes going to be unsatisfactory and the agent will get 'punished' even though the fault is not his or hers. So long as the agent cares only about his or her expected salary, this does not matter. But almost everyone cares not just about his or her expected earnings but also about the range of possible variation in the earnings. That is, they are risk averse. They evaluate a risky income stream in terms not of the expected value but of the expected value less a discount, the size of which depends on the variability of the income stream.

For this reason a sharp incentive scheme may be too costly for the principal since the agent will discount it by the amount of risk he or she has to bear. Since the principal is likely to be less risk averse than the agent (e.g. because he or she is wealthier and better able to cope with risk), the solution lies in offering an incentive scheme that lies somewhere between a completely flat salary and a sharp incentive scheme where the agent bears all risk. Different forms of profit sharing and bonuses are examples of such incentive schemes. This solution comes at a cost. The agent still has to bear more risk than is optimal, since otherwise he or she will not put in extra effort. That means the principal has to pay him or her a higher expected salary to offset the discount due to risk aversion, which is costly from the principal's point of view. Also, it is possible that the principal will have to be reconciled to the agent putting in a low or moderate effort level, if the extra wage cost in order to give incentives does not justify the gain in expected profits to the principal from the high effort level.

Risk aversion is not the only possible reason why it is hard to implement a 'perfect' incentive scheme. Another reason is limited liability. Suppose the agent is not risk averse but must be given some minimum amount of salary due to labour regulations or social norms.

---

[4] For example, if the salary is $1,000 a month if the outcome is satisfactory and 0 otherwise, then working hard entails an expected salary of $750 and not working hard yields an expected salary of $500. So long as the cost of working hard does not exceed $250 in monetary terms, the agent will work hard.

This puts a lower bound on how much the agent can be penalized if the outcome is unsatisfactory. It restricts the use of incentive mechanisms such as performance bonds. Given that the agent cannot be penalized very much if the outcome is unsatisfactory, the only way to induce the agent to put in effort is to reward the agent when the outcome is satisfactory. But from the principal's point of view, punishment is cheaper than rewards. As a result, the principal might want to induce a lower effort level than that which would be possible under perfect monitoring to economize on rewards given out to agents.

Revisionist perspectives

The classical principal–agent model is well suited to analyse situations where there is a single principal dealing with a single agent as performance can be measured even though the measure is noisy and the agent is entrusted with a single task. Clearly, these assumptions do not apply to many situations and accordingly the incentive theory has been extended to deal with these situations. Below we briefly discuss some of the major directions in which the basic principal–agent model has been extended (see Dixit 2002 for a detailed review).

Measurability
In many cases the measurement of performance is very difficult. For example, how does one measure the performance of a teacher? The task of a teacher is to provide 'good education', but this is much harder to measure than, say, production in an assembly line, sales, or provision of banking services or even some public services such as garbage removal or power supply. This means that in these cases it would be hard to find good performance measures. If performance measures are noisy, then making rewards sensitive to performance does not give effective incentives and imposes unnecessary risk on the employee. In these situations, the solution is to offer a flat incentive scheme and introduce a subjective performance evaluation. If the agent's performance is considered satisfactory by the principal (but hard to quantify and explicitly introduced in the contract), he or she will be given a payrise in the future or a promotion.

Multi-tasking
Most jobs involve several tasks. If some of these have good performance measures and not others, then making an agent's pay sensitive to

the good performance measures will cause him or her to substitute effort away from the other tasks and could result in a loss of efficiency. To continue with the example of teaching, good education involves students being able to achieve high scores in standardized tests but also encouraging a spirit of creativity, curiosity and the inculcation of good values. The former is easy to measure but if teachers are rewarded just on the basis of the performance of students in tests, this might lead to an excessive focus on examination skills at the expense of the other components of a good education. This makes provision of incentives hard when employees have to perform multiple tasks (Hölmström and Milgrom 1991). Similarly, if hospitals are given incentives to cut costs, they are going to sacrifice quality by refusing to treat certain types of illnesses or being excessively selective in using expensive medical procedures.

Multiple agents

Sometimes several agents are involved in a task and it is hard to separate the contribution of one agent from the other. This is referred to as the problem of moral hazard in teams (Hölmström 1982). In this situation, in addition to the principal–agent problem between the principal and the team of agents taken together, there is also a free-rider problem among the agents. In other words, since individual contributions cannot be separated and so incentives of each individual agent will depend on the performance of the team, each agent will supply less effort than if performance depended only on his or her own effort.

Multiple principals

In some organizations an agent works for multiple principals who may not share the same objectives. In a profit-maximizing firm one would expect that in the ultimate analysis, only the net profits matter. But clearly members of the organization at the top of the hierarchy may have their private agendas as well, and due to principal–agent problems between the owners and these individuals, the divergence of objectives may not be eliminated through incentive schemes. For example, the head of the engineering division may be driven by an objective of coming up with an innovation that will be his or her or the department's ticket to fame. But the head of the sales division may be concerned only with sales. Also, a doctor can be concerned with the success of a particular treatment method. This can be in conflict with the interests of the hospital management (or tax payers at large) who would like to minimize costs. This can also be in conflict with patients, who might not wish to be subjects of experimentation. Similarly, a teacher might want to put more emphasis on learning using expensive teaching aids, as opposed to imparting mechanical test-taking skills. This might make the (enlightened) parents happy, but the school principal or management might care more about the average test record of their students, and tax payers may be more concerned about the expenses. Since each principal would like to induce the agent to put more effort into activities that he or she cares about more, if the incentive schemes are not chosen to maximize the joint payoffs of the principals, there will be inefficiencies over and above the basic agency costs because of the lack of cooperation and coordination among the principals.

Implicit incentives
The classical principal–agent model takes the view that the agent works exclusively for the principal and has rewards set inside the organization. However, in practice, principal–agent relationships are set in a market context. The market determines the outside option of the agent. Also agents may have one eye on the market when they choose how much effort to put in – the rewards may come from the market rather than from the current principal. An agent who is viewed as performing well will command a higher market price in future periods. Hence incentives become implicit (see Dewatripont et al. 1999). In this instance, the principal loses some control over the incentive schemes that can be offered due to the operation of market forces.

Empirical evidence

Empirical evidence on the standard economic approach to principal–agent problems is relatively thin, especially in comparison with the extensive theoretical literature (see Prendergast 1999; Chiappori and Salanie 2003 for excellent surveys). There are two key issues that empirical research has focused on. First, do incentive schemes affect performance? Second, are incentive schemes optimally chosen? Prendergast (1999) in his survey concludes that while the answer to the first question is, in general, yes, the answer to the second question is mixed and inconclusive.

The main difficulty is what empirical economists call the problem of 'identification'. It is rare to find changes in incentives which occur for genuinely exogenous reasons. As a result, if one compares across two sets of incentive schemes and measures the difference in performance, it is not clear whether one is picking up the effects of the variation in the incentive schemes or differences in the two environments or the characteristics of the agents. For example, if we observe one firm using high-powered incentive schemes and also having higher measures of productivity compared with another firm, we cannot conclude that greater incentive pay raises productivity. It could be that more productive agents self-select to work in firms that offer greater incentive pay. This problem of selection can contaminate evidence. Although overall the evidence does point out a positive effect of incentive pay on performance, the selection effect can be important in specific cases. For example, Lazear (2000) looks at how windshield fitters respond to the introduction of piece-rate incentives. He finds a significant effect that can be largely explained by the selection of different individuals in piece-rate jobs.

The three Ms approach

In this section we report on our ongoing work (Besley and Ghatak 2003; 2005) which builds an approach to the principal–agent problem with some distinctive features. This approach can be applied to the design of incentive schemes in public and private organizations.

There are three key elements in our approach: missions, motivation and matching. A mission consists of the attributes of a project that make some principals and agents value its success over and above any monetary income they receive in the process. This could be based on what the organization does (charitable versus commercial), how it does it (environment friendly or otherwise), who is the principal (kind and caring versus strict profit-maximizer) and so on. Motivation is any value in excess of the monetary rewards from doing something that a principal and agent may derive. This can be viewed as job satisfaction and is likely to be greater if things are done in the way an individual likes. For example, a sales representative in the Body Shop may put in extra effort since she is opposed to animal testing and has strong pro-environment views. Matching is the process by which firms bring together like-minded principals and agents. Because they share similar views on missions and therefore are motivated not just by the monetary rewards, the principal–agent problem is alleviated and the need to give explicit incentives (which are costly for reasons discussed above) is lessened. We discuss these concepts in greater detail below.

Missions

The mission of the organization displaces the conventional notion of profit maximization. The idea that missions are important in public organizations is not a new one. It is a central plank of James Q. Wilson's celebrated study of public bureaucracies (Wilson 1989: 95). He defines a mission as a culture 'that is widely shared and warmly endorsed by operators and managers alike'. It is an important and frequent theme in the literature on non-profit organizations (see, for example, Sheehan 1996). It is the nature of the activities in question and not whether the service is provided publicly or privately that unites mission-oriented organizations.

While the notion of missions is somewhat vague compared with notions like profit, we believe that it is an important departure when thinking about organizations that are not directly responsive to market forces. Missions can also be important in more standard private-sector occupations. Firms frequently profess that their goal is to serve customers rather than to make their shareholders as rich as possible. One can question whether these firms are genuinely committed to these missions or whether these are just a veil for some other underlying self-interested behaviour. However, there need not be any incompatibility between profit maximization and commitment to specific missions. For example, firms that adhere to norms of corporate social responsibility and adopt business practices that seemingly sacrifice some profits (e.g. adopting environment-friendly technologies) may actually be better off doing so in net terms, since they would attract workers who share the same mission preference.[5] If principals and agents share a view of the mission, it is likely that an effective mission will economize on monetary incentives.

We assume that the mission of the organization is determined by the principals in the organization. This can be a heterogeneous group with

---

[5] Analogously, such firms may be able to attract customers who may be willing to pay a higher price to 'consume' the mission along with the product. In Besley and Ghatak (2004) we analyse corporate social responsibility from this point of view.

overlapping responsibilities. For example, in the case of a school, the principals are the parents, the government and the head teacher. Preferences over missions can be heterogeneous. For example, some parents may value high levels of discipline. There could also be disagreement on the right curriculum choices such as the weight to be attached to music teaching or languages. An important role of the management in a mission-oriented organization is to foster a congruent outlook. Thus as Miller (2002: 446–7) argues in the context of her case studies of twelve non-profit organizations: 'Non-profit board members do not expect conflict between the executive director and the purpose for which the organization was created. The board believes that the executive management will not act opportunistically and that what management actually does is to ensure good alignment and convergence in its relationship with principals.'

Changing the mission of an organization in a way that is not favoured by the agents can reduce the efficiency of the organization. In that sense, the approach shows why mission-oriented organizations are conservative and slow moving since there is a rigidity built in from the types of agents who are attracted to the organizations. Organizations without mission-oriented agents, such as private firms, are likely to be more flexible and adaptable.

Motivation

A key assumption in the principal–agent model is that performance benefits from the effort put in by agents and that this effort is costly and that the agents in question have to be motivated to put in effort. But rewards for putting in effort are not always purely monetary – agents may be motivated because they care about the output that is being produced. However, such non-monetary rewards depend on the way in which the organization is structured. For example, teachers may care about teaching a curriculum that they think is most conducive to learning. Thus, the mission of the organization can affect the degree to which agents are willing to commit costly effort.

When goods are produced with external benefits (i.e. benefits that exceed the market value of the good or the service being produced), individuals who work in the production of these goods may factor the value of the output that they produce into their decision to work in that sector and into the amount of effort that they put in. This is the labour market equivalent of the idea that individuals engage in private supply of public goods and those with the highest valuation of public goods may have the greatest interest in contributing. The model could also be one in which individuals are 'altruistically' motivated or in which they get a 'warm glow' from doing social good.[6] In the former case, the level of the good being produced matters to the individual, but not who provides it. This can lead to free-riding. In the latter case, it's not the level of the goods but how much the individual contributes that matters. It is clear that, on either of these views, the value of what they do should be attached to the job that they do, and not the sector in which they do it. Thus, if a nurse believes that nursing is an important social service with external benefits, it should not matter whether he or she is employed by the public or private sector except in so far as this affects the amount of the benefit that he or she can generate.

The general point here is that a system of organization and remuneration for the provision of goods and services will have to take into account not only how on-the-job incentives affect those in the sector but also who is attracted to work there. This might alleviate the need to give high-powered incentives. François (2000) has shown that government bureaucrats are not residual claimants, which implies that they can commit to a 'hands-off' policy that elicits greater effort from workers who have 'public service motivation'. However, if individuals differ in terms of how motivated they are and in addition have heterogeneous mission preferences, it is important to examine the process by which agents are matched to an organization.

Matching

Matching is the process by which principals and agents come together to create an organization. Matching serves an allocative role in bringing consumers to providers ('product market matching') and workers to providers ('labour market matching').

If consumers care about the missions adopted in organizations, then allowing them to choose between providers with different missions is a potentially important source of welfare improvements. This argument

---

[6] These ideas are also related to the strong professional ethics that govern the behaviour of workers in the production of collective goods. Such ethical codes de-emphasize narrow self-interest.

applies to both the private and the public sector. There is no reason why a consumer could not exercise choice between two competing hospitals or schools in much the same way that they choose a TV or a car. This application of private goods choice to public services underpins the standard argument for voucher provision of public services.

If workers care about missions in organizations, then principals and agents can match with one another on the basis of the perceived mission of the organization. This is a natural consequence of organizations being mission oriented. This matching increases efficiency in the operation of organizations since the returns from putting in effort are higher when agents share the same goals as those espoused by the organization. This process of selection at the entry point alleviates the need to use explicit financial incentives on the job.

Applications

In this section we discuss how the above general approach can be applied to specific issues. We begin by discussing the role of incentives in different kinds of organizations. Second, we discuss differences between public and private organizations. Third, we discuss different views of the role of competition and finally, incentives to innovate.

The role of incentives

The standard principal–agent model underpins the classic economic view of organization design. However, some of the business school literature on the firm (see, for example, Harvard Business School 2003) has tended to emphasize the importance of motivation in the firm without paying sufficient attention to the problem of getting incentives right. Moreover, this more hands-on literature also gives a much bigger role to selection of individuals whose motivations cohere with those of the organization. This view is therefore quite compatible with the three Ms approach that we have outlined.

Akerlof and Kranton (2003) have developed a view of organizations based on the sociological notion of identity. In their view organizations develop identities and people conform to these identities in effective organizations. They emphasize the role of entry rituals in socializing individuals into the appropriate identity. Like the three Ms approach, they put much less weight on the role of monetary incentives in organization design. Akerlof and Kranton cite Max Weber's notion of the importance of vocation. According to Weber, an office is a vocation: 'Entrance into an office is an acceptance of the fealty to the purpose of the office.' Akerlof and Kranton remark that if Weber's observation reflects the behaviour of most jobholders, 'the standard economic theory of behavior in organizations (principal–agent theory) has missed most of what causes them to function'.

Which of these views is most appropriate to understanding any particular production process will vary a great deal by type of organization. We are not claiming that monetary incentives as modelled in the classical principal–agent problem are never relevant, even though economists have perhaps overplayed their significance. The three Ms approach is able to bring a traditional economic view and a more sociological view of incentives closer together.

Public versus private organizations

Public-sector reform is one of the key policy areas where issues of risk management and incentives in general are important. At the heart of many debates is an issue of whether the public and private sectors are fundamentally different in important ways. Under the auspices of the New Public Management model (see, for example, Barzelay 2001; Hood et al. 1999) there has been a huge focus on bringing the practice of incentive pay into the public sector.

The New Public Management model has two key components. First, it stresses an administrative philosophy with a central role for hands-on management and a focus on measurable results (targets) and re-orienting public service provision towards consumers. It also stresses themes such as transparency and accountability. Second, it is a style of organizing public service delivery with a focus on the role of executive agencies, contracting out and quasi-markets. A simplistic view of principal–agent relationships would support this as the *sine qua non* of effective organization. However, our analysis calls this into question.

One possibility is that ideas of mission and a culture of control based on limited monetary incentives are indeed peculiar to the public sector. This view was embodied in the idea of the Whitehall village. Thus, Hood et al. (1999: 74) characterize Whitehall in terms of:

The traditional picture of a village world regulated in a relatively informal way through largely unwritten rules, a compliance culture and low relational distance between regulator and regulated still appeared to capture much of the style of regulation within Whitehall a quarter of a century after Heclo and Wildavsky's study.

The debate between these competing visions of public management can be thought of in terms of the three Ms framework. The Whitehall village model has strong use of missions, weak need for monitoring and emphasizes matching and socialization in controlling organizations. By contrast, the New Public Management model emphasizes weak mission preference and heavy use of monitoring and incentive pay.

The importance of mission in effective public organization is a dominant theme of the literature on public bureaucracies – see, for example, Wilson (1989). This suggests that a view of public organization with a strong emphasis in mission in aligning incentives makes a lot of sense in this context. This explains well why models of organization that de-emphasize the standard principal–agent concerns are found in this literature. The attack on this conception by public choice theorists like Niskanen (1971) fundamentally questions whether there are any key differences in motivation between public and private employees. While this is difficult to test systematically, there is evidence from the literature on non-profit organizations that motivation differs between individuals who work in for-profit and not-for-profit organizations.

What is clear is that there is no particular reason to believe that there is something special about publicly owned organizations. Motivation seems much more likely to attach to what an organization tries to achieve – the extent to which it works in the public interest. While the ownership structure may be a correlate of this, it is not what matters per se. Thus, if there are differences in organizational structure between different organizational forms, we would expect them to be more broadly correlated with the way in which organizations operate. For example, we would not expect large differences between state and private schools and public and private hospitals.

The role of competition
We have not so far discussed the role of competition in affecting incentives and organization performance. However, the forces of competition are frequently appealed to in improving organizational effectiveness.

In traditional principal–agent models there are two effects that determine how competition affects incentives in organizations (see Schmidt 1997). Since the agent is rewarded out of any rents that the principal earns in the market place, competition that limits rents will tend to reduce incentive pay and hence organizational efficiency. However, competition may often reduce the probability that an inefficient organization will survive. If the agent earns a rent from working for the principal, this liquidation effect will tend to increase organizational efficiency.

In situations where there are many agents completing similar tasks, there is a potential role for competition based on benchmarking of performance – so-called 'yardstick competition'. A good example of this is the use of league tables in the regulation of schools and hospitals.

The three Ms approach suggests that the role of competition in improving organizational efficiency can also work through improved matching in the labour market. Agents who are poorly matched will have higher incentive pay and lower levels of productivity. Matching reduces the misalignment in missions and hence increases efficiency.

Innovation in organizations

Organizations are frequently under pressure to seek out new ways to please customers and to improve efficiency. The forces that shape an organization's responsiveness to such opportunities are an important source of long-run advantage. In the standard principal–agent approach of agents with preferences over pecuniary aspects of their jobs, innovation incentives are achieved by paying for adaptability pure and simple.

The three Ms approach complicates matters. Since agents have an interest in the mission of the organization, they may also have a direct preference over innovations in so far as the latter interact with mission preferences. Thus, a new method of teaching in a school may appear attractive to one educationist but may be viewed by some teachers as interfering with their educational goals.

Thus the three Ms approach does lead to some understanding of organizational conservatism that does not appeal to emotions and innate conservatism. In other words, conservatism is quite consistent with a rationally based view of organization design. To the extent that the forces in the three Ms approach are different across different types of organization, we would expect organizational conservatism to differ too.

The approach also reveals that the efficiency of innovation needs to be considered in a broader framework – a narrow financial criterion may be a misleading basis for advocating efficiency improvements if there is demotivation because agents are less in tune with organizational goals. These considerations need to be added to the purely financial criterion and brought into the criteria for efficient innovation.

Conclusion

This chapter has discussed economic approaches to risk management and organization design. The three Ms approach provides a means of thinking through some issues that fall outside the ambit of the standard economic approach. Yet it maintains the spirit of many key ideas in principal–agent theory. The approach also helps to bridge the gap between thinking about incentives in economics and in other branches of the social sciences. Much remains to be done to further this agenda. But it provides a better understanding of the limitations of focusing only on monetary incentives and an appreciation of the role of selection or matching in better aligning the objectives of a firm's employees with those of the owner or the manager.

7 | Mathematizing risk: models, arbitrage and crises

DONALD MACKENZIE

Two moments in the financial history of high modernity: Monday, 17 August 1998. The government of Russia declares a moratorium on interest payments on most of its rouble-denominated bonds, announces that it will not intervene in the markets to protect the exchange rate of the rouble, and instructs Russian banks not to honour forward contracts on foreign exchange for a month. Elements of the decision are a surprise: countries in distress usually do not default on domestic bonds, since these can be honoured simply by printing more money. That Russia was in economic difficulties, however, was well known. Half of its government income was being devoted to interest payments, and investors – some fearing a default – had already pushed the yield on GKOs, short-term rouble bonds, to 70 per cent by the beginning of August. Nor is the news on 17 August entirely bad: Russia manages to avoid a default on its hard currency bonds. And Russia, for all its size and nuclear arsenal, is not an important part of the global financial system. 'I do not view Russia as a major issue,' says Robert Strong of Chase Manhattan Bank. Wall Street is unperturbed. On 17 August, the Dow rises almost 150 points.[1]

---

[1] See Dunbar (2000: 200–201) and Lowenstein (2000: 144); the quotation from Strong is taken from the latter. Earlier versions of this paper were presented to the Colloque International, Centre Alexandre Koyré, 'Modèles et Modélisations, 1950–2000: Nouvelles Pratiques, Nouveaux Enjeux', and to London School of Economics, Centre for the Analysis of Risk and Regulation, Workshop on 'Organisational Encounters with Risk'. I am indebted to a critic of the latter version for helpful comments. The former version has now been published in the *Revue d'Histoire des Sciences*. The research reported here was supported originally by DIRC, the Interdisciplinary Research Collaboration on the Dependability of Computer-Based Systems (UK Engineering and Physical Sciences Research Council grant GR/N13999). It is being continued with the support of a professorial fellowship awarded by the UK Economic and Social Research Council (RES-051-27-0062).

Tuesday, September 11, 2001. Two hijacked planes destroy the World Trade Center in Manhattan, and a third hits the Pentagon, the heart of American military power. Thousands – the exact number only slowly becomes known – die. It is a blow to the heart of the global financial system, both geographically and economically: the American economy, the world's largest, has already been sliding into recession. Within seconds of the news reaching Chicago, S & P index futures fall 3 per cent and before further panic becomes evident, the markets close. Says a hedge fund manager: 'This is your one-in-a-billion scenario. … You have to wonder about all the derivatives. Anyone who has leveraged positions may be destroyed.'[2]

Now let us move forward a month from those two events. Thursday, 17 September 1998: the Russian default has amplified through the financial system. 'It's like a blanket of fear has descended over the market,' said one options trader (Lowenstein 2000: 168). The prices of risky assets have, in general, plummeted: for some assets, a market scarcely exists because no one will buy at other than distressed prices. At the core of the spreading crisis is one of the world's most sophisticated hedge funds, Long-Term Capital Management (LTCM). LTCM's large, complex portfolio, which had been constructed to be extremely safe, is losing value almost every day: around $500 million has been lost over the previous week. It is becoming clear that LTCM's bankruptcy is inevitable, with imponderable consequences. If it failed, as William J. McDonough, President of the Federal Reserve Bank of New York, later put it, 'there was a likelihood that a number of credit and interest rate markets would experience extreme price moves and possibly cease to function for a period of one or more days and maybe longer' (McDonough 1998: 1052). Should that have happened, said Alan Greenspan, Chairman of the Federal Reserve, it 'could have potentially impaired the economies of many nations, including our own' (Greenspan 1998: 1046).

Thursday, 11 October 2001: the war in Afghanistan has scarcely begun and its outcome is still unclear. Economic indicators increasingly point to recession. Yet the main global equity markets, having plunged

---

[2] See, for example, Chaffin and Clow (2001), from whom the quotation is taken. A derivative is an asset (such as a swap or option: see below), the value of which depends on the price of another, 'underlying' asset or on the level of an index or interest rate.

following the September 11 atrocities, have recovered to the level they were at prior to that dreadful morning: 'Within the space of a month, equity markets seem to have gone from assuming that the effects of the terrorist attacks would be politically and economically catastrophic to assuming that, after allowing for the easing of monetary policy, the effect will be neutral or broadly positive' (Coggan 2001). The bonds of 'emerging market' countries have fallen, but by a surprisingly small average 2.5 per cent. Joyce Chang, analyst at J. P. Morgan, comments that 'the sell-off has been very orderly compared with other crises' (Ostrovsky and Wiggins 2001). The US government bond market has been hit both financially and in human terms: the broker and market-maker Cantor Fitzgerald, with its offices high in the World Trade Center, has suffered dreadfully. But even a week after the atrocities, it is becoming clear that the crisis in the bond market is less severe than three years previously. 'Traders stressed ... that the bond market was not undergoing the turmoil it endured in 1998 after the Long-Term Capital Management hedge-fund crisis. ... "The market is by no means locked up," ' said one (Wiggins and Boland 2001).

The chain of events set in motion on September 11 has not yet run its course. Here, I shall use its early phase simply as a counterpoint to the 1998 crisis. It may seem callous to discuss the financial consequences of an event whose human aspects were so dreadful, but I make no apologies for doing so. Economic crises, after all, have their own way of killing: undramatic, unnoticed, individual; through despair, dislocation and disease. Their effects are at their worst not in the heartland countries of the global financial system but in its peripheries. Understanding the robustness of the financial system in the face of shocks of different kinds is not unimportant.

Because LTCM was at their heart, the events of August and September 1998 also have a significance of quite a different kind. The near-failure of LTCM (it was rescued from bankruptcy by a consortium of the world's leading banks coordinated by the Federal Reserve Bank of New York) has been taken as a verdict upon the modern theory of finance and on the mathematical models at its core. Among LTCM's partners were Robert C. Merton and Myron Scholes, winners of the 1997 Nobel Prize in Economics for their fundamental contributions to the theory of finance, and others in the firm were also well versed in the theory and had often been important contributors to it. Typical is the conclusion of the most influential work on LTCM:

The professors ... sent their mathematical Frankenstein gamely into the world as if it could tame the element of chance in life itself. No self-doubt tempered them; no sense of perspective checked them as they wagered such staggering sums. (Lowenstein 2000: 235)

To those, like myself, on the more 'humanistic', qualitative rather than quantitative side of the social sciences, such a conclusion is seductive. But as I have investigated the episode and its intellectual and economic context, I have learned that Lowenstein's verdict, comforting as it is to those with my inclinations, is false. Indeed, ultimately it trivializes what took place. If LTCM really had been guilty of blind faith in mathematical models and of reckless risk taking, its crisis would have been predictable and of little interest. But it was guilty of neither and its fate is therefore the more interesting. We need a far more nuanced view of finance theory, of mathematical models of financial risk, of LTCM and of the events of 1998. This chapter, which represents work in progress rather than any definitive statement, attempts to sketch this more nuanced view.

Four sections follow this introduction. The first describes the development of the modern theory of finance, focusing especially on the crucial role in that theory of arbitrage.[3] Arbitrage is the exploitation of differences between the prices of the same or similar assets; it is the key mechanism that drives prices towards their theoretical values. This section of the chapter may be somewhat 'tough going' for readers without a background in finance. They can be reassured that all that is required to understand the later parts of the chapter is the overall gist of this section (in particular the pivotal assumption that arbitrage will close price discrepancies), not its details. The second section explores the possibility that finance theory is performative: that it helps bring into being the world that its models posit rather than simply describing an already-existing external world. The third section describes LTCM, its trading strategies and the crisis of 1998. The fourth section suggests some general conclusions about the 1998 encounter with risk, the contrast with 2001, and financial models, imitation and arbitrage.

---

[3] For a brief history of finance theory that emphasizes the centrality of arbitrage, see Harrison (1997), and for a more extensive history, see Bernstein (1992). One of the few sociological studies of arbitrage is Beunza and Stark (2004).

Arbitrage and models of financial markets

The invocation of arbitrage as a mechanism in models of financial markets can be traced most centrally to the Nobel Prize-winning work of Franco Modigliani and Merton Miller, who demonstrated that in a 'perfect market' (Modigliani and Miller 1958: 268) the total value of a firm is not affected by its 'capital structure', that is, by its degree of leverage, the extent to which it chooses to finance its activities by the issuance of debt such as bonds rather than stock. What was of significance was not just Modigliani and Miller's proposition, but the way they proved it: a way that has become known as 'arbitrage proof'. They showed that if two firms with different capital structures but identical expected future income streams were valued differently by the market, 'arbitrage will take place and restore the stated equalities'. In other words, 'an investor could buy and sell stocks and bonds in such a way as to exchange one income stream for another stream, identical in all relevant respects but selling at a lower price. … As investors exploit these arbitrage opportunities, the value of the overpriced shares will fall and that of the underpriced shares will rise, thereby tending to eliminate the discrepancy between the market values of the firms' (Modigliani and Miller 1958: 269).

The key papers initiating the use of 'arbitrage proof' to determine the price of derivatives were by Fischer Black, Myron Scholes and Robert C. Merton (Black and Scholes 1973; Merton 1973), work that in 1997 won Nobel Prizes for Scholes and Merton (Black died prematurely in 1995). The problem solved by Black, Scholes and Merton was the pricing of options: contracts that confer the right, but not the obligation, to buy ('call') or sell ('put') a given asset at a given price, at (or up to) a given expiry date. Again assuming a perfect market (no transaction costs and, for example, the capacity both to borrow and to lend at the riskless rate[4] of interest), they showed that an option on an asset such as stock could be replicated completely by a continuously adjusted portfolio of the asset and cash, so long as the returns on the asset followed the by-then-standard model of a log-normal[5] random walk

---

[4] The 'riskless rate' is the rate of interest paid by a borrower whom lenders are certain will not default. The yield of bonds issued in their own currency by major governments is typically taken as an indicator of the riskless rate.

[5] If stock price changes themselves were normally distributed, there would be a non-zero probability of negative prices and limited liability means that stock prices cannot be negative. Log-normality of price changes was a more attractive

in continuous time.[6] If the price of the asset diverges from the cost of
the replicating portfolio, arbitrageurs will buy the cheaper and short
sell[7] the dearer of the two, and they will continue to do so until equality
is restored. More generally, Black, Scholes and Merton's analyses
suggested a methodology for the rational pricing and hedging of derivative products of all kinds: identify the replicating portfolio of more
basic assets (if it exists) and use its cost to work out the price of the
derivative and (if desired) to hedge its risks. This methodology is, as
noted in the introduction, key not just to the academic study of derivatives but also to the practice of derivatives markets.

Commentary on LTCM's crisis has often drawn a connection
between the events of August and September 1998 and the assumption
of log-normality in Black-Scholes-Merton option pricing: some of the
price movements of those months were indeed wildly improbable on
the hypothesis of log-normality (see MacKenzie 2003a). To focus upon
log-normality, however, is to focus on a less-than-central aspect of
Black, Scholes and Merton's contribution to finance theory: that
stock price changes were not in practice log-normal was known even
in 1973, when their work was published. As Bouleau (1998: 63) puts it,
the 'epistemological rupture' is the idea of the replicating portfolio and
consequent possibility of pricing by arbitrage. Merton himself, and
other finance theorists such as Steve Ross, John Cox, Mark
Rubinstein and William Sharpe, soon showed how to extend the
basic framework of Black-Scholes-Merton derivative pricing to worlds
in which the dynamics of asset pricing was not log-normal.

The work of Black and Scholes on option pricing was first circulated
in October 1970.[8] By 1979, J. Michael Harrison and David M. Kreps
had established the form of derivative pricing theory that is most
attractive to mathematicians (Harrison and Kreps 1979; Harrison
and Pliska 1981). Crucial was the link they drew to the theory of
martingales. (A martingale is a stochastic process for which expected
future values of a variable, conditional upon its current value, are its

assumption because it avoided this problem (a variable is log-normal if its
  logarithm follows a normal distribution).
[6] I am here oversimplifying a complex historical development: see MacKenzie
  (2003b).
[7] To 'short sell' or 'short' an asset is to sell an asset one does not own, for example
  by borrowing it, selling it and later repurchasing and returning it.
[8] This version is in box 28 of the Fischer Black papers at MIT (Institute Archives,
  MC505).

current value. Loosely – there are deep mathematical complications here – a martingale is a 'fair game': in a game of chance which is a martingale, a player's expectation of gain or loss is zero.) Others had previously realized that financial markets could be modelled as martingales, but it was Harrison and Kreps (and Stanley R. Pliska) who brought to bear the full power of modern martingale theory. Martingale theory freed option pricing from dependence upon any *particular* stochastic process: it could encompass the log-normal random walk posited by Black, Scholes and Merton; the Poisson, 'jump', process investigated by Cox, Ross and Merton; and the finite-time models of Sharpe, Cox, Ross and Rubinstein.

Harrison and Kreps showed that in a 'frictionless' market with no opportunities for arbitrage, there existed an 'equivalent martingale measure', a way of assigning probabilities to the path followed by the price of an asset such that the arbitrage-imposed price of a derivative contract on that asset was simply the conditional expectation of its payoff discounted back to the present. If the market was complete – in other words, if every contingent claim[9] could be replicated – then the equivalent martingale measure was unique. Harrison and Kreps's conclusions gave general form to perhaps the most surprising of the findings of the work of Black, Scholes and Merton: that pricing by arbitrage proof meant that all sorts of complications, notably the degree of risk aversion of investors, could be ignored and derivatives could be priced as if all investors were risk neutral. (To get a sense of what 'risk neutrality' means, imagine being offered a fair bet with a 50 per cent chance of winning $1,000 and a 50 per cent chance of losing $1,000, and thus an expected value of zero. If you would require to be paid to take on such a bet you are 'risk averse'; if you would pay to take it on you are 'risk seeking'; if you would take it on without inducement, but without being prepared to pay to do so, you are 'risk neutral'.)

These 1970s' developments in derivative pricing theory were greatly elaborated in the 1980s and 1990s, as any textbook of mathematical finance (e.g. Hull 2000) reveals and, as noted above, were drawn on heavily in the rapidly growing derivatives markets. The theory of derivatives developed by Black, Scholes and Merton, and added to by

---

[9] A contingent claim (such as an option) is a contract the value of which depends on some future state of the world (for example, the value of an option at its expiry depends on the price of the underlying asset).

Cox, Ross, Rubinstein, Harrison, Kreps and others, forms an essential part of this huge high-modern industry, guiding participants both in the pricing of derivative products and in hedging the risks involved. The theory and its accompanying mathematical models are built deep into the economic structure of high modernity.

'Arbitrage proof' thus plays a central role in the theory of derivatives. Arbitrage is also highly significant in the justification of the overall notion of 'market efficiency', which has shaped not just financial economics but also, via the plausibility it lends to notions of rational expectations, economics as a whole, and has helped derivatives markets to grow by providing legitimacy. Options, for example, are not new products: they have been traded since the seventeenth century. They had often been the object of suspicion, however, because they looked dangerously like wagers on price movements. The argument that derivatives could contribute to market efficiency, and were not simply vehicles for gambling, was key to the gradual removal in the 1970s and 1980s of legal barriers to derivatives trading (MacKenzie and Millo 2003).

A financial market is 'efficient' if prices in it reflect all available information (Fama 1970). The idea of market efficiency is the key overall foundation of orthodox modern financial economics, as well as contributing to the perceived legitimacy of actual markets. But what might make markets efficient? For some of the central figures in modern financial economics, to assume that all investors are perfectly rational and perfectly well informed has been just too heroic. It is, for example, difficult on that assumption to explain the high volumes of trading in the financial markets. If markets are efficient, prices already incorporate all publicly available information, and so if all traders are perfectly rational and perfectly well informed, why should they continue to trade once they have diversified their portfolios satisfactorily? 'Noise trading,' said Fischer Black (1986: 531) 'provides the essential missing ingredient. Noise trading is trading on noise as if it were information. People who trade on noise are willing to trade even though from an objective point of view they would be better off not trading. Perhaps they think the noise they are trading on is information. Or perhaps they just like to trade.'

If the empirical presence of noise trading and other departures from rationality is hard to deny, and if its denial leads to incorrect predictions (markets with far less trading than in reality), does this then mean that the thesis of market efficiency must be rejected and some version of 'behavioural finance' adopted?[10] Not so, argues Steve Ross (2001: 4):

> I, for one, never thought that people – myself included – were all that rational in their behavior. To the contrary, I am always amazed at what people do. But, that was never the point of financial theory.
>
> The absence of arbitrage requires that there be enough well financed and smart investors to close arbitrage opportunities when they appear. … Neoclassical finance is a theory of sharks and not a theory of rational homo economicus, and that is the principal distinction between finance and traditional economics. In most economic models aggregate demand depends on average demand and for that reason, traditional economic theories require the average individual to be rational. In liquid securities markets, though, profit opportunities bring about infinite discrepancies between demand and supply. Well financed arbitrageurs spot these opportunities, pile on, and by their actions they close aberrant price differentials. … Rational finance has stripped the assumptions [about the behaviour of investors] down to only those required to support efficient markets and the absence of arbitrage, and has worked very hard to rid the field of its sensitivity to the psychological vagaries of investors.

Performing theory

Orthodox modern finance economics, including the theory of derivatives, is elegant and powerful. What is the relationship of that theory and its accompanying models to 'reality'? They are, of course, an abstraction from it and known to be such by all involved: see, for example, Black (1988). Neither finance theorists nor sophisticated practical users of financial models believe in the literal truth of the models' assumptions.[11] Does that lack of verisimilitude mean that, as much of the commentary on LTCM (such as Lowenstein 2000) suggests, the theory is a hopelessly flawed endeavour? Two points suggest not. The first was spelled out by Milton Friedman in his famous essay 'The methodology of positive economics' (Friedman 1953). The test of an economic theory, Friedman argued, was not the accuracy of its

---

[10] In 'behavioural finance', market participants are assumed to be less than entirely rational, for example to be subject to various systematic biases, normally psychological in their nature.

[11] See the interviews drawn on in MacKenzie (2003a, 2003b) and MacKenzie and Millo (2003).

assumptions but the accuracy of its predictions. That viewpoint has
become fundamental not just to modern neoclassical economics but
also to finance theory: indeed, one of the distinguishing features of the
modern theory of finance is that it abandoned the earlier attitude that
the job of the scholar in finance was accurately to describe what people
in the finance industry actually did. When the Black-Scholes-Merton
option-pricing model, for example, was first propounded in the early
1970s, its assumptions were wildly unrealistic. Not only was it already
known by then that empirical stock price distributions had 'fat tails' (in
other words, that the probabilities of extreme events were considerably
greater than implied by the log-normal model), but transaction costs
were high (not zero as assumed in the model), there were significant
restrictions on short-selling stocks, etc. By the late 1970s and early
1980s, however, the differences between empirical option prices and
best-fit Black-Scholes theoretical prices were remarkably good, with
residual discrepancies typically less than 2 per cent (Rubinstein 1985).
'When judged by its ability to explain the empirical data,' commented
Steve Ross (1987: 332), Black-Scholes-Merton option-pricing theory
and its variants formed 'the most successful theory not only in finance,
but in all of economics'. (Interestingly, the fit between empirical data
and the Black-Scholes-Merton model deteriorated after 1987, but that
is a matter which for reasons of space must be set aside here: see
Rubinstein 1994; MacKenzie and Millo 2003.)

The second point is that the empirical accuracy of finance theory's
typical assumptions has increased considerably since the 1970s. This is
perhaps most apparent in regard to the speed of transactions (the
Black-Scholes-Merton option-pricing model assumes the possibility
of instantaneous adjustment of the replicating portfolio) and transaction costs. Because of technological change and institutional reform (in
particular, the abolition of fixed commissions on the New York Stock
Exchange and other leading exchanges), for major players in the main
stock markets transaction costs are now close to zero[12] and significant
adjustments to portfolios can now be made, if not instantaneously at

[12] Among the reasons is that brokers will offer to transact large trades effectively
free of commission because of the informational advantages such transactions
offer them. Note, however, that slippage (see text) is still a significant issue and it
can also be seen as a transaction cost.

least in seconds. Finance theory models are still idealizations of market realities, but less radical idealizations than they were in the early 1970s.

Has the crucial assumption that price discrepancies will be closed by arbitrage, like the other assumptions of finance theory, also become more true with the passage of time? The prevalence of arbitrage opportunities is a more difficult point to investigate than, for example, the decline in transaction costs. There is a strong incentive to exploit such opportunities rather than to reveal them in the academic literature, so they may be under-reported. Conversely, however, what may *appear* to be an arbitrage opportunity may actually disappear as soon as one seeks to exploit it. The typical mechanism by which this happens is what market participants call 'slippage': the movement of prices against one as soon as one starts to trade in significant quantities. Because of slippage and other practicalities, one cannot simply investigate statistically: in a sense, to determine the presence of arbitrage opportunities one must become an arbitrageur. As Ross puts it: 'To find the [arbitrage] opportunities one must put oneself in the shoes of the arbitrageurs which is difficult and expensive' (2001: 4).

The testimony of actual arbitrageurs (in interview)[13] is not entirely unequivocal, but all tend to agree that arbitrage opportunities that are relatively easy to identify tend to diminish. The action of arbitrageurs may not close them completely – there may be a kind of 'predator–prey' dynamics (see below) in which as arbitrage opportunities diminish so too does the commitment of arbitrage capital to exploiting them – and the expansion of the global financial system into new geographical territories and new products creates new opportunities to replace diminished ones. But, overall, it seems reasonable to conclude that in the core financial markets of the Euro-American world the assumption that price discrepancies will be closed by arbitrage has a tendency to become more realistic.

Note that some of the increasing realism of the assumptions of finance theory is due to the very development and acceptance of the theory. As Callon (1998) has pointed out, economic theory has a performative dimension. It does not simply describe an already-existing external world, but can help that world come into being. (The classic study of neoclassical economics creating a market in its own image is Garcia 1986.) Part of the process by which finance theory's models

---

[13] For these interviews, see note 11.

gained verisimilitude had nothing directly to do with those models, but was the result of the role of technological change in speeding transactions and reducing transaction costs. However, part of it was the result of the role of free-market economics (to which finance theory was a significant contributor) in legitimating the removal of what were increasingly seen as regulatory 'barriers'. Yet another part of the process was the mutually reinforcing interaction between financial economics and the 'financial' view of the firm as oriented above all to maximizing shareholder value (see Whitley 1986a, 1986b).

Performative aspects of financial economics can also be found in more detailed matters. Take, for example, option-pricing theory. The close empirical fit between the pattern of observed option prices and the Black-Scholes-Merton model resulted in part from the use of option-pricing theory to detect and exploit arbitrage opportunities.[14] In addition, the Black-Scholes-Merton analysis and subsequent developments of it enable the risks involved in derivatives portfolios to be decomposed mathematically. Many of these risks are mutually offsetting, so the residual risk that requires to be hedged is often quite small in relation to the overall portfolio, and the transaction costs incurred in doing so are limited. So the Black-Scholes-Merton assumption of zero transaction costs is now close to true for the hedging of derivatives by major investment banks – in part because the use of that theory and its developments by those banks allows them to manage their portfolios in a way that minimizes transaction costs.

If finance theory already had its performative aspects by 1980, by the 1990s it was, as noted above, built into the very fabric of the high-modern financial world. Thus Walter (1996: 904) describes the role of Itô's lemma, the key bridging result between 'ordinary' calculus and the stochastic calculus of Merton's version of option-pricing theory and its many more recent developments. Without the lemma, 'no trading room

---

[14] The classic arbitrage was 'spreading': using option-pricing theory to identify relatively 'over-priced' and relatively 'under-priced' options on the same underlying asset, selling over-priced options and hedging their risk by buying under-priced ones. The effect of the strategy was to push prices in the direction of satisfying the key econometric test (Rubinstein 1985) of the validity of the Black-Scholes-Merton model: that the 'implied volatilities' of all the options with the same expiry on the same underlying asset should be identical. This is discussed in more detail in MacKenzie and Millo (2003), which also examines why option prices since 1987 differ from prices prior to 1987 in this respect.

could now manage its options market positions'.[15] The key players in the markets of high-modern finance perform not just general notions of market efficiency but highly sophisticated mathematical formulations. Martingale theory, for example, is no longer simply 'pure mathematics' but is performed in flesh, blood and silicon in the markets. Finance theory is a world-making, and not just a world-describing, endeavour.

Long-Term Capital Management

LTCM was an investment partnership set up in 1993 by John Meriwether, previously head of Salomon Brothers' bond arbitrage desk and a senior manager in the bank.[16] Meriwether recruited to LTCM from Salomon and elsewhere an impressive team of experienced traders and specialists in mathematical finance: among its partners were Merton and Scholes, whose work on option-pricing theory is described above. Much of LTCM's trading was with leading banks and it largely avoided risky 'emerging markets', preferring well-established ones such as those in government bonds of the leading industrial nations (though active in the United States and Japan, as Salomon had been, LTCM was more heavily involved than Salomon had been in European bond markets), in swaps,[17] in options, in mortgage derivatives and in certain very restricted categories of stock.[18] Following the tradition established by Meriwether at Salomon, the fund eschewed speculation based upon intuitive hunches. It sought pricing discrepancies around which to base arbitrage strategies and generally constructed its positions so as to be insulated from overall stock market movements and interest rate changes.

[15] My translation. In fact, there may be rather greater dependence on discrete-time models such as Cox-Ross-Rubinstein than on continuous-time models to which Itô's lemma applies (see MacKenzie and Millo 2003), but Walter's generic point is undoubtedly correct.

[16] This section draws on an earlier treatment of LTCM (MacKenzie 2000), but that treatment is in some respects in error. MacKenzie (2003a) discusses the LTCM case fully – it contains, for example, quantitative tests of the explanation of 1998 that is sketched here – and it should be consulted for details, discussion of sources, etc. In the interests of brevity, I describe here only the outline of the episode.

[17] A 'swap' is a contract to exchange two income streams, for example fixed-rate and floating-rate interest on the same notional principal sum.

[18] See, for example, the list of LTCM's major positions on 21 August 1998 given in Perold (1999: C6–C7).

LTCM's market positions were varied, but a common theme underlay many of them. Using theoretical reasoning, extensive practical experience and databases of prices the firm would identify pairs of assets, the prices of which ought to be closely related, which should over the long run converge (and in some cases *had* to do so), but which for contingent reasons had diverged: perhaps one was temporarily somewhat easier to trade than the other and therefore more popular, or perhaps institutions had a particular need for one rather than the other. The fund would then buy the underpriced, less popular asset and borrow and sell the overpriced, more popular asset (or take positions equivalent to these by use of derivatives, especially swaps). The close relation between the two assets would mean that general market changes such as a rise or fall in interest rates or in the stock market would affect the prices of each nearly equally, and long-run convergence between their prices would create a small but very low-risk profit for LTCM. By 'levering' its own capital – in other words, performing arbitrage using borrowed funds and/or securities – LTCM could turn this small profit into a larger one; this also increased risk, but only to modest levels. The partnership knew perfectly well that over the short and medium term prices might diverge further, but the probabilities and the consequences of them doing so were carefully calculated by a statistical 'value-at-risk' model, which measured the potential losses from adverse market movements (by the late 1990s such models were used by all the sophisticated institutional participants in the financial markets).

Pace standard accounts of LTCM, however, the firm did not simply assume that past price patterns would continue into the future, nor did it display an uncritical attitude to its risk model. Observed volatilities and correlations were increased by explicitly judgement-based 'safety factors' to take account of possible changes in markets and of possible deficiencies in the model. A consequence of this conservatism was that LTCM's risk model predicted risk levels that were substantially higher than those actually experienced (until the 1998 crisis). The model predicted an annual volatility of net asset value of 14.5 per cent while the actual volatility was 11 per cent, and both figures were considerably less than the 20 per cent volatility that investors in LTCM had been warned to expect. LCTM also 'stress-tested' its trading positions to gauge the effect on them of extreme events not captured by standard statistical models or by recent historical experience, events such as the failure of European economic and monetary union or stock exchanges crashing by a third in a day. LTCM balanced its portfolio to minimize the consequences of such events and sometimes purchased explicit protection against their consequences. With a considerable presence in the Italian capital markets, for example, LTCM decided it was prudent to buy protection against bond default by the government of Italy.

Was what LTCM did 'arbitrage'? LTCM certainly described its activities as such and in so doing it was simply adopting the standard financial-market usage of the term. However, LTCM needed to deploy some of its own capital as a foundation for borrowing, and its need to apply a value-at-risk model makes clear that its trading involved risk (albeit apparently modest risk), when in orthodox finance theory arbitrage is defined as being profitable trading that demands no net capital and is entirely free from risk. An economist might therefore respond that a case study of LTCM's risky trading has no bearing on our understanding of arbitrage as a riskless theoretical mechanism.

However, among LTCM's major positions (and one of the two most serious sources of loss) was a close real-world counterpart of the arbitrage that imposes Black-Scholes option pricing, the central theorem of the economics of derivatives. This position, taken on in 1997, responded to a price discrepancy developing in the market for stock index options with long expirations. As the name suggests, an index option is one in which the underlying 'asset' is not the stock of an individual corporation but the level of a broad stock market index. Increasingly, banks and insurers in Europe and the United States were selling investors products with returns linked to gains in equity indices but also a guaranteed 'floor' to losses. Long expiry options were attractive to the vendors of such products as a means of hedging their risk, but such options were in short supply. The price of an option is dependent upon predictions of the volatility of the underlying asset, and market expectations of that volatility ('implied volatility') can be deduced from option prices using option-pricing theory – indeed, that is one of the most important uses of the theory. In 1997, however, the demand for long-expiry options had pushed the volatilities implied by their prices to levels that seemed to bear little relation to the volatilities of the underlying indices. Five-year options on the S & P 500 index, for example, were selling at implied volatilities of 22 per cent per annum and higher, when the volatility of the index itself had for several years fluctuated between 10 per cent and 13 per cent, and the implied volatilities of shorter-term options were also much less than 20 per cent per annum (Perold 1999: A7–A8). LTCM therefore sold large quantities of five-year index options, while hedging the risks involved with index futures and sometimes short-expiry options. In effect, then, LTCM responded to the discrepancy in prices by selling the options and 'buying' and adjusting the replicating portfolio. Complications such as the use of short-expiry options aside, LTCM was conducting the arbitrage that option-pricing theory posits.

The event that triggered LTCM's crisis was the decision of the Russian government on 17 August 1998 to default on rouble-denominated bonds and in effect to devalue the rouble while permitting Russian banks temporarily not to honour foreign-exchange forward contracts. LTCM had only a minor exposure to Russia, but the precise form of Russia's actions caused significant losses to other hedge funds and Western banks. A hedge fund called High Risk Opportunities failed, and unfounded rumours began that Lehman Brothers, an established investment bank, was also about to do so. Suddenly, market unease turned into self-feeding fear. A 'flight to quality' took place as a host of institutions sought to liquidate investments that were seen as difficult to sell and potentially higher risk and to replace them with lower-risk, more liquid alternatives. Because LTCM's arbitrage generally involved holding the former and short selling the latter, the result was a substantial market movement against the fund.

A similar flight to quality was, for example, triggered by the attacks of September 11 (2001). The key difference between the events of 1998 and 2001 is that the 1998 flight to quality was amplified, overlain and in some instances contradicted by a much more specific process.[19] LTCM's very success had encouraged imitation: other hedge funds

[19] In a minority of instances, LTCM (and, most likely, its imitators) held the *more* liquid asset and was short the illiquid one. In Germany and France, for example, LTCM held (highly liquid) government bonds, hedged by paying fixed interest in (less liquid) interest-rate swaps. This kind of case is crucial in allowing the effects of a flight to quality to be distinguished analytically from those of the more specific process discussed in the text. Swap spreads (the difference between the fixed interest rate at which swaps can be entered into and the yield of government bonds of equivalent maturity denominated in the same currency) should rise in a flight to quality. They did indeed do so sharply in the United States, United Kingdom and Sweden in 1998, but much less so in Japan (where LTCM had no net position), while in France and Germany they fell during much of the crisis. For further details, see MacKenzie (2003a).

and many of the world's leading banks, notably Wall Street investment banks, had either taken up similar arbitrage trading or devoted more capital to it. In aggregate, this body of arbitrageurs held positions broadly similar to those of LTCM, but some of them had greater exposure to Russia than LTCM had. To cover losses incurred there, they had to liquidate other positions similar to LTCM's. As the prices of these moved against the arbitrageurs, they found themselves having to liquidate further positions, thus worsening price pressures, and so on. The arbitrage 'superportfolio' (the aggregate of arbitrage positions similar to LTCM's) began to unravel.

Paradoxically, the process seems to have been intensified by risk management practices in banks. Banks employ value-at-risk models not just as LTCM did (to gauge the overall risks faced by the fund) but also as a management tool (see, for example, Dunbar 2000). By allocating value-at-risk limits to individual traders and trading desks, banks can prevent the accumulation of over-risky positions while giving traders flexibility within those limits. In 1996, the importance of value-at-risk models was increased when the Basel Committee on Banking Supervision permitted banks to use these models to help determine capital adequacy ratios. This reduced the amount of capital that banks had to set aside, but had the consequence that as volatility increased and prices moved against a bank, it could ultimately face a choice between setting aside more capital and liquidating its positions. In August 1998, many seem to have opted for liquidation. Value-at-risk became a stop-loss rule: the traders involved had no alternative but to try to cut their losses and sell, even if it was an extremely unfavourable time to do so. In August 1998, widespread efforts, apparently often driven by risk models, to liquidate broadly similar positions in roughly the same set of markets, in a situation in which those who might otherwise have bought such assets were also trying to sell, intensified the adverse market movements that were the initial problem. Crucially, these various processes unravelling the arbitrage superportfolio led to greatly enhanced correlations between what historically had been only loosely related markets, across which risk had seemed to be reduced by diversification.

When used as management tools, value-at-risk models (intended to describe the market as if it were an external thing) thus became part of a process that magnified adverse market movements, which reached levels far beyond those anticipated by these models. LTCM's loss in

August 1998 was a –10.5σ event on the firm's risk model and a –14σ event in terms of the actual previous price movements: both have probabilities that are vanishingly small. Value-at-risk models with stop-loss rules, other forms of stop-loss, management nervousness, hedge fund managers' fears of investor withdrawals, the need to liquidate positions to meet such withdrawals, cover losses and meet margin calls – all these seem to have combined to cause a failure of arbitrage. As 'spreads' (the difference between prices of related assets) widened and thus arbitrage opportunities grew more attractive, arbitrageurs did not move into the market, narrowing spreads and restoring 'normality'. Instead, potential arbitrageurs continued to flee, widening spreads and intensifying the problems of those which remained, such as LTCM.

LTCM, however, was constructed so robustly that these problems, though they caused major losses, were not fatal. In September 1998, though, LTCM's difficulties became public. On 2 September, Meriwether sent a private fax to LTCM's investors describing the fund's August results and seeking to raise further capital to exploit what (quite reasonably) he described as attractive arbitrage opportunities.[20] The fax was posted almost immediately on the Internet and seems to have been read as evidence of desperation. The nervousness of the markets crystallized as fear of LTCM's failure. Almost no one could be persuaded to buy, at any reasonable price, an asset that LTCM was known or believed to hold because of the concern that the markets were about to be saturated by a fire sale of the fund's positions. In addition, LTCM's counterparties – the banks and other institutions that had taken the other side of its trades – protected themselves as much as possible against LTCM's failure by a mechanism that seems to have sealed the fund's fate. LTCM had constructed its trades so that solid collateral, typically government bonds, moved backwards and forwards between it and its counterparties as market prices moved in favour of one or the other. Under normal circumstances, when market prices were unequivocal, it was an eminently sensible way of controlling risk. But in the fear-chilled, illiquid markets of September 1998, prices lost their character as external facts. LTCM's counterparties marked against LTCM: that is, they chose prices that were predicated on LTCM's failure. That minimized the consequences for their balance

---

[20] The fax is reproduced in Perold (1999: D1–D3).

sheets of LTCM's failure by getting hold of as much of the firm's collateral as possible, but made that failure inevitable by draining the firm of its remaining capital.

Conclusion

The crisis of 1998 was not the result of reckless risk taking on LTCM's part, nor of blind faith in models. The background to the crisis was a flight to quality involving sharp rises in the relative prices of safe and liquid instruments and sharp declines in those that were perceived as risky and illiquid. But the flight to quality was only part of the process that generated the crisis. A similar flight took place in September 2001, but its effects were different and more limited. By then, the capital devoted to the kind of convergence and relative value arbitrage pursued by LTCM was tiny by comparison with three years previously (perhaps a tenth as large). There was no massive superportfolio of overlapping arbitrage positions and no major internal mechanism amplifying the crisis.[21] No major hedge fund failed; no investment bank – not even Morgan Stanley, a major occupant of the World Trade Center – was threatened. The overall returns for September 2001 of JWM Partners, the successor fund set up by John Meriwether and several of his former colleagues at LTCM, were 'basically flat'. August and September 1998 devastated the world of the arbitrageurs; September 2001 was but a relatively minor disturbance of it.

LTCM's success, and imitation of that success by others, had created by the summer of 1998 a 'global microstructure' (in the sense of Knorr

---

[21] There was a bottleneck in the US repo market caused by disruption to the Bank of New York, the main Treasury bond settlement agent, whose headquarters were close to the World Trade Center. (Repo is a contract in which party A borrows money from party B to buy securities such as bonds. B holds the securities as collateral for the loan.) On 4 October 2001, the Treasury Department decided on an *ad hoc* auction of $6 billion of ten-year bonds to alleviate the bottleneck (Ip and Zuckerman 2001). On September 11 – in response to earlier stock market falls, not the terrorist attacks – the UK Financial Services Agency had also suspended another potential source of amplification, the 'resilience test' imposed on UK insurance companies. The test requires insurers to be able to meet their obligations following a 25 per cent drop in share prices and an increase of 3 percentage points in interest rates. The Agency's fear was that the test would force insurers to sell into an already falling market, so exacerbating its fall (Bolger 2001).

Cetina and Bruegger 2002). A superportfolio had been created, in part deliberately (because of conscious imitation of LTCM), in part inadvertently (independent discovery of, and efforts to exploit, the same pricing anomalies). Once the holders of part of this superportfolio had to unwind their positions, they caused price movements that impacted negatively on the other holders of the portfolio. LTCM was structured precisely so as to avoid having to liquidate positions in the face of such pressures and indeed it did not do so on any large scale (although the sheer size of its positions would in any case have made it extremely difficult to liquidate them quickly). But the large losses LTCM suffered in August 1998 set in motion, in September, what was in effect a run on the bank. The prophecy of LTCM's failure became self-fulfilling (Merton 1949), or at least would have done so had the Federal Reserve not intervened.

Debate over the adequacy of mathematical models of financial risk, or about the efficient market hypothesis and wider theoretical framework of modern financial economics, has a curiously static, ahistorical character.[22] Financial economics, and the models it proposes, affect the reality that it and they analyse. Most of the time, I would conjecture, the effects of this reflexive connection serve to increase the veracity of finance theory's assumptions and the accuracy of its models' predictions. For example, as noted above, the availability of the Black-Scholes-Merton model of option prices, predicated as it was on the assumption that arbitrage would close pricing discrepancies, assisted arbitrageurs in identifying, exploiting and thus reducing those discrepancies. The model's practical adoption, in other words, helped make it more true. The events of 1998, in contrast, suggest a reflexive loop that was counterperformative rather than performative. The exploitation of arbitrage opportunities, using mathematical models (albeit ad hoc models, often quite simple and typically involving estimated parameters), grew to such a level that it became unstable. As spreads began to widen, instead of arbitrageurs entering the market to reduce them, they found themselves forced to flee the market, thus widening spreads. The assumption that arbitrage would close pricing discrepancies was,

---

[22] See, for example, the most important recent contribution to this debate (Shleifer 2000). On many particular topics, including the limits of arbitrage (see below), it is insightful. But Shleifer's central question, the validity of the efficient market hypothesis, is largely construed as if that question had an ahistorically correct answer, at least for the past thirty years. Almost certainly, it does not.

paradoxically, undermined by the very popularity that arbitrage had come to enjoy.

Part of the process that undermined arbitrage in 1998 was identified and modelled in a prescient article by Andrei Shleifer and Robert Vishny (1997: see also Shleifer 2000). While, in economic theory, arbitrage may be riskless, real-world arbitrage often involves risk and often cannot be conducted entirely using borrowed capital. If those who invest in arbitrageurs (hedge fund investors, senior management in investment banks, etc.) are influenced by the performance of these investments, then a price movement against arbitrageurs can become self-reinforcing, as the latter are forced by investor withdrawals to abandon even excellent arbitrage opportunities. Another, more explicitly sociological part of the process leading to the crisis of 1998 was, as I have suggested, imitation. Imitation – 'herd behaviour' it is sometimes called – in financial markets is often noted but is typically assumed to be the characteristic of naïve, uninformed, lay investors and to be irrational. If the hypothesis presented here is correct, however, the preconditions of the 1998 crisis were created by skilled, professional investors imitating each other. Nor, furthermore, should we regard imitation as necessarily irrational. André Orléan suggests an appropriate metaphor. Imagine you and another person are in a room in which a fire breaks out. The room has two exits, one which leads to a dead-end (if you take it, you will die) and one through which you can safely escape, but you do not know which is which. Nor do you know whether the other person knows. With no time to communicate, you decide simply to imitate the other person, following him or her through whichever door he or she chooses. It is herd behaviour – at least with a herd numbering two – but is it irrational? No, says Orléan. If the other person knows which exit leads to safety, one has assured one's safety. If he or she does not know, you are no worse off than if you had on your own taken a random decision (Orléan 1998: 39).[23] Relative-value arbitrageurs in August 1998, and a wider range of market participants in September 1998, were in a sense in the room postulated by Orléan,

---

[23] Fans of the television game show *Who wants to be a millionaire?* will note the structural parallel with the option of the contestant, who has to choose the right answer among four possibilities, to 'ask the audience': in other words, to poll the studio audience. 'Ask the audience' is a valuable resource – participants can use it only once – because the answers of those who do not know will tend to distribute randomly, so the most popular answer is probably right.

with the added complication that the safety of the different courses of action was not a given, but was affected by the ensemble of their own behaviour. Their behaviour was rational, but in a profound sense it was also social.

The key, fatal consequence of imitation was the disastrous increase in correlations of August and September 1998. LTCM's arbitrage positions were geographically diverse, in disparate asset classes and in spreads that at the level of economic 'fundamentals' were often quite unrelated. Yet correlations that had historically been at the level of 0.1 or lower jumped during the crisis to around 0.7 as the holders of the imitative superportfolio started to liquidate its components simultaneously. This – the 'social', imitative, correlational nature of financial risk – interestingly is the lesson that LTCM's principals have learned from their 1998 encounter with risk. The risk model of LTCM's successor fund, JWM Partners, incorporates the possibility that an extreme event can trigger all correlations to become 1.0. Paradoxically, though, the very fact of the unpopularity of relative-value and convergence arbitrage since 1998 meant that even the extreme event of September 11 did not provoke the imitation-based, superportfolio crisis that JWM's risk modelling now anticipates.

Arbitrage is an historically situated process in two senses. First, as noted above, there is an interaction between arbitrage as market practice and arbitrage as theoretical presupposition, an interaction that generally is performative. Second, however, there is an interaction between the popularity of arbitrage and its success. Mostly, this interaction is also positive: arbitrage's success leads it to become more widely practised. But there is perhaps a potential instability, akin to the sudden tipping point in models of predator–prey dynamics.[24] If arbitrageurs are foxes and arbitrage opportunities are rabbits, then a small number of foxes will flourish in a world of many rabbits. Arbitrageurs make markets more efficient, just as in conventional ecological thinking predators are necessary to 'nature's balance', preventing prey populations from outstripping the resources on which

---

[24] I owe the analogy to a conversation with Doyne Farmer (see also Farmer 1998). It is not a complete analogy: it fails fully to capture the processes of August and September 1998, which, as noted in the text, were characterized by an increase, not a decrease, in arbitrage opportunities. The years from 1994 to early summer 1998, however, were characterized by an increase in arbitrage leading to a diminution in arbitrage opportunities: see MacKenzie (2003a).

they in turn depend. But just as fox populations can outstrip those of rabbits and suddenly collapse, so arbitrage can become too popular. That in a sense was the cause of the encounter with risk in 1998: LTCM on its own could have survived the events of that year, but in a world of imitators it could not survive without recapitalization. After a collapse of predator numbers, predation can again become a flourishing activity. So, it seems, with arbitrage. The crisis of 1998 greatly reduced the amount of capital devoted to convergence and relative-value arbitrage. Subsequently, arbitrage seems once again to have become stably profitable, surviving the crisis of September 2001 without difficulty.

How do the two aspects of the historical situatedness of arbitrage interact? The answer may vary from market to market and between pricing discrepancies of different types, and in any case I can only speculate, but one possibility is this: that in some circumstances[25] arbitrage can succeed reliably as a practical activity only when the amounts of capital devoted to it are insufficient substantially to close pricing discrepancies. So any historical tendency for arbitrage to make markets more efficient may remain only that: a tendency, always vulnerable to reverse.

---

[25] See Shleifer and Vishny (1997: 49–54) for some interesting suggestions in respect to the bearing on these circumstances of the risk they analyse of investors withdrawing capital from arbitrage in response to adverse price movements.

8 Interdependencies within an organization

HOWARD KUNREUTHER AND
GEOFFREY HEAL

T HE World Trade Center terrorist attacks of September 11 raise a set of challenges that organizations face in dealing with low-probability events that have catastrophic consequences. More specifically, there are certain bad events that can occur only once. Death is the clearest example: an individual's death is irreversible and unrepeatable. With respect to firm behaviour, bankruptcy is the obvious analogue.[1] This chapter explores the impact that the possibility of an extreme event, such as bankruptcy, has on the propensity of different parts of an organization to take risks.

A key point to emphasize at the outset is that the economic incentive for any division in an organization to invest in risk-reduction measures depends on how it expects the other divisions to behave in this respect. Consider Division 1. If it thinks that the other divisions will not invest in protection, this reduces Division 1's incentive to do so. However, should Division 1 believe that the others are taking appropriate steps to mitigate their risks, it may be best for Division 1 to do so as well. In other words there may be situations where no one invests in protection, even though all divisions would be better off if they had incurred this

Earlier versions of this paper have been presented at the workshop 'Organizational Encounters with Risk' at the London School of Economics (LSE) 3–4 May 2002 and the Risk Symposium 'Formulating Policy to Deal with Contemporary Environmental Risks' at Ohio State University (OSU) on 13 May 2002 and the Decision Processes Workshop at the University of Pennsylvania. We appreciate the helpful comments by Jim Ament and Paul Kleindorfer as well as those participating in the above workshops. We acknowledge support for this research from the US Environmental Protection Agency under Cooperative Agreement CR 826583 with the University of Pennsylvania, the Wharton Risk Management and Decision Processes Center, the Columbia University Earth Institute and the National Science Foundation.

[1] By the term *bankruptcy* we mean the complete financial failure of a firm (Chapter 7 of the US Bankruptcy Code), not the reorganization of an insolvent firm (Chapter 11 of the US Bankruptcy Code). We would like to thank Richard Shell for pointing this out to us.

cost. As will be shown, this situation does *not* have the structure of a prisoner's dilemma game, even though it has some similarities.

The fundamental question that motivates our research is: 'Do organizations such as chemical firms and airline companies, and decision makers such as computer network managers, invest in security to a degree that is adequate from either a private or social perspective?' In general the answer is 'no'. We will then explore the obvious next question: 'What should we do about this?'

Common features of the problem

There are several versions of this problem and all have certain features in common. We have already indicated one of these: a payoff that is discrete. A bad event either occurs or it does not and that is the full range of possibilities. You die or you live. A firm is bankrupt or not. A plane crashes or it doesn't. It is not useful in these examples to differentiate the outcomes more finely.

Another feature common to the problems that we consider is that the risk faced by one agent depends on the actions taken by others. In other words there are externalities. The risk that a corporate divisional manager faces of his company being sent into bankruptcy depends not only on how he manages his divisional risks but also on how other division heads behave. The risk of an airline's plane being blown up by a bomb depends on the thoroughness with which other airlines inspect bags that they transfer to this plane.

Finally, there is a probabilistic element in all of these situations. In contrast to the standard prisoner's dilemma paradigm where the outcomes are specified with certainty, the interdependent security problem involves chance events. The question addressed is whether to invest in protection when there is some probability, often a very small one, that there will be a catastrophic event that could be prevented or mitigated. The risk depends in part on the behaviour of others. The unfavourable outcome is discrete in that it either happens or it does not.

Importance of problem structure

These three factors – non-additivity of damages, dependence of risks on the actions of others, and uncertainty – are sufficient to ensure that there can be an equilibrium where there is under-investment in risk-prevention measures. The precise degree of under-investment depends on the nature of the problem. We focus here on the possibility of a firm's bankruptcy due to a catastrophic loss to one of its plants or divisions. An example would be a Bhopal-like accident to a chemical plant where the losses are so large that it causes bankruptcy to the entire operation. Another example is an ownership group such as Lloyd's which controls a number of syndicates all operating in a semi-autonomous fashion. If one of the syndicates experiences a severe enough loss it can lead the ownership group to declare bankruptcy. In 2002 Arthur Andersen was sent into bankruptcy by the actions of its Houston branch. Several years ago Barings was likewise destroyed by the actions of a single trader in its Singapore division.

In each of these cases we had multi-unit organizations in which the risk of bankruptcy faced by any unit was affected by its own choices and by the choices made by other units. In such a situation the incentive that any unit has to reduce bankruptcy risks is lessened by the knowledge that others are not doing so. A culture of risk taking can spread through the organization because knowledge that a few groups are taking risks reduces the incentives that others have to manage them carefully.

As noted above, there can be a stable equilibrium where all agents choose not to invest in risk-reduction measures, even though all would be better off if they did invest. An interesting property of some of these equilibria is the possibility of *tipping*, as described by Schelling (1978). More specifically, how can we ensure that enough agents will invest in security so that all the others will follow suit?

Characterizing the problem

We now set out formally the framework within which we study interdependent security (IDS), utilizing chemical plant protection as an example. We first investigate the two-agent problem and then extend this to multiple agents.

Chemical plant protection: the two-agent problem

Consider two identical, independently operating divisions in the BeSafe chemical firm: A_1 and A_2, each maximizing its own expected returns and having to choose whether to invest in a protective measure. Such an investment would reduce the probability of a catastrophic chemical accident to one of its plants. Let p be the probability of an accident that bankrupts the division and $q \leq p$ be the probability that the accident bankrupts the entire firm. Note that q and p are not independent of each other. The loss from an accident to the participants in the division is L. One should view L as the costs that managers and other employees of the division will incur if their division goes bankrupt. These include the search costs for new employment and other negative features associated with losing one's job, including loss of reputation.[2] The expected loss from such a catastrophic accident to the participants in the division is thus pL. If the division has invested in protective measures at an upfront cost of c, then the chances of this accident are reduced to zero.[3]

Suppose Division 1 has invested in protection. There is still an additional risk q that BeSafe will go bankrupt if Division 2 has not taken this precautionary measure. In other words, the employees in Division 1 may lose their jobs because of the carelessness of Division 2. In this sense Division 2 can contaminate other parts of the organization by not protecting its plants against a catastrophic accident. Similarly, Division 1 can contaminate Division 2 if it fails to adopt adequate protection.

Let Y be the assets of each division before any expenditure on protection or any losses during the year from the risks faced. Employees in each division are assumed to receive bonuses at the end of the year that are proportional to the size of the division's ending assets. The cost of investing in security is $c < Y$.

Assume that each division has two choices: invest in security, **S**, or do not invest, **N**. We can construct a simple 2×2 matrix illustrating what happens to the expected returns of each division as a function of the choices each one makes. The four possible paired outcomes are shown in Table 8.1.

To illustrate the nature of the expected returns consider the upper left-hand quadrant where both divisions invest in security (**S, S**). Then each division incurs a cost of c and faces no possible catastrophic accidents so that each of their net returns is $Y - c$.

---

[2] See Greenwald and Stiglitz (1990) for a discussion of the costs of bankruptcy that professional managers in firms suffer should the firm go bankrupt.

[3] We have assumed the risk to be zero to simplify the exposition. The qualitative results do not change if there is still a positive probability of an accident with a loss of L after precautionary measures have been adopted.

Table 8.1: Expected returns associated with investing and not investing in security

		Division 2 (A_2)	
		S	N
	S	$Y - c, Y - c$	$Y - c - qL, Y - pL$
Division 1 (A_1)			
	N	$Y - pL, Y - c - qL$	$Y - [pL + (1 - p)qL],$ $Y - [pL + (1 - p)qL]$

If A_1 invests and A_2 does not, this outcome is captured in the upper right-hand quadrant (S, N). Here A_1 incurs an investment cost of c but there is still a chance q that a catastrophic accident will occur in A_2 causing BeSafe to go bankrupt so that A_1's expected loss from damage originating elsewhere is qL. This type of contamination imposed by A_2 on A_1 is referred to in economics as a *negative externality*. A_2 incurs no cost of protecting itself and faces no risk of bankruptcy from A_1, but does face the risk of damage originating in one of its plants with an expected loss of pL. The lower left quadrant (N, S) has payoffs which are just the mirror image of these.

Suppose that neither division invests in protection (N, N) – the lower right-hand quadrant in Table 8.1. Then each has an expected return of $Y - pL - (1 - p)qL$. The expected losses can be characterized in the following manner. The term pL reflects the expected loss originating from an accident in one's own division. The second term reflects the expected loss from an accident originating at the other division that bankrupts the firm (qL) and is multiplied by $(1 - p)$ to reflect the assumption that bankruptcy to a division can occur only once. In other words, the risk of contamination matters to a division only when that division does not have a catastrophic accident originating at home.

Since each division wants to maximize the expected returns to its employees, the conditions for it to invest in protection against a catastrophic accident are that $c < pL$ and $c < p(1 - q)L$. The first constraint is exactly what one would expect if BeSafe consisted of a single division: that is, the cost of investing in protection must be less than the expected cost to its employees from a catastrophic accident. Adding a second division tightens the constraint by reflecting the possibility of contamination from others. This possibility reduces the incentive to

Table 8.2: Expected returns associated with investing and not investing in security – illustrative example: $p = .1$, $q = .05$, $L = 1000$ and $c = 98$

		Division 2 (A_2)	
		S	N
Division 1 (A_1)	S	$Y - 98$, $Y - 98$	$Y - 148$, $Y - 100$
	N	$Y - 100$, $Y - 148$	$Y - 145$, $Y - 145$

invest in protection. Why? Because in isolation, investment in protection buys the employees in the division freedom from bankruptcy. With the possibility of contamination from others it does not. Even after investment there remains a risk of bankruptcy emanating from the other division. Investing in protection buys you less when there is the possibility of contamination from others.

This solution concept is illustrated with a numerical example. Suppose that $p = .1$, $q = .05$, $L = 1000$, $c = 98$. The matrix in Table 8.1 is now represented as Table 8.2.

One can see that if A_2 has protection (S), it is worthwhile for A_1 to also invest in security since its expected losses will be reduced by $pL = 100$ and it will spend 98 on the security measure. However, if A_2 does not invest in security (N), there is still a chance that A_1 incurs a loss. Hence the benefits of security to A_1 are only $p(1 - q)L = 95$ which is less than the cost of the protective measure. So A_1 will *not* want to invest in protection. In other words, either both divisions invest in security or neither of them does so. These are the two Nash equilibria for this problem.

The multi-agent IDS case

The results for the two-agent IDS case carry over to the most general settings with some increase in complexity. The incentive for any agent to invest in protection depends on how many other agents there are and on whether or not they are investing. Other agents who do not invest reduce the expected benefits from one's own protective actions and hence reduce an agent's incentive to invest. In this section we review briefly the main features of the general case, without providing detailed proofs of the results. Those can be found in Kunreuther and Heal (2003) and Heal and Kunreuther (2003).

Suppose there are now n identical divisions. Each has a probability p of a catastrophic accident that can cause bankruptcy to the division and $q \leq p$ that the accident bankrupts BeSafe if it does *not* invest in security systems. This probability is zero if it invests. If a division does not invest in protection, it can contaminate all the other divisions. Let $X(n, j)$ be the total expected negative externalities due to contamination from others imposed on a division which has invested in security when j of the other $n - 1$ divisions have also taken this step.

If none of the other divisions is protected, the condition for any division to invest in protection is given by the following: $c < p[L - X(n, 0)]$. Let c^* be the value of c where the division is indifferent between investing and not investing in protection when j of the other divisions have invested in security. In other words $c^* = p[L - X(n, j)]$. If there are no negative externalities because all the divisions have invested in security, then $c^* = pL$ which is the same as if the division were operating in isolation. As more divisions do not invest in protection then c^* decreases, so that the division is less likely to take security measures if it is maximizing the expected returns of its employees.

Now suppose that the number of divisions (n) in the organization gets large. When none of the other $n - 1$ divisions invests in protection, the negative externalities to a division that has installed protection have been shown by Kunreuther and Heal (2003) to approach $X(n, 0) = L$. This implies that the expected loss to any division approaches L as a result of contamination from all the other unprotected divisions. In this situation $c^* = 0$ and there is no cost incentive for any division to invest in protecting itself against a catastrophic accident.

Here is the intuition for this somewhat surprising result. If one division is unprotected, then if it incurs a catastrophic accident, there is a probability q that the firm will go bankrupt. One weak link in the organization compromises all the other divisions. In other words, one unprotected division endangers all of the other divisions in the firm even if they have all invested in security. The more divisions that have not invested in protection, the greater the chances that the employees of any division will be looking for another job even if their own plants are secure from a catastrophic accident. As more divisions decide not to invest in security (i.e. take action **N**), the probability of a catastrophic accident becomes very large and there is no economic incentive for your division to undertake protection. In the limit this probability approaches 1 and $c^* = 0$.

Proposed risk management solutions for the IDS problem

The above example suggests that there are limited economic incentives for divisions in firms to invest in protection against low-probability events that could bankrupt their company if they believe that other divisions in their organization will not do so. In this section we examine the following two questions:

- How can a firm encourage its divisions to invest in protection through internal rules?
- What role can government regulations coupled with third-party inspections and insurance play in encouraging firms to invest in protection?

Internal organizational rules

In a large firm with many divisions there is likely to be a need for some type of coordinating mechanism from top management if each division's objective is to maximize the expected returns of its own employees. A key question in this regard is how companies which advertise 'Safety is our most important product' operationalize this slogan.

A natural way for a company to deal with this situation is to form a centralized management committee (CMC) that specifies a set of rules requiring each division to take measures that make sense from the firm's point of view. In their classic book on the behavioural theory of the firm, Cyert and March (1963) noted that organizations normally develop a set of standard operating procedures to guide the actions of different divisions or groups.

In the context of the above IDS example, the CMC of BeSafe could institute a specific rule that would require the division to invest in any protective measure where the expected benefits to the firm exceeded the costs of the measure. More specifically, if the cost of the protective measure, c, was greater than its expected benefits to the division, pL, then the investment would not be cost effective from the division's vantage point. However, it might be cost effective from the perspective of the entire organization. In this case the central organization could provide subsidies to the appropriate division to encourage it to invest in safety. A challenge for the CMC is to determine the appropriate subsidy to give a division and to find appropriate sources for these funds.

Role of third-party inspections, insurance and regulations

If divisions within firms are reluctant to adopt protective measures to reduce the chances of catastrophic accidents, there may be a role for government standards and regulations. One reason for involving the public sector is that some of the consequences of a chemical accident will affect nearby residents but the industrial facility will not be held fully liable for these impacts. For example, suppose property values in the surrounding area fall or there are disruptions in community life because of an accident. The firm causing the accident will not be legally responsible for these losses.

One way for the government to enforce its regulations is to turn to the private sector for assistance. More specifically, third party inspections coupled with insurance protection can encourage divisions in firms to reduce their risks from accidents and disasters. Such a management-based regulatory strategy shifts the locus of decision-making from the regulator to firms who are now required to do their own planning as to how they will meet a set of standards or regulations (Coglianese and Lazer 2001).

The passage of Section 112(r) of the Clean Air Act Amendments (CAAA) of 1990 offers an opportunity to implement such a programme. This legislation requires facilities to perform a hazard assessment, estimate consequences from accidents and submit a summary report to the US Environmental Protection Agency (EPA) called the Risk Management Plan (RMP) (Belke 2001). The challenge facing the EPA is how to encourage compliance with these regulations so that firms will be operating in a safer manner than they otherwise would be. There is some urgency for a type of decentralized procedure with appropriate incentives due to the EPA's limited personnel and funds for providing technical guidance and auditing regulated facilities. Chemical firms, particularly smaller ones, have little financial incentive to follow centralized regulatory procedures if they estimate that the likelihood they will be inspected by a regulatory agency is very small and/or they know the fine should they be caught will be low. In such cases they may be willing to take their chances and incur the fine should they violate the existing rule or regulation and be caught.

Third-party inspections in conjunction with private insurance is a powerful combination of two market mechanisms that can convince many firms of the advantages of implementing RMPs to make their plants safer and encourage the remaining ones to comply with the regulation to avoid being caught and fined. The intuition behind using third parties and insurance to support regulations can be stated rather simply. One of the biggest concerns of the EPA is that it doesn't have enough resources to audit all firms and their divisions subject to the RMP rule. Low-risk divisions, which the EPA has no need to audit, cannot credibly distinguish themselves from the high-risk ones without some type of inspection. By delegating part of the inspection process to the private sector through insurance companies and third parties, the EPA provides a channel through which the low-risk divisions in firms can speak for themselves. If a division chooses not to be inspected by third parties, it is more likely to be a high-risk rather than a low-risk one. If it does get inspected and shows that it is protecting itself and the rest of the organization against catastrophic accidents, it will pay a lower premium than a high-risk division which is not undertaking these actions. In this way the proposed mechanism not only substantially reduces the number of inspections the EPA has to undertake but also makes the audits more efficient.

Kunreuther et al. (2002) show more formally how such a programme could be implemented in practice. They provide supporting evidence from pilot studies undertaken in Delaware and Pennsylvania in which the Department of Environmental Protection in these two states worked closely with the insurance industry and chemical plants in testing out the proposed programme.[4] The centralized management committee of a firm should support this programme for two reasons. It gives them a rationale for hiring third party inspectors from outside to make sure their divisions are operating in a safe manner. It also increases the firm's expected profits by reducing the negative externalities that divisions create due to their fear of being contaminated by others.

---

[4] For more details on these pilot studies see McNulty et al. (1999) and US Environmental Protection Agency (2001).

Extending the analysis

The choice as to whether to protect against events where there is interdependence between your actions and those of others raises a number of interesting theoretical and empirical questions. We discuss some of these in this concluding section of the chapter.

Tipping behaviour

Suppose that divisions in a company are heterogeneous so that they have different risks and costs associated with their activities. In the case of a chemical firm some divisions may be responsible for plants that have a much higher risk of a large-scale accident than plants operated by other divisions. In an investment banking firm, the trading division is likely to take more risks with its activities than the mergers and acquisition division. The actions taken by Nick Leeson and the traders he hired at the Barings Futures Singapore office were primarily responsible for bringing down Barings Bank.[5]

Heal and Kunreuther (2003) have shown that there may be one division in the firm occupying such a strategic position that if it changes from not investing to investing in protection, all others will find it in their interests to follow suit. Even if there is no single division that can exert such leverage, there may be a small group. More specifically, the division that creates the largest negative externalities to others in the firm should be encouraged to invest in protective behaviour not only to reduce these losses but also to induce other divisions to follow suit.

This type of tipping behaviour is in the spirit of the many interesting examples described in Schelling (1978) where there is a sudden change from one equilibrium to another due to the movement of a few agents (e.g. the sudden change in the racial composition of a neighbourhood). Tipping behaviour implies that one needs to focus on only certain parts of an organization to convince others that it is in their economic interest to follow suit. It suggests that it is particularly important to persuade some key players to manage risks more

---

[5] For a more detailed analysis of the nature of the decision process by Leeson and how it caused Barings' downfall see Chapter 1 of Hoch and Kunreuther 2001.

carefully. Working with them may be a substitute for working with all the divisions in the firm.

Principal-agent problems

A key aspect of the IDS problem is that it is difficult to motivate individuals or groups to take certain actions that are in the best interest of the firm should others decide not to follow suit. This raises a set of challenges for aligning the incentives between the principal (e.g. a firm) and its agents (e.g. the divisions in the firm). The most obvious way to encourage these divisions to invest in protection is to utilize either formal rules promulgated by a CMC of the firm or through regulations from a government agency such as the EPA.

The standard principal–agent models discussed in the literature are predicated on the use of economic incentives to agencies so they will undertake specific actions that are in the best interest of the firm. Multi-agent versions of the principal–agent problem assume there is interdependency between agents (e.g. production decisions in one division impact on the production decisions of another).[6] Solutions to the firm's problem then require an understanding of the impact of incentives on individual agents as well as the anticipated behavioural responses of these agents to each other. While some of the multi-agent design literature on collective choice (e.g. Groves 1979) has addressed the issue of externalities across agents, there has been no work undertaken to date on how to deal with the type of interdependent security problems described in this chapter.

For the IDS problem there is a need to provide either special economic incentives to key units in the organization to induce tipping behaviour or to apply a subsidy or impose a tax on all the agents. For example, if the CMC taxed all divisions a certain amount when they did not adopt cost-effective protective measures, each of them would want to invest in these actions if the penalty was high enough (Kunreuther and Heal 2003). More generally, there is a need to develop principal–agent models that examine the efficacy of alternative policy

---

[6] For a comprehensive treatment of principal–agent models see Kreps (1990, Chapter 16). For a discussion of multi-person principal–agent problems, see Kleindorfer et al. (1993, Chapter 7). There is also a rich literature on the design of organizational incentives to account for interdependency problems across divisions. This includes the well-known work of Groves (1979) and Hölmström (1982), with more recent contributions summarized in Gibbons (1998).

instruments that the principal could apply when there are contamination effects between agents.

Multi-period and dynamic models

Deciding whether to invest in protection normally involves multi-period considerations since there is an upfront investment cost that needs to be compared with the benefits over the life of the protective measure. A division that invests in a protective measure knows that this action promises to offer benefits for a number of years. Hence it needs to discount these positive returns by an appropriate interest rate and specify the relevant time interval in determining whether or not to incur this investment cost. There may be some uncertainty with respect to both of these parameters.

From the point of view of dynamics, the decision to invest depends on how many others have taken similar actions. How do you get the process of investing in security started? Should one subsidize or provide extra benefits to those willing to be innovators in this regard to encourage others to take similar actions? The nature of the decisions undertaken by divisions and the CMC of the firm will undoubtedly be different in a dynamic environment where learning can take place than in the one-period model developed in this chapter.

Examining alternative decision rules

Individuals and firms often utilize simplified decision rules when determining what courses of actions to follow. One rule that managers often follow is a threshold model of choice whereby action is taken only if the chance of some event occurring is above a critical probability level. If the perceived probability is below this level, it is assumed that this event is not worth worrying about.

Empirical research has provided evidence that decision makers use threshold-like models in making their decisions. In a laboratory experiment on purchasing insurance, many individuals bid zero for coverage, apparently viewing the probability of a loss as sufficiently small that they were not interested in protecting themselves against it (McClelland et al. 1993). Similarly, many homeowners residing in communities that are potential sites for nuclear waste facilities have a tendency to dismiss the risk as negligible (Oberholzer-Gee 1998).

In interviews with managers at the Chemco Company after the Bhopal disaster, Bowman and Kunreuther (1988) discovered that the firm had an informal rule that it would concern itself with the dangers of specific chemicals only if the probability of an accident was above a certain threshold level.

Suppose a manager utilizes the following rule for his or her division: invest in protection only if the probability (p) of having a catastrophic accident that causes the division to go bankrupt is greater than some pre-specified value. One could estimate what this threshold probability would have to be so that the division's behaviour would be consistent with maximizing the expected returns of its employees.

Consider Division 1 of the firm. Let n^* be the number of other divisions which do not invest in protection against catastrophic accidents. One can determine how this threshold probability would be affected as n^* changes. Define p_n^* to be the probability where Division 1 would be indifferent between investing and not investing in protection if it were maximizing the expected returns of its employees.

Suppose $n^* = 0$ so that all other divisions have invested in protection. Division 1 will be indifferent between investing and not investing in protection if $p_0 L = c$. Hence $p_0 = c/L$. If $n^* = 1$ the situation in this case is equivalent to the case in a two-division firm where Division 2 does not invest in protection. Now the decision rule for Division 1 to be indifferent between investing and not investing in protection is $p_1(1 - q) = c/L$. Hence $p_1 > p_0$. As the value of n^* increases, there will be more divisions which can contaminate others so that the perceived probability of an accident in one's own division will have to be higher for the division to want to incur the costs of protection. In other words, as n^* increases, p_n^* also increases.

This rule implies that the more divisions do not invest in protection, the less likely it is that any division will invest in protection for any given value of p. The division thus uses the same line of reasoning in specifying a threshold probability as when it maximizes the expected returns of its employees: investing in protection does less good for the division, the more divisions that have their plants unprotected against a catastrophic accident that could bankrupt the firm.

Role of coordinating mechanisms

Suppose that one was investigating the IDS problem in the context of firms in an industry rather than divisions in a firm. An example would be the airlines where each company is concerned that an uninspected bag transferred from another airline could contain a bomb. One way to convince the *n* airlines that it would be in everyone's best interests to invest in baggage security would be to utilize some official organization to coordinate these decisions. For example, the International Air Transport Association (IATA), the official airline association, has indicated on its website that since September 11 it has 'intensified hand and checked baggage processing'. IATA could have made the case to all the airlines that they would be better off if each one of them utilized internal baggage checking so that the government would not have had to require this.

An association can play a coordinating role by stipulating that any member has to follow certain rules and regulations, including the adoption of security measures, and has the right of refusal should they be asked to do business with an agent that is not a member of the association and/or has not subscribed to the ruling. IATA could require all bags to be reviewed carefully and each airline could indicate that it would not accept in-transit bags from airlines that did not adhere to this regulation.

Apparently IATA follows this type of policy in agreements regarding pricing policies. If an airline does not belong to IATA and you want to transfer to this airline from an originating IATA airline, the originating airline will not make a reservation for you. Furthermore, an IATA airline will not honour a non-IATA airline ticket unless it conforms to the IATA tariff conference.[7]

Estimating the risk of an accident

The IDS model we have developed assumes that the probability and outcomes of a particular event are well specified. In reality there is considerable ambiguity associated with these data. There is thus a need to examine the impact of ambiguity on decisions on whether or not to invest in protective measures. Furthermore, there is a need to collect better data on the risk in order to estimate the chances and consequences of a catastrophic accident.

At the time of writing the Wharton Risk Management and Decision Processes Center is engaging in two types of data-collection efforts in

---

[7] See the IATA website at http://www.iata.org/membership/steps.asp#10

this regard with the US Environmental Protection Agency. The first of these uses accident history data from the US chemical industry, while the second is concerned with the performance of management systems designed to improve the environmental, health and safety (EH&S) performance of companies.

Accident history data have been collected on the performance of the US chemical industry for the period 1995–2000 under Section 112(r) of the Clean Air Act Amendments of 1990. Every chemical facility in the United States was required to provide these data for any listed chemical (140 toxic and inflammable chemicals in total) above threshold quantities. Elliott et al. (2003) indicate how these data can be used to analyse potential relationships between the following factors:

- the characteristics of the facility itself, including facility location, size and the type of hazard present (as characterized by the chemicals and process used, the training and management systems in place, and other facility-specific characteristics);
- the nature of regulations in force that are applicable to this facility and the nature of enforcement activities;
- the level of pressure brought on the facility to operate safely and to inform the community of the hazards it faces.

These same data can be linked to financial information so one can analyse the association, if any, between the financial characteristics of the parent company of a facility and the frequency or severity of accidents. Similarly, the property damage estimates, and associated indirect costs from these, can be used to assess the consequences of EH&S incidents on overall company performance and provide valuable insights for insurance underwriting for such accidents. Finally, the same data can be used to assess worst-case consequences from such incidents, including those that might arise from site security risks associated with terrorism.[8]

The second data-collection project is a study of near misses in organizations and the systems that have been put into place to report and analyze these data. Near misses are defined as incidents that, under different circumstances, could have resulted in major accidents. Linking these data on accident precursors to the Accident History database in RMP*Info may enable one to identify categories of

---

[8] For recent details on this aspect of the chemical Accident History database in RMP*Info, see Kleindorfer et al. (2003).

precursors that give early warnings of the potential for major accidents. Audit tools and other aspects of near-miss management can then focus not just on emergency response but on the range of prevention and mitigation activities before the fact that can help avert major disasters.[9] Even with these data, there will still be considerable uncertainty regarding the estimates of risks associated with these low-probability events.

Evaluating similarities and differences between IDS problems

Two common features of IDS problems are the possibility that other agents can contaminate you and your inability to reduce this type of contagion through investing in security. An agent is thus discouraged from adopting protective measures when it knows others have decided not to take this step. Below we list some other problems besides bankruptcy that satisfy these conditions and deserve more detailed analysis.

- Investing in airline security such as baggage-checking systems.
- Making buildings more secure against attacks.
- Investing in sprinkler systems to reduce the chance of a fire in one's apartment.
- Making computer systems more secure against terrorist attacks.
- Investing in protective measures for each part of an interconnected infrastructure system so that services can be provided to disaster victims after the next earthquake.
- Reducing production disruption by focusing on weak links in the supply chain.

In each of these examples there are incentives for individual units or agents not to take protective measures, but there are large potential losses to the organization and to society from their failure to do so. Furthermore, the losses are sufficiently high that they are non-additive.

IDS problems can be contrasted with other types of protective measures that do not have these features. Two that are discussed in more detail in Kunreuther and Heal (2003) are theft protection and vaccination. In the case of theft protection, if you install an alarm system that you announce publicly with a sign, the burglar will look for greener

---

[9] For details on the Wharton Near-Miss Management Project, see Phimister et al. (2003).

pastures to invade.[10] With respect to vaccines, if you knew everyone else had been vaccinated, there would be no point in being vaccinated since you could not catch the disease.[11]

Conclusion

The events of September 11 have highlighted the importance of addressing the questions associated with interdependent security. There are enormous challenges in modelling the nature of the interaction between agents that need to be addressed through future theoretical and empirical studies. By developing a richer set of models and testing them through controlled experiments and field studies we will increase our understanding of the way agents behave and their relationship to models of choice, such as the one developed in this chapter.

The models discussed above all assume that individuals make their decisions by comparing their expected benefits with and without protection to the costs of investing in security. With respect to protective measures there is empirical evidence from controlled field studies and laboratory experiments that many individuals are not willing to invest in security for a number of reasons that include myopia, high discount rates and budget constraints (Kunreuther et al. 1998).

There is a need for developing IDS models that incorporate these behavioural features as characterizing individual choice processes. For example, if one was to determine the expected benefits of an investment today on expected profits over a T-period horizon, one would then compare the fixed cost c with the discounted expected benefits during the next T periods. The division would be less likely to incur this investment cost if it is myopic so it only takes into account the benefits over a $T^* < T$ period horizon. A more realistic model of interdependent security that incorporated these behavioural factors, relevant constraints and people's misperceptions of the risk may suggest a different set of policy recommendations than those implied by a rational model of choice. For example, if agents were reluctant to invest in protection

---

[10] Ayres and Levitt (1998) have demonstrated the social benefits of protection when individuals invest in unobservable precautionary measures such as the LoJack car-retrieval system that criminals cannot detect.

[11] See Hershey et al. (1994) for a more detailed discussion of the role that free-riding plays in vaccination decisions.

because they were myopic, then some type of loan may enable them to discern the long-term benefits of the protective measure. A long-term loan would also help relieve budget constraints that may deter some individuals or firms from incurring the upfront costs of the risk-reducing measure.

To conclude, there is a need to re-examine the role of the public and private sectors in developing efficient and equitable strategies for providing protection against catastrophic events so as to reduce their likelihood of occurrence and their potential consequences. This is a rich area for future research.

Restoring reason: causal narratives and political culture

SHEILA JASANOFF

D o human societies learn? If so, how do they do it, and if not, why not? The American activist singer and song writer Pete Seeger took up the first question in the 1950s (Seeger 1955)[1] in a song whose concluding lines circled hauntingly back to its opening and whose refrain – 'When will they ever learn?' – gave anti-war protest in the 1960s a musical voice. Seeger's answer was, apparently, 'never'. Like many a pessimist before and since, Seeger saw human beings as essentially fallible creatures, doomed to repeat history's mistakes. But modern societies cannot afford to stop with that unregenerative answer. The consequences of error in tightly coupled, high-tech worlds could be too dire (Perrow 1984). If we do *not* learn, then it behoves us to ask the next-order questions. Why do we not? Could we do better?

For social analysts, part of the challenge is to decide where to look for answers. At what level of analysis should such questions be investigated? Who, to begin with, learns? Is it individuals or collectives, and if the latter, then how are knowledge and experience communicated both by and within groups whose membership remains indeterminate or changes over time? Organizational sociologists from Max Weber onwards have provided many insights into why collectives think alike. Especially illuminating is the work on group socialization, routinization and standardization (Bowker and Star 1999; Vaughan 1996; Short and Clarke 1992; Clarke 1989; Bourdieu 1980; Foucault 1979; Weber 1946). This literature focuses on the inculcation of disciplined habits and practices among a group's human members, leading to common

I would like to thank Bridget Hutter, Mike Power and Stefan Sperling for helpful comments on an earlier draft.
[1] 'Where Have All the Flowers Gone?' was arguably Pete Seeger's best-known song. It was inspired by a Ukrainian folk song quoted in Mikhail Sholokov's epic 1928 war novel *And Quiet Flows the Don*. The opening lines were:
   Where have all the flowers gone, long time passing?
   Where have all the flowers gone, long time ago?

styles of thought and modes of behaviour. To these observations, studies of technological systems have added a material dimension. Theorists of the left, from Karl Marx to more recent scholars such as David Noble (1977) and Langdon Winner (1986a), have looked to the power of capital (or other hegemonic formations such as colonialism and the state) to explain the design of obdurate technological systems that constrain group behaviour. Everyday metaphors – such as 'built-in', 'path-dependent' or 'hard-wired' – underscore a widespread popular awareness that material structures can shape a society's developmental trajectories in ways that seem, for all practical purposes, inevitable.

The problem from the standpoint of learning is that the better we get at creating and, secondarily, explaining stability in groups and systems, the harder it seems to make or to account for change. If human collectives are bound by deeply socialized practices and rituals, and rigidly constrained by the technological infrastructures of their lives, how can they break out of those iron cages to craft safer, more supple and more sustainable forms of life? How, more particularly, do new ideas find toeholds and footholds, let alone *take* hold, in settings configured by and for outworn modes of thinking and knowing, as well as their material embodiments? To make progress, it would seem, we need more dynamic models of the ways in which people arrive at common understandings of their condition, about what works as well as what has failed to work. How are such shared beliefs about the causes of success and failure constructed in advanced technological societies? And if we penetrate to the heart of that puzzle, can we also ask how systematic beliefs and forms of life may be *re*constructed to let in new interpretative possibilities?

Put differently, stories about learning are, at one and the same time, epistemological stories. They are narratives of how people acquire trustworthy knowledge from experience – and how they either fit new knowledge to old mindsets or transform their cognitive habits, individually and collectively, so as to arrive at radically altered understandings. In modern life, moreover, those understandings encompass not only how people wish to order their relations with each other but also how they go about living with the products of their technological inventiveness.

In this chapter, I look at the nation state as an important analytic unit within which to explore the problem of such collective learning. There are several reasons for this choice. First, we know from several decades of cross-national research that risk issues are framed for public policy through nation-specific institutional and political forces that influence what is seen as potentially harmful and how such harms should be avoided (Jasanoff 1995; Jasanoff 2005; Vogel 1986). Accordingly, learning about risk often happens within a framework structured by the dynamics of national politics. Second, the cultures or styles of decision making within nation states affect the production of policy-relevant knowledge and discourse and thereby set the habits of thought and language that shape the possibility of learning. For example, the vulnerability of US decision makers to legal challenge is associated with a preference in that country for seemingly objective and rational analytic tools, such as quantitative risk assessment (Porter 1995; Jasanoff 1986). But these techniques, in turn, frame which risks U.S. decision makers are likely to take note of and the parameters within which they will seek prevention or remediation (Winner 1986b: 138–54). Third, in a time of growing recognition that not only elites but broader publics, too, are key players in processes of learning, the nation state offers a critically important site for examining how citizens make sense of threats and disasters. Public ways of knowing, which I have elsewhere termed civic epistemologies (Jasanoff 2005), are constituted, displayed, and reaffirmed within the decision-making processes of states, including those aimed at the management of risk and prevention of harm.

To illustrate these points, I adopt a comparative approach, looking at three episodes of learning following technological catastrophes in India, Britain and the United States. On the surface, the examples chosen from each country have little substantively in common: a chemical disaster in India (Bhopal), a food safety crisis arising from industrial agriculture in Britain ('mad cow' or BSE) and a terrorist tragedy exposing vulnerabilities in civil aviation and urban infrastructure in the United States (9/11). They are, however, comparable in other salient respects that bear on learning. Each was perceived as a problem of national proportions with international ramifications, calling for solutions at national and supranational levels. Each precipitated years of public inquiry into the causes of what had happened, as well as public efforts to prevent similar disasters from occurring in the future; in that respect each event was a site of learning, as well as a site of memory.[2] In

---

[2] Historians use the term 'site of memory' to refer to places, including the imaginative spaces of works of art and literature, where communities repose, and reify, their memories of significant past events. While this is not the place for a fuller

each case, the power of the state was invoked in distinctive ways to organize the search for truth, with important implications for the 'truths' that were revealed in the process. In each, too, policy closure of a formal kind was achieved, although the underlying narratives of cause and responsibility remained significantly, and stubbornly, more open-ended.

Through a comparison of these three national policy-learning exercises, I hope to show that civic epistemology is, in a sense, foundational to contemporary political cultures and helps define the trajectories of learning within a given polity. I focus my analysis on one aspect of learning only: the efforts to determine a causal agent or agents in each instance, since identifying causes is a prerequisite to any subsequent efforts to target solutions and remedies. Who, or what, in short was held responsible for the breakdowns that precipitated each crisis or catastrophe, and how did those findings, and their ambiguities, shape subsequent policy responses? I relate the answers to these questions, in turn, to the cultures of knowledge making that steered national learning processes towards particular conclusions. A point that emerges from this comparison is that the particularity of national civic epistemologies lies, in part, in the boundary that each framework constructs between factual and moral causes or, put differently, between responsibility and blame.

India: Bhopal gas disaster

On the night of 3 December 1984, barely a month after the traumatic assassination of Prime Minister Indira Gandhi, India experienced the worst industrial accident ever recorded. The scene of the disaster was a pesticide plant run by Union Carbide in Bhopal, the capital of the central Indian state of Madhya Pradesh. Water seeping into a storage tank of liquid methyl isocyanate (MIC) – no one knew exactly how – released the chemical in a lethal gaseous form over the sleeping city. Though exact casualty figures will never be known, up to 3,500 people were estimated to have died from the immediate effects of toxic

discussion of history and memory, I note that the construction of memory is integral to the process of learning and that public policy – which is often based on an authoritative analysis of past events – therefore can be seen as an important site of memory in modern societies.

exposure and as many as 150,000 people were permanently injured or disabled.

A tragedy of this magnitude necessitated prompt remedial action by the state and the Indian government did respond quickly. Action was complicated, however, by the heterogeneity of the network within which the events unfolded, a network that joined together in an unprecedented web of cross-national interactions, corporate entities, legal systems, medical experts, regulatory authorities and countless local victims (Jasanoff 1994; on technological networks, see Bijker et al. 1987). At the level of physical causation, the story was clear to all: deadly toxic gas escaping from an identified source had killed or injured large numbers of people living in the vicinity. At a systemic or moral level, responsibility was much harder to assign.

In the days, months and years that followed the disaster, the Indian government and other affected actors had to come to grips with the complexity of the ties that bound them, and these efforts led to vastly divergent causal accounts. To what extent, for instance, was legal ownership relevant to liability and how did it intersect with blame? Union Carbide, the parent company, disavowed responsibility for events occurring at a facility managed by its Indian subsidiary, almost half-owned by the Indian state, and entirely overseen by local staff and personnel. Whose neglect or failure, moreover, had precipitated the tragedy? Union Carbide officially maintained that it was an act of sabotage by a disgruntled employee – a theory that absolved the company of any legal or moral liability (Kalelkar 1988). At the opposite extreme, many Indian critics blamed a global power structure that permitted uncaring multinationals like Union Carbide to perpetrate 'genocide' on unsuspecting citizens of developing societies (Visvanathan 1985). Which of these views prevailed, if either, clearly had huge implications for future policy.

Medical science, too, failed to deliver univocal answers to important issues of causation. In the chaos following the gas release, both affected bodies and their specific afflictions remained unrecorded. MIC's irritant properties at very small doses were well known, and thousands of instantaneous deaths provided sombre evidence of the chemical's lethal potency at higher exposure levels. But the long-term effects on people who had been more peripherally affected remained unestablished for decades. Because MIC was dangerous to handle, no studies had been done on its effects at low doses on the nervous system, the respiratory tract, vision or digestion, let alone on the psychological effects of being a gas survivor. Then, too, national and local medical authorities clashed with the victims in interpreting their symptoms and tendering appropriate remedies. A bitter technical confrontation erupted within days of the accident, centring on whether MIC had broken down into cyanide in victims' bodies, causing symptoms that sufferers claimed were alleviated by the antidote thiosulfate (Jasanoff 1994: 185–7). Experts sent in by the Indian government denied the victims' claims of cyanide poisoning and debunked community efforts to act on an officially discredited theory. Ensuing governmental action to block thiosulfate distribution and to arrest and detain physicians offering the treatment left a legacy of distrust that persisted into the present century.

Legal disputes growing from the disaster proved as thorny as they were inconclusive. An initial descent on Bhopal of prominent American trial lawyers, scenting huge damage awards, prompted the Indian government, under the so-called Bhopal Act, to assume the sole right to represent all claimants under an extended *parens patriae* doctrine. A New York federal court refused to allow the case against Union Carbide to be tried in the United States, as India had requested, on the ground that adequate justice could be done by the Indian legal system, even though no industrial accident on remotely this scale had ever troubled the subcontinent's courts. The complex legal skirmishes led in 1989 to an out-of-court settlement of $470 million by Union Carbide, brokered by the Indian Supreme Court. It was closure of a kind – indeed, even a vindication of sorts for Bhopal victims if measured against the substantially smaller $180 million settlement in May 1984 in the Vietnam veterans' lawsuit against manufacturers of Agent Orange (Schuck 1986). But from the victims' social and psychological standpoint the closure was anything but settling. In exchange for money, the Indian government dropped all criminal charges against the company, thereby permanently foreclosing what many saw as the only morally supportable response to Union Carbide's negligence. The settlement swept under the carpet the political economic critique that had framed the accident as a natural consequence of deep structural imbalances in the world. For those who saw both the state and the multinational corporation as shoring up the corrupt structures of global inequality, the mere transfer of millions of dollars from one to another equally non-accountable actor brought cold comfort. Money alone could not remedy what some saw as a moral catastrophe.

The Bhopal disaster, then, opened up a nested set of possible causes – from individual malice to corporate negligence and from state failure to global political economy – without leading to a broad societal consensus on any one of these. The lack of resolution was poignantly in evidence during a field trip to Bhopal that I made with a colleague in the summer of 2004, almost twenty years after the original catastrophe.[3] By sheer coincidence, only in the week of our visit did the Indian government release the last instalment of the Bhopal settlement, ending years of confrontation over whether state authorities or victims were entitled to increases in the fund through interest accumulation and fluctuating exchange rates. Local newspapers reported that the payouts would produce a short-term increase in sales of cell phones, scooters and other consumer goods, while patient groups maintained that the funds were barely sufficient to cover the long-term costs of medical treatment and rehabilitation.

The funds will be paid out in due course, but the sense of justice denied still burns strong in many of Bhopal's gas-affected citizens, some of whom were children when the disaster happened. The recently fenced-in plant sits abandoned, in a densely populated, still unmodernized part of the city, home to grazing cows and memorialized only by a nondescript stone statue of a female figure near its entrance gate. At community centres and health clinics run by veteran activists, people whose lives were permanently scarred by the events of 1984 wait for a fuller redress that may never come. One of our informants stated that, for him, this case would not truly close until Warren Anderson, Union Carbide's chief executive in 1984, served at least one symbolic day behind bars. Another activist leader focused on corporate responsibility from a different angle, describing the strategies that he and his associates were following to hold Union Carbide's new owner, Dow Chemical, responsible for environmental damage caused by the plant. *These* claims, he insisted, had not been formally extinguished by the 1989 settlement and his group was pursuing political and legal opportunities in India and the United States in an effort to bring Union Carbide, through Dow, to book for offences that had never been properly accounted for.

---

[3] I was accompanied by Stefan Sperling, whose anthropological perspective has greatly enriched my own policy analytic interpretation of the lack of closure in Bhopal. We are particularly indebted to Abdul Jabbar and Satinath Sarangi for their time and generosity in offering personal interviews, supporting materials and introductions to others in the gas-affected communities of Bhopal.

To the extent that Bhopal victims' groups continue to assert successful claims against the Indian state, it is not so much through official
recognition of their health and safety claims as through the authenticity
of their suffering. Twenty years after the precipitating events, after
several changes of government and the assassination of Rajiv Gandhi,
during whose prime ministership the Bhopal settlement was negotiated, victims' demonstrations seem still to have power to elicit
responses from the state. One activist leader described, for example, a
successful hunger strike that he and two colleagues had conducted in
Delhi to persuade the government that the Bhopal Act did not pre-empt
private litigation against Dow for environmental damage around the
Union Carbide plant. What proved compelling in this case was not a
factual demonstration of how bad things are in Bhopal, but the expres-
sive voice of a community which, through the uniqueness of its experience, gained and retains moral claims on a nation's conscience –
regardless of any divergences in their reading of the 'facts'.

The tragic open-endedness of the Bhopal case so many years later
speaks to features of public knowledge making in India that we will
return to later in this chapter. For now, let us flag chiefly the lack of
anything approaching a definitive epistemological resolution: a time
and place when all the major participants came together to agree on a
common understanding of what had actually happened and what
should be done on the basis of that shared knowledge. In the absence
of such a moment of truth, multiple narratives of responsibility and
blame continue to flourish in Bhopal, on the look-out for new external
audiences or events to legitimate them. Yet this very lack of resolution
can be seen as a form of learning – not the kind that necessarily leads to
regulatory change or institutional reform, though both did happen in
the disaster's wake (Jasanoff 1994), but rather the kind that, through
its very incompleteness, reveals the impossibility of taming a cataclys-
mic event through necessarily imperfect managerial solutions. The
open-endedness of learning at Bhopal offers in this sense its own
redemption, by negating the possibility of forgetfulness.

Britain: BSE, food safety and the restoration of trust

If Bhopal burst upon the stage of world history in a single night of death
and destruction, Britain's bovine spongiform encephalopathy (BSE or
'mad cow') crisis crept slowly into public consciousness over the course

of much of a decade. The earliest signs of trouble appeared in the mid-1980s. Cows began to sicken mysteriously; they staggered and drooled as if gone mad and eventually died. The epidemic had affected 160,000 animals by 1996. This was bad news enough for the export-oriented British beef cattle industry, but regulators sensed the shadow of something worse around the corner. If whatever ailed the cows were to cross the species barrier and infect people, Britain might be faced with a public health disaster of unprecedented proportions. The Ministry of Agriculture, Fisheries and Food (MAFF), the agency responsible for both agricultural productivity and food safety regulation, took up the dual challenge for policy: to diagnose and stop the spread of illness in cattle and to allay the incipient official concern that people, too, might be at risk from BSE.

The second issue presented MAFF with a basic logistical difficulty. How could the ministry launch an inquiry into a public health hazard of potentially epidemic scale (beef was, after all, Britain's staple meat) without causing mass panic and so destroying an industry already burdened by the direct costs of coping with BSE in cows? Faced with this dilemma, MAFF followed the traditional British strategy of containment. A small, trusted body of experts, headed by Oxford Vice Chancellor Sir Richard Southwood, an eminent zoologist and policy adviser, was convened to recommend what actions should be taken both to assess the risks to public health and to stop the spread of infection. The committee was alarmed at the rapid and uncontrolled industrialization of animal husbandry, including the 'unnatural' practice of feeding ground meat and bone meal to cattle that most probably had caused the spread of BSE. Yet the face the state turned towards the public was one of calm reassurance, with both advisers and officials stating that the risk of disease transmission from cows to humans was too small for concern. The infective agent might have jumped the species barrier once, from sheep to cows, but the Southwood committee saw little need to worry about a second jump from ruminants to human beings (MAFF 1989).

MAFF's confidence, together with that of its advisers, that BSE would not affect humans, and could be controlled in cattle through incremental restrictions on possibly infected cuts of meat, turned out to have been misplaced. An empiricist culture of governance, never too happy with speculative judgements, could not write off the possibility of harm without seeking further evidence. British authorities began to monitor suspicious cases of human death from an illness known as Creutzfeld-Jakob disease (CJD) and by 1996 enough instances of a new variant (vCJD) had been found to persuade them that the unthinkable had happened: 'mad cow' disease had crossed into people and it was essential to make that news public. On 23 March, Stephen Dorrell, the Secretary of State for Health, announced to Parliament that ten deaths from vCJD had been identified in Britain. Against earlier expert predictions, it appeared that as many as several hundred thousand unsuspecting Britons might now be at risk of an irreversible and fatal degenerative brain disease caused by the same infectious agent as BSE.[4] The panic that MAFF had so assiduously sought to prevent suddenly gripped not only Britain but also the European Union and Britain's non-European trading partners, most of whom immediately banned imports of British beef. Within Britain, too, the giant food industry took potentially contaminated beef off the shelves and turned to safer sources, such as Argentinian meat for use in McDonald's hamburgers. The episode cost the UK public sector alone £4 billion. More important, if less tangible, was the ensuing 'civic dislocation' (Jasanoff 1997) that caused citizens to turn away from government as a source of credible health and safety information and made the restoration of trust an urgent priority for Labour following its decisive electoral victory in 1997.

If neither Union Carbide nor the Indian state had wanted to resolve the multiple factual conflicts around the Bhopal gas disaster, the same could not be said of Tony Blair's new Labour government and BSE. The government promised a full public inquiry, Britain's favoured mechanism for ascertaining the facts after any major breakdown or controversy. A lengthy process headed by Lord Phillips of Worth Matravers, a Law Lord, concluded in 2000 that MAFF and its technical advisers had made substantial errors of judgement, on the basis of imperfect understandings of the facts and of available policy options (Lord Phillips 2000). The inquiry identified MAFF's culture of secrecy (exceptional even in British terms) as an underlying problem that had prevented timely disclosure of risks and aggressive pursuit of scientific knowledge and policy alternatives. These findings dealt a final blow to a ministry that had for years been under fire for its lack of transparency and close

---

[4] By the end of 2002, 129 people would be diagnosed with confirmed and probable cases of the disease (Andrews et al. 2003).

ties to agribusiness. MAFF was dissolved, its responsibilities were transferred to other bodies, such as the expanded Department of Environment, Food and Rural Affairs, and a new advisory committee, the Food Standards Agency, was formed to provide more transparent, consumer-oriented advice to government on matters of food safety.

From the standpoint of public knowledge making, however, what interests us most is the Phillips inquiry's strategy for determining who was to blame for the BSE fiasco. Was it a failure of knowledge and competence, and if so of individuals or institutions? The committee was on surest ground when it concluded that MAFF and its advisers had acted contrary to widely accepted principles or easily accessible public knowledge – put differently, when people seemed to have violated canons of common sense. Thus, in one instructive passage, the committee said:

… we do not consider that the [Southwood] Working Party correctly applied the ALARP [as low as reasonably practicable] principle. Animals with BSE that had developed clinical signs of the disease were to be slaughtered and destroyed. No steps were to be taken, however, to protect anyone other than babies from the risk of eating potentially infective parts of animals infected with BSE but not yet showing signs. It is true that infectivity of the most infective tissues – the brain and spinal cord – rises significantly shortly before clinical signs begin to show. It is also true that there were reasons to think that babies might be more susceptible to infection than adults. *But we do not consider that these differences justified an approach that treated the risk from eating brain or spinal cord from an animal incubating BSE as one in respect of which there were no reasonably practical precautions that need be taken.* [my emphasis]

To empiricist judicial minds, trained in common law notions of reasonableness, it seemed obvious that infectivity could never be contained within strict physical demarcations (brain and spinal cord), any more than some beef-eating populations (adults in this case) could be declared absolutely unsusceptible to risk. Responsible experts, the inquiry concluded, should have known that risk in a population extends across a continuum, from zero to certain harm, with corresponding opportunities for graduated precautionary action. It was plainly unreasonable, then, to target for protection only the high end of the risk continuum: babies exposed to brain and spinal cord tissue from infected but pre-symptomatic cattle. Other consumers, too, should have been provided for under the accordion-pleated principle of 'as low as reasonably practicable' risk reduction. MAFF's advisers had not acted commonsensically enough.

When it came to assigning individual responsibility, however, the committee was noticeably more hesitant. Expert bodies might be held accountable to widely accepted public health principles, such as ALARP, just as they might be expected to craft regulatory responses carefully fitted to the uncertainties of the situation. But individual public servants could not be deemed at fault for errors of fact or judgement so long as they were acting in good faith, according to their best understanding of their duties. The following observations from the Phillips inquiry are instructive [paragraph numbers indicated; my emphasis throughout]:

- It is inevitable that an Inquiry such as ours focuses on what went wrong. The main point of having the Inquiry is to find out what went wrong and to see what lessons can be learned from this. *This can be harsh for individuals. Their shortcomings are put under the spotlight. The overall value of the contributions that they have made is lost from view.* We do not wish our Report to produce this result ... (Lord Phillips 2000: 1245).

- Those who were most active in addressing the challenges of BSE are those who are most likely to have made mistakes. As was observed in the course of the Inquiry, 'if you do not put a foot forward you do not put a foot wrong.' In this context we think it right to single out for mention Mr Meldrum. Mr Meldrum was Chief Veterinary Officer in Great Britain for almost the whole of the period with which we are concerned. He involved himself personally in almost every aspect of the response to BSE. *He placed himself at the front of the firing line so far as risk of criticism is concerned* (Lord Phillips 2000: 1250).

- *We are satisfied that where Mr Meldrum perceived the possibility of a significant risk to human health he gave this precedence over consideration of the interests of the livestock industry* (Lord Phillips 2000: 1256).

- We have criticized the restrictions on dissemination of information about BSE in the early stages of the story, which were motivated in part by concern for the export market. We suspect that this may have reflected a culture of secrecy within MAFF, which Mr Gummer sought to end with his policy of openness. *If those we have criticized were misguided, they were nonetheless acting in accordance with what they conceived to be the proper performance of their duties* (Lord Phillips 2000: 1258).

- For all these reasons, while we have identified a number of grounds for individual criticism, we suggest that *any who have come to our Report hoping to find villains or scapegoats, should go away disappointed* (Lord Phillips 2000: 1259).

Evident in these quotations is a firm commitment to protecting public servants against undue censure for honest mistakes. This protectiveness is understandable in a political culture that values learning from experience – in which both experts and civil servants have traditionally risen to power and influence not merely, nor mainly, on the strength of technical credentials, but by showing that they have served the public interest to the best of their abilities (Jasanoff 1994, 2005). It would not do, in this context, to make 'villains or scapegoats' of people who may have displayed intellectual shortcomings, but only through having placed themselves 'at the front of the firing line' of criticism, or who may have been misguided, but were acting throughout 'in accordance with what they conceived to be the proper performance of their duties'. To penalize such people simply because of mistakes would be to deprive the state of a cadre of dedicated public servants that the nation could ill afford to lose. Unlike some national elites, who stand *above* the people in skills and knowledge, British public servants ideally stand *for* the polity. They are people in and out of government who not only possess the virtue of selflessness but who, through experience and service, have earned the right to see and know for the wider public – who embody, in other words, their nation's civic epistemology, its capacity for generating reliable collective knowledge.

A change of government and a major public inquiry led in Britain to serious institutional redesign, most notably through the dissolution of a long-established ministry. At the same time, as we will see below, it left untouched core beliefs about the best way to preserve trust in government and to construct credible public knowledge for purposes of collective action.

United States: 9/11, aeroplanes and the failure of intelligence

The terrorist attacks of September 11 (2001) on the United States were, on one level, vastly different in kind from the methyl isocyanate and

BSE disasters. Although the death toll of nearly 3,000 was close to the loss of life sustained in Bhopal, the event that came to be known as 9/11 was universally seen, unlike the two earlier tragedies, as having been caused by intentional human malice. The nineteen young Muslim terrorists who were among the dead that day were bent on killing Americans and destroying major symbols of American economic and political might, the twin towers of New York's World Trade Center, the Pentagon, and possibly the White House or the Capitol. The attacks were immediately compared with the Japanese assault on Pearl Harbor that brought the United States into the Second World War. Framed as an act of war, 9/11 led in turn to military retaliations against Afghanistan, the prime training ground of the Al-Qaeda terrorist network, and Iraq, a country inimical to US interests in the world but not connected, according to official findings, with the 9/11 attacks.

Yet contained within the script of 9/11 was what we may with little stretch of the imagination view as a 'normal' technological disaster in the sense discussed by Perrow (1984). It involved the use of commercial airliners as weapons aimed at large buildings – thereby subverting the normal operations of two of modernity's most foundational technological systems, transportation and urban infrastructure. Unsurprisingly, the 9/11 Commission's sweeping remit under its authorizing statute of 2002 included a look at the security of commercial aviation. One of the Commission's prime tasks was to determine how four aeroplanes could have been hijacked from three US airports and crashed into national landmarks, and how to keep such incidents from occurring again. Indeed, the final report's first chapter is entitled, in words drawn from the first transmission from the hijacked American Airlines Flight 11, ' "We have some planes" '(9/11 Commission 2004). The chapter offers a blow-by-blow reconstruction of what happened on board each of the four doomed airliners and how aviation authorities had tracked but failed to intercept the planes.

True to the practices of a country in which open information is believed to be the cornerstone of political empowerment and rational policy making, the 9/11 Commission identified problems in the US intelligence system as the major reason for the surprise attacks. The report highlighted many institutional deficits that had prevented information from being shared in timely fashion and so had kept the big-picture threat of Al-Qaeda from emerging with the kind of clarity that might have prompted preventive action. Important among these deficiencies, the report concluded, were the organizational barriers that kept two of the nation's foremost intelligence-gathering outfits, the Federal Bureau of Investigation (FBI) and the Central Intelligence Agency (CIA), from effectively sharing information related to terrorism. To counter those failures of coordination, the Commission recommended the appointment of a single national intelligence director, whose job would be to pull the intelligence capabilities scattered among fifteen separate federal agencies into a functioning, organic whole. It was neither the processes of information collecting, nor the nature of the information collected, that the Commission blamed. The fault was attributed instead to the absence of a single synthesizing institution that could absorb the available information and convert it into a credible, reliable assessment of the risk of terrorism.

Here and there in the report are suggestions that the Commission understood the difficulty of building such an all-seeing, or all-knowing, eye within the government. In a chapter called 'Foresight – and Hindsight', the Commission noted that the failures that had led to 9/11 included not only those of policy, capabilities and management, all of which presumably could be corrected through familiar changes in organization and governance, but also those of imagination, a far more difficult virtue to cultivate inside the routines of administrative practice (9/11 Commission 2004: 339). Observing that '[i]magination is not a gift usually associated with bureaucracies', the chapter went on to say:

It is therefore crucial to find a way of routinizing, even bureaucratizing, the exercise of imagination. Doing so requires more than finding an expert who can imagine that aircraft could be used as weapons. Indeed, since Al Qaeda and other groups had already used suicide vehicles, namely truck bombs, the leap to the use of other vehicles such as boats (the *Cole* attack) or planes is not far-fetched. (9/11 Commission 2004: 344)

But here we confront a paradox. If it did not take *much* imagination to conceive of what happened on 9/11, why did the Commission identify lack of imagination as a key factor leading to the attacks? And if the use of aircraft as weapons could have been foreseen so easily, why did the relevant authorities fail to exercise the modest amount of imagination needed to forestall that event?

The answer that emerges on the page following the above quote is telling: for imagination is here reduced, for all practical purposes, to routine administrative analysis. The Commission identifies four fairly uncontroversial analytic steps that the Counterterrorism Center (CTC) might have taken but did not: analysis from the enemy's perspective; development of tell-tale indicators; requirements for monitoring such indicators; and identifying systemic defences within terrorist-controlled aircraft. None of these elements is presented as new or path-breaking. Indeed, they had become standard, the Commission suggests, in the years after Pearl Harbor, and CTC's error lay in not using them well or at all. The methods 'did not fail', the report concludes, 'they were not really tried' (9/11 Commission 2004: 347–8). The alleged failure of imagination, then, was little more than a failure to do conventional risk assessment in the national security arena, in accordance with long-established codes of practice.

The irony of this move – beginning with an ambitious attempt to chart new conceptual territory but returning to fighting yesterday's war on yesterday's terms – did not go unnoticed. A commentary on the 9/11 report by Judge Richard Posner, an acerbic social critic and one of America's foremost apostles of the free market, blamed the Commission for proposing a solution that did not follow from its own analysis (Posner 2004). His own suggestions, based as he said on the Commission's findings, were more modest, specifically targeted and often technological. For example, with regard to airline safety, Posner called for better passenger and baggage screening, secure cock-pit doors and override mechanisms to enable hijacked planes to be controlled from the ground. He also recommended more effective border controls, including biometric screening, and improved building evacuation plans, which he felt had received too little attention.

At bottom, however, Posner's disagreements with the Commission rested on ideological foundations. Accusing the Commission of 'herd thinking' and a lean towards centralized planning, Posner charged that the proper solution to 9/11 was not a unified intelligence system of questionable efficacy that aggrandized the state. Consistent with market principles, Posner's view seemed to be that the bottom-up forces of individual or small-scale entrepreneurship would do better at producing robust collective defences than top-down state coordination of all information sources:

The Commission thinks the reason the bits of information that might have been assembled into a mosaic spelling 9/11 never came together in one place is that no one person was in charge of intelligence. That is not the reason. The reason or, rather, the reasons are, first, that the volume of information is so vast that even with the continued rapid advances in data processing it cannot be collected, stored, retrieved and analyzed in a single database or even network of databases. Second, legitimate security concerns limit the degree to which confidential information can be safely shared, especially given the ever-present threat of moles like the infamous Aldrich Ames. And third, the different intelligence services and the subunits of each service tend, because information is power, to hoard it. (Posner 2004: 11)

Posner concluded that, ultimately, there is very little a society can do to prevent truly novel risks like 9/11; it is therefore wasteful to engage in too much front-end planning to keep such surprises from happening.

In this respect, Posner's dissent from the Commission's conclusions echoes what another market libertarian, the late political scientist Aaron Wildavsky (1988), had said almost two decades earlier about the futility of advance planning against environmental and other hazards. In both Posner's and Wildavsky's estimation, post-hoc deter-minations of causality, coupled with precisely targeted remedies, will serve society better than trying to predict harms in advance and pre-dicting erroneously. Underlying both positions is a deep, and thor-oughly American, suspicion of the state and its capacity to see, or know, for the people; in a culture committed to the discourse of transparency, the state arguably has no privileged position from which to see any differently than its individual members, who can see well enough for themselves.

Causal analysis and civic epistemology

What light do these three national disasters, and subsequent attempts to make sense of them, shed on our initial question: do human societies learn and, if so, how do they do it? As we have seen, all three events gave rise to long, costly, anguished efforts to identify the causes of tragedy and affix responsibility accordingly. For this purpose, it proved necessary in all three cases to produce bodies of communal knowledge that would underwrite and make plausible the causal analysis that the state wished to embrace for itself and to have its citizens endorse. In this section we ask how each effort reflected or reinforced established national approaches to public knowledge making or, in other words, each nation's characteristic civic epistemology. To what extent were the explanations given for each event stamped or shaped by cultural commitments to particular ways of knowing?

As I have argued elsewhere (Jasanoff 2005), the credibility of governmental actions in contemporary knowledge societies depends crucially on the public evaluation of competing knowledge claims and the consequent production of reliable public knowledge. The concept of civic epistemology acknowledges the centrality of this dynamic. It refers to the mix of ways in which knowledge is produced, presented, tested, verified and put to use in public arenas. These public knowledge-ways, moreover, are not universal but are grounded in historically conditioned practices that may vary from one national context to another. Seen in this light, civic epistemology is a constitutive element of political culture. In any functioning political community, including importantly the nation state, we can identify distinctive, shared understandings among citizens and rulers about what makes some sorts of knowledge claims or modes of reasoning seem more credible than others; public explanations, in turn, achieve robustness by meeting entrenched, institutionalized, cultural expectations about how to produce authoritative knowledge.

Cross-national comparisons, conducted thus far mostly among Western countries, have shown five dimensions of possible variation in the practices of civic epistemology: (1) the dominant styles of public knowledge making; (2) the methods of ensuring accountability; (3) the practices of public demonstration; (4) the preferred registers of objectivity; and (5) the accepted bases of expertise (Jasanoff 2005). Reviewing our three cases of causal analysis in the light of these factors reveals interesting contrasts that resonate with and extend earlier comparative research. These contrasts are summarized in Table 9.1 and elaborated in greater detail below.

The organization of post-disaster inquiries in each country conformed to well-known national *styles of public knowledge making*. In India, the state took early control over medical and legal fact-finding following a disastrous accident, but, significantly, was unwilling or unable to establish a process for making those facts authoritative.[5] In

---

[5] Some of the Indian government's difficulties may relate to the complexities of being embroiled in transnational litigation against Union Carbide, but other considerations had to do with avoiding potential liability for what had happened under its watch in Bhopal. These issues bear more detailed investigation than I am able to provide within the limits of this chapter. For additional perspectives, see Jasanoff (1994).

Table 9.1: Civic epistemology: a comparative overview

	India	Britain	US
Form of post-disaster inquiry	Social protest	Judicial inquiry	Bipartisan national commission
Public knowledge making (style of)	Contentious; movement-based	Embodied; service-based	Pluralist; interest-based
Public accountability	Fluid assumptions; political	Assumptions of trust; relational	Assumptions of distrust; legal
Demonstration	Elite knowledge vs. authentic experience	Common sense empiricism	Socio-technical experiments
Objectivity (strategy for)	Contested; view from somewhere	Negotiated; view from everywhere	Analytic; view from nowhere
Expertise (basis for)	Institutional or political position	Experience	Formal analytic methods

the absence of a definitive public inquiry, multiple accounts of suffering and blame continued to circulate, prompting, as we have seen, new claims and counter-claims as much as two decades after the original tragic event. Factually as well as morally, the Bhopal disaster refused to close; indeed, it spawned a tradition of social protest that promised to outlast the immediately affected generation and to reframe a case of failed industrial risk management as a question of global inequity and injustice. In Britain, by contrast, a judicial inquiry presided over by a Law Lord produced a consensual account of the facts and broad agreement on the institutional changes needed to prevent a recurrence – most particularly, the disbanding of the seriously discredited MAFF. Unlike the BSE inquiry, which followed an adjudicatory model, the US 9/11 Commission drew its authority from bipartisan representation and a politically negotiated unanimity. Not surprisingly, the Commission's primary policy recommendation, the centralization of intelligence gathering, took the form of a managerial fix that sidelined politics and values and quickly won the approval of both major political parties.

The methods for ensuring *accountability* in public knowledge production varied as much across the three cases as did the inquiry processes. In Bhopal, the company, the government and the victims were sceptical about each other's approaches to fact-finding and this mutual suspicion never resolved itself. Union Carbide continued to insist on the sabotage theory, although the victims ridiculed it; the government continued to deny some of the victims' health claims and pegged compensation to administrative classifications rather than to subjective assessments of harm; and the victims continued to insist that they and their offspring had been irreparably damaged in ways not fully accounted for by official medical experts or financial reckonings. In marked contrast, the BSE inquiry produced a relatively uncontested version of the facts and a correspondingly uncontroversial allocation of responsibility. It held accountable institutional actors who, like MAFF or the Southwood working party, had failed to act on the basis of common knowledge and common sense. On the other hand, the inquiry exonerated individuals who, like Mr Meldrum, had made mistakes while sincerely carrying out their duty. For the 9/11 Commission, accountability was more a matter of following the appropriate analytic routines so as to ascertain objective facts; inexcusable error lay in agencies like the CTC not using information to the fullest and not pushing analysis far enough to uncover in-principle knowable truths.

Participants in knowledge making in all three countries relied on different forms of public *demonstration* to legitimate their particular epistemologies. In India, the company and the government used formal legal procedures to reach a settlement designed to make further fact-finding unnecessary. But the settlement never completely assuaged the victims' sense of injury and as late as 2004 activist groups were still staging acts of conscience such as hunger strikes to win benefits from the state. Victims who never experienced the consolation of a day in court won instead a lifelong hearing in the courts of public opinion, in India and beyond. In Britain, the risk of interspecies BSE transmission was publicly admitted only after epidemiological research uncovered evidence of a new pathology. Similarly, British authorities proved reluctant to set upper bounds on the number of possible human infections until they had accumulated several years of data on proved and probable incidents of vCJD. On both issues, certainty was achieved only on the basis of proofs that everyone found persuasive. In the United States, the two 9/11 explanations that gained widest support were, on one hand, the massive failure of intelligence and, on the other, the lack of suitable technological fixes such as biometric passports and better baggage screening. Both are consistent with a civic culture in which breakdowns in social order are frequently framed as technological failures. By the same token, technology, whether social (like intelligence gathering) or material, is the preferred American means of problem solving and US rulers frequently gain support by demonstrating, through public socio-technical experiments, that their policies work (Ezrahi 1990).

National strategies for establishing the *objectivity* of official fact-finding also differed among the three cases. In post-Bhopal India, the major actors each claimed primacy for their own forms of knowledge, but on divergent grounds. Thus, the Indian government used its experts to produce official counts of death and injury, but these were disputed by the victims and their representatives, who preferred to rely on subjective experience backed by community-based clinical observations. Union Carbide also stuck by the opinions of its own experts, particularly on the issue of sabotage, implying that neither Indian officialdom nor the victims could be trusted to produce an unbiased appraisal of the facts. If the Indian knowledge claims represented a view from *somewhere* – that is, from a partisan political standpoint – post-BSE Britain took pains to construct the view from *everywhere*, a consensual account that brooked no real dissent. Discernible within the inquiry findings, moreover, was an acceptance of some truths as self-evident, for example when the committee agreed that infectivity rises shortly before clinical signs of disease appear and that babies are likely to be more susceptible to infection than adults. Statements such as these bear the stamp of a culture that readily accepts the possibility of communal vision. The 9/11 Commission, too, forged a common position, but it did so by sticking close to a dry reconstruction of the events and carefully excluding areas of possible partisan contention. The faults it found, similarly, were those of inadequate analysis and information processing rather than of moral or political short-sightedness (as in Bhopal) or of ignoring obvious facts (as in the BSE case). This approach to objectivity corresponds most nearly to what the philosopher Thomas Nagel (1989) has termed the 'view from nowhere' – that is, a view that is self-consciously shorn of interest or positional bias.

Finally, the three case studies of causal learning illustrate different notions of what constitutes legitimate *expertise*. In the aftermath of Bhopal, it became clear that the major parties were willing neither to trust each other's experts nor to accept any adjudication of the relative merits of their claims as dispositive. There was, in short, no shared credibility economy (Shapin 1995) in which experts for the warring interests could negotiate their cognitive differences and arrive at a common understanding. Expertise remained irretrievably tied to the parties' institutional positions; valid knowledge, then, was not knowledge detached from political engagement but knowledge gained as an extension of politics.

The BSE case, by contrast, displayed at many levels Britain's cultural commitment to a transcendental notion of embodied expertise – that is, expertise acquired through experience, with the expert's standing deriving not only from superior technical abilities but also from a proven record of public service (Jasanoff 1997). Lord Phillips, Sir Richard Southwood and Mr Meldrum all conformed to this image of the expert who stands above special interests, and the inquiry committee's refusal to identify any 'villains or scapegoats' indicated a deep reluctance to question the merits of that kind of expertise. Individuals may have erred when they acted outside the bounds of common sense, but they were not held, for that reason, morally blameworthy. For the 9/11 Commission, which similarly blamed no individuals personally, the chief failure lay in the system's inability to process information in accordance with appropriate frameworks of analysis. Experts, under this reading, were people possessing the necessary technical skills to read the tea leaves of passing events. Their job was to foster, through impersonal analysis and appropriate organizational routines, the sort of preventive imagination that the Commission found so sadly lacking in the disastrous lead-up to 9/11.

Conclusion: learning cultures

Bhopal, the BSE crisis and 9/11 were disasters on a scale that engaged entire nations in processes of collective self-examination and efforts at preventive learning. I have suggested that these efforts unfolded within, and were constrained by, the national traditions of producing and evaluating public knowledge that I have termed civic epistemologies. These institutionalized ways of coming to terms with communal experience are a feature of contemporary political cultures. They at once provide the means of sense making in tangled circumstances and discipline, to some extent, the kinds of reasoning that are considered robust or plausible within a functioning political community. The causes identified and the people or institutions held responsible in each case reflected national commitments to holding still, or *not* questioning, certain features of each nation's political culture, along with a willingness to undertake some forms of institutional reform or policy change.

The cases help us address a major problem identified at the beginning of this chapter: how do we account for learning within extremely stable organizational settings, including nation states, that devote considerable energy and resources to withstanding change? The answer has to do, in part, with the heterogeneity of 'culture' as displayed in these cases. Civic epistemology, in particular, is not a seamless way of knowing shared by all participants in a political community. Far from it. In India, for instance, all those who grappled with the consequences of Bhopal were engaged in producing public facts; yet their notions of how to make facts count and be authoritative were, and remained, apart. There was, to be sure, a formal financial settlement of claims, but this did not constitute closure with respect to the moral narratives of suffering and blame that continued to circulate in India long after the events of December 1984. Events as much as two decades after the date of the accident suggest that the state and its citizens recognized the power of moral arguments to spill over and outlast resolutions reached solely on the basis of factual determinations or administrative convenience.

Britain and the United States both appointed official bodies to inquire into the causes of the BSE fiasco and 9/11 respectively, but while both processes effectively shifted the ground from moral blaming to institutional failure, neither succeeded in fully closing off alternate readings of the events. Closure on facts and evidence was perhaps most complete in Britain, but even in that relatively consensual environment disagreement quickly appeared over the adequacy of the government's policy response. Criticism of the Food Standards Agency and the later vehement controversy over genetically modified crops suggest that state and citizens remained sharply divided over crucial aspects of how to produce authoritative knowledge and robust explanations in areas of high uncertainty. In the United States, Posner's dissent from the 9/11 Commission points to a similar persistence of multiple epistemologies within a single political system. Posner's argument centred, after all, on the state's capacity to serve as a consolidated nerve centre for anti-terrorist intelligence. In questioning the feasibility of that role, Posner spoke for critics from the right and left of the political spectrum who place more faith in local knowledge and decentralized action than in centralized managerial solutions based on seeing like a state (Scott 1998).

Learning from disaster emerges out of these stories as a complex, ambiguous process – conditioned by culture, yet not easily forced into univocal, totalizing, national narratives. It is in the raggedness of accounting for tragic experience that the possibility of cultural reinvention ultimately resides. Comparisons of the sort undertaken here help reveal the cracks in the paving stones of culture from which creative gardeners can coax into bloom new shoots of understanding and self-awareness.

Bibliography

9/11 Commission (2004) *Final Report of the National Commission on Terrorist Attacks upon the United States*. Washington DC: US Government Printing Office.

Abbott, A. (1988) *The System of Professions: an essay on the division of expert labor*. Chicago: University of Chicago Press.

Agency for Healthcare Research and Quality (AHRQ) (2003) *Evidence-based practice centers: overview*. AHRQ Publication No. 03-P006, March. Rockville MD: Agency for Healthcare Research and Quality. http://www.ahrq.gov/clinic/epc/ Last viewed on 4 August 2004.

Ahrens, T. C. and Chapman, C. (2000) 'Occupational identity of management accountants in Britain and Germany', *European Accounting Review*, 9 (4): 477–98.

Akerlof, G. A. and Kranton, R. E. (2003) 'Identity and the economics of organizations', *Journal of Economic Perspectives*, 19 (1): 9–32.

Allred, A. D. and Tottenham, T. O. (1996) 'Liability and indemnity issues for integrated delivery systems', *St. Louis University Law Journal*, 40: 457.

Altman, L. K. (2003) 'Even elite hospitals aren't immune to errors', *New York Times*, 23 February, section 1, p. 16.

American Medical Association (AMA) (1996) *Directory of Practice Parameters*. Chicago, IL: AMA.

(2004) 'Chronology of AMA history: 1900–1920'. http://www.ama-assn.org/ama/pub/category/1924.html Last viewed on 4 August 2004.

Andrews, N. J., Farrington, C. P., Ward, H. J. T., Cousens, S. N., Smith, P. G., Molesworth, A. M., Knight, R. S. G., Ironside, J. W. and Will, R. G. (2003) 'Deaths from variant Creutzfeldt-Jakob disease in the UK', *Lancet*, 361: 751–2.

Annas, G. J. and Grodin, M. A. (eds.) (1992) *The Nazi Doctors and the Nuremberg Code: human rights in human experimentation*. New York: Oxford University Press.

Ayres, I. and Braithwaite, J. (1992) *Responsive Regulation*. Oxford: Oxford University Press.

Ayres, I. and Levitt, S. (1998) 'Measuring the positive externalities from
    unobservable victim precaution: an empirical analysis of Lojack',
    Quarterly Journal of Economics, 113: 43–77.
Ayres, J. (1994) 'The use and abuse of medical practice guidelines', *Journal of
    Legal Medicine*, 15: 421–43.
Baker, T. and Simon, J. (2002) (eds.) *Embracing Risk: the changing culture of
    insurance and responsibility*. Chicago, IL: University of Chicago Press.
Bardach, E. and Kagan, R. (1982) *Going by the Book: the problem of
    regulatory unreasonableness*. Philadelphia PA: Temple University Press.
Barzelay, M. (2001) *The New Public Management – improving research and
    policy dialogue*. Berkeley CA: University of California Press.
Battaglia, B. P. (1997) 'The shift toward managed care and emerging liability
    claims arising from utilization management and financial incentives
    arrangements between health care providers and payers', *University of
    Arkansas Little Rock Law Journal*, 19: 156–217.
Baucus, M. and Dworkin, T. M. (1991) 'What is corporate crime? It is not
    illegal corporate behaviour', *Law and Policy*, 13 (3): 231–44.
Beamish, T. D. (2002) *Silent Spill: the organization of industrial crisis*.
    Cambridge, MA: MIT Press.
Beaumont, P. B., Leopold, J. W. and Coyle, J. R. (1982) 'The safety officer: an
    emerging management role?', *Personnel Review*, 11 (2): 35–8.
Beck, U. (1992) *Risk Society: towards a new modernity*. London: Sage
    Publications.
Beecher, H. K. (1966) 'Ethics of clinical research', *New England Journal of
    Medicine*, 274 (24): 1354–60.
Belke, J. (2001) 'The case for voluntary third party risk management
    program audits'. Unpublished. Paper presented at the Process Plant
    Safety Symposium of the American Institute of Chemical Engineers,
    23 April.
Berg, M. (1997) *Rationalizing Medical Work: decision support techniques
    and medical practices*. Cambridge, MA: MIT Press.
Bernstein, P. L. (1992) *Capital Ideas: the improbable origins of modern Wall
    Street*. New York: Free Press.
Besley, T. and Ghatak, M. (2003) 'Incentives, choice and accountability in
    public service provision', *Oxford Review of Economic Policy*,
    19 (2): 235–49.
    (2004) 'The economics of corporate social responsibility'. Unpublished.
    London School of Economics and Political Science.
    (2005) 'Competition and incentives with motivated agents', *American
    Economic Review*, 95 (3), June.
Better Regulation Task Force (2004) *Avoiding Regulatory Creep*. London:
    Cabinet Office Publications.

Beunza, D. and Stark, D. (2004) 'Tools of the trade: the socio-technology of arbitrage in a Wall Street trading room', *Industrial and Corporate Change*, 13.

Bijker, W., Hughes, T. and Pinch, T. (eds.) (1987) *The Social Construction of Technological Systems*. Cambridge, MA: MIT Press.

Black, F. (1986) 'Noise', *Journal of Finance*, 41: 529–43.

(1988) 'The holes in Black-Scholes', *Risk*, 1 (4): 30–2.

Black, F. and Scholes, M. (1973) 'The pricing of options and corporate liabilities', *Journal of Political Economy*, 81: 637–54.

Black, J. (2002) 'Regulatory conversations', *Journal of Law and Society*, 29 (1): 163–96.

Bolger, A. (2001) 'Move to aid life assurers in falling market', *Financial Times*, 12 September, p. 23.

Bosk, C. (1979) *Forgive and Remember: managing medical failure*. Chicago: University of Chicago Press.

Bouleau, N. (1998) *Martingales et marchés financiers*. Paris: Jacob.

Bourdieu, P. (1980) *The Logic of Practice*. Palo Alto, CA: Stanford University Press.

Bourrier, M. (1999) *Le nucléaire a l'épreuve de l'organisation*. Coll. Le Travail Humain. Paris: Presses Universitaires de France.

Bowker, G. C. and Star, S. L. (1999) *Sorting Things Out: classification and its consequences*. Cambridge, MA: MIT Press.

Bowman, E. and Kunreuther, H. (1988) 'Post Bhopal behavior of a chemical company', *Journal of Management Studies*, 25: 387–402.

Braithwaite, J. and Drahos, P. (2000) *Global Business Regulation*. Cambridge: Cambridge University Press.

Braithwaite, J. and Fisse, B. (1985) 'Varieties of responsibility and organisational crime', *Law and Policy*, 7 (3): 315–43.

Brunsson, N. and Jacobsson, B. (2000) *A World of Standards*. Oxford: Oxford University Press.

Butterworth, M. (2000) 'The emerging role of the risk manager', in J. Pickford (ed.) *Mastering Risk, Volume 1: Concepts*. London: Financial Times / Prentice Hall, pp. 21–5.

Bynum, W. F. (1988) 'Reflections on the history of human experimentation', in S. F. Spicker, I. Alan, A. deVries and H. T Engelhardt Jr. (eds.) *The Use of Human Beings in Research*. Boston: Kluwer Academic Publishers, pp. 47–90.

Callon, M. (1998) *The Laws of the Markets*. Oxford: Blackwell.

Campion, F. D. (1984) *The AMA and the U.S. Health Policy Since 1940*. Chicago: Chicago Review Press.

Carroll, J. S. and Perin, C. (1995) *Organizing and Managing for Safe Production: new frameworks, new questions, new actions*. Cambridge,

MA: Sloan School of Management, Massachusetts Institute of Technology.

Carson, W. G. (1982) *The Other Price of Britain's Oil*. Oxford: Martin Robertson.

Chaffin, J. and Clow, R. (2001) 'Markets closed as they count the cost', *Financial Times*, 12 September, p. 2.

Chiappori, P. A. and Salanie, B. (2003) 'Testing contract theory: a survey of some recent work', in M. Dewatripont, L. Hansen and S. Turnovsky (eds.) *Advances in Economics and Econometrics*, vol. 1. Cambridge: Cambridge University Press.

Clarke, L. (1989) *Acceptable Risk? Making decisions in a toxic environment*. Berkeley, CA: University of California Press.

(1992) 'Context dependency and risk decision making', in L. Clarke and J. F. Short (eds.) *Organizations, Uncertainties, and Risk*. Boulder, CO: Westview Press, pp. 27–38.

(1993) 'The disqualification heuristic', in W. Freudenberg and T. Youn (eds.) *Research in Social Problems and Public Policy*, vol. 5. Greenwich, CT: JAI Press.

(1999) *Mission Improbable: using fantasy documents to tame disaster*. Chicago: University of Chicago Press.

Coggan, P. (2001) 'Rally may have sting in the tail', *Financial Times*, 12 October, p. 25.

Coglianese, G. and Lazer, D. (2001) *Management-based Regulation: using private sector management to achieve public goals*. Regulatory Policy Program Working Paper. Cambridge MA: John F. Kennedy School of Government, Harvard University.

Colebatch, H. K. (1989) 'The concept of regulation in the analysis of the organised world', *Law and Policy*, 11 (1): 71–237.

Collins, H. M. (1985) *Changing Order: replication and induction in scientific practice*. London: Sage.

Columbia Accident Investigation Board (2003) *Report*, vol. 1. Washington, DC: US Government Printing Office.

Committee of Sponsoring Organizations of the Treadway Commission (COSO) (2003) 'Enterprise risk management framework: exposure draft', http://www.coso.org/

(2004) *Framework for Enterprise Risk Management*. Jersey City, NJ: COSO.

Conference Board of Canada (2001) *A Composite Sketch of a Chief Risk Officer*. Ottawa: Conference Board of Canada.

Cutter, S. L. (1993) *Living With Risk*. Sevenoaks: Edward Arnold.

Cyert, R. and March, J. (1963) *A Behavioral Theory of the Firm*. Englewood Cliffs, NJ: Prentice-Hall.

Dewatripont, M., Jewitt, I. and Tirole, J. (1999) 'The economics of career concerns', *Review of Economic Studies*, 66 (1): 189–217.

Deyo, R. A., Psaty, B. M., Simon, G., Wagner, E. H. and Omenn, G. S. (1997) 'The messenger under attack: intimidation of researchers by special-interest groups', *New England Journal of Medicine*, 336: 1176–9.

Dezalay, Y. (1995) 'Introduction: professional competition and the social construction of transnational markets', in Y. Dezalay and D. Sugarman (eds.) *Professional Competition and Professional Power*. London: Routledge, pp. 1–21.

Di Mento, J. F. (1986) *Environmental Law and American Business: dilemmas of compliance*. New York: Plenum Press.

Dickinson, G. M. (2001) 'Enterprise risk management: its origins and conceptual foundation', *Geneva Papers on Risk and Insurance – Issues and Practice*, 26 (3): 360–6.

Dietz, T. and Rycroft, R. W. (1987) *The Risk Professionals*. New York: Russell Sage.

Dixit, A. (2002) 'Incentives and organizations in the public sector: an interpretive review', *Journal of Human Resources*, 37 (4): 696–727.

Dobbin, F., Dierkes, J., Kwok, Man-Shan and Zorn, D. (2001) 'The rise and stagnation of the COO: fad and fashion in corporate titles', Princeton: Department of Sociology, Princeton University.

Douglas, M. (1986) *How Institutions Think*. Syracuse, NY: Syracuse University Press.

(1987) *How Institutions Think*. London: Routledge.

(1999) 'Les risques du fonctionnaire du risque: la diversité des institutions et la répartition des risques' [The risks of the risk officer: diversity of institutions and the distribution of risks], *La Revue Alliage*, 40: 61–74.

Douglas, M. and Wildavsky, A. (1982) *Risk and Culture*. Berkeley, CA: University of California Press.

Dracup, K. (1996) 'Putting clinical practice guidelines to work', *Nursing*, 26 (2): 41–7.

Dunbar, N. (2000) *Inventing Money: the story of Long-Term Capital Management and the legends behind it*. Chichester: Wiley.

Dunsire, A. (1993) 'Modes of governance', in J. Kooiman (ed.) *Modern Governance: new government-society interactions*. London: Sage, pp. 21–34.

Durieux, P., Chaix-Couturier, C., Durand-Zaleski, I. and Ravaud, P. (2000) 'From clinical recommendations to mandatory practice: the introduction of regulatory practice guidelines in the French healthcare system', *International Journal of Technology Assessment in Health Care*, 16 (4): 969–75.

Edelman, L. B., Petterson, S., Chambliss, E. and Erlanger, H. S. (1991) 'Legal ambiguity and the politics of compliance: affirmative action officers' dilemma', *Law and Policy*, 13 (1): 74–97.

Edelman, L., Riggs Fuller, S. and Mara-Drita, I. (2001) 'Diversity rhetoric and the managerialization of law', *American Journal of Sociology*, 106 (6): 1589–1641.

Elliott, M., Kleindorfer, P. and Lowe, R. (2003) 'The role of hazardousness and regulatory practice in the accidental release of chemicals at US industrial facilities', *Risk Analysis*, 23 (5): 883–96.

Emanuel, E. J., Wendler, D. and Grady, C. (2000) 'What makes clinical research ethical?', *Journal of the American Medical Association*, 283 (20): 2701–11.

Epstein, S. (1996) *Impure Science: AIDS, activism, and the politics of knowledge*. Berkeley, CA: University of California Press.

Ericson, R. V. and Doyle, A. (2003) (eds.) *Risk and Morality*. Toronto: University of Toronto Press.

  (2004) *Uncertain Business: risk, insurance and the limits of knowledge*. Toronto: University of Toronto Press.

Ericson, R. V., Doyle, A. and Barry, D. (2004) *Insurance as Governance*. Toronto: University of Toronto Press.

Ericson, R. V. and Haggerty, K. D. (1997) *Policing the Risk Society*. Toronto: University of Toronto Press.

Ermann, M. D. and Lundman, R. J. (2002) (eds.) *Corporate and Governmental Deviance: problems of organizational behavior in contemporary society*. New York: Oxford University Press.

Evidence-based Practice Centers (2003) *Overview*. AHRQ Publication no. 03-P006. Rockville MD: Agency for Healthcare Research and Quality. http://www.ahrq.gov/clinic/epc/ Last viewed on 4 August 2004.

Ewick, P. and Silbey, S. S. (1998) *The Common Place of Law: stories from everyday life*. Chicago: University of Chicago Press.

Ezrahi, Y. (1990) *The Descent of Icarus: science and the transformation of contemporary democracy*. Cambridge, MA: Harvard University Press.

Faden, R. R. and Beauchamp, T. L. in collaboration with King, N. M. P. (1986) *A History and Theory of Informed Consent*. New York: Oxford University Press.

Falkenstein, E. (2001) 'The risk manager of the future: scientist or poet?', *RMA Journal*, 18–22, February.

Fama, E. F. (1970) 'Efficient capital markets: a review of theory and empirical work', *Journal of Finance*, 25: 383–417.

Farmer, J. D. (1998) *Market Force, Ecology, and Evolution*. Working Paper 98-12-117E. Santa Fe, NM: Santa Fe Institute.

Fennell, P. (1988) *Investigation into the King's Cross Underground Fire*. London: HMSO.

Field, K. and Lohr, J. (1992) *Guidelines for Clinical Practice: from development to use*. Washington, DC: National Academy Press.

Fishkin, C. A. (2001) 'Are you the risk manager of tomorrow?', *RMA Journal*, 23 (7), February.

Fisse, B. and Braithwaite, J. (1983) *The Impact of Publicity on Corporate Offenders*. Albany, NY: State University of New York Press.

Fligstein, N. (1990) *The Transformation of Corporate Control*. Cambridge, MA: Harvard University Press.

Foucault, M. (1979) *Discipline and Punish: the birth of the prison*. New York: Random House.

François, P. (2000) 'Public service motivation as an argument for government provision', *Journal of Public Economics*, 78: 275–99.

Freudenberg, W. R. (2003) 'Institutional failure and organizational amplification of risks: the need for a closer look', in N. Pidgeon, R. Kasperson and P. Slovic (eds.) *The Social Amplification of Risk*. Cambridge: Cambridge University Press, pp. 102–20.

Frey, B. and Jegen, R. (2001) 'Motivation crowding theory', *Journal of Economic Surveys*, 15 (1): 589–611.

Frey, B. S. (1997) *Not Just for the Money: an economic theory of personal motivation*. Cheltenham: Edward Elgar Publishing.

Friedman, M. (1953) 'The methodology of Positive Economics', in *Essays in Positive Economics*. Chicago: University of Chicago Press, pp. 3–43.

Gabe, J. (1995) 'Health, medicine and risk: the need for a social approach', in J. Gabe (ed.) *Medicine, Health and Risk: sociological approaches*. Oxford: Blackwell.

Galanter, M. (1999) 'Do the "haves" still come out ahead?', *Law & Society Review*, 33 (4): 1113–23.

—— (1974) 'Why the "haves" come out ahead: speculations on the limits of legal change', *Law and Society Review*, 9: 95–160.

Garcia, M.-F. (1986) 'La construction sociale d'un marché parfait: le marché au Cadran de Fontaines-en-Sologne', *Actes de la Recherche en Sciences Sociales*, 65: 2–13.

General Accounting Office (GAO) (1997) 'Managed care: explicit gag clauses not found in HMO contracts, but physician concerns remain', GAO/HEHS-97-175, Washington, DC: GAO (www.gao.gov).

Gibbons, R. (1998) 'Incentives in organizations', *Journal of Economic Perspectives*, 12 (Fall): 115–32.

Glanz, J. (2001) '1978 study had troubles like a fatal Hopkins test', *New York Times*, 26 July, p. A18.

Gosfield, A. G. (1989) 'Physicians and the PRO's third scope of work', *Medical Staff Counselor*, 3 (4): 1–10.

Gould, S. J. (2000) 'Syphilis and the shepherd of Atlantis', *Natural History*, 109: 38–42, 74–82.

Government Accountability Office (GAO) (2001) *Executive Guide: maximizing the success of chief information officers*. Washington DC: General Accounting Office.

Graham, I., Calder, L., Hébert, P., Carter, A. and Tetroe, J. (2000) 'A comparison of clinical practice guideline appraisal instruments', *International Journal of Technology Assessment in Health Care*, 16 (4): 1024–38.

Greenhouse, C. J. (1989) 'Just in time: temporality and the cultural legitimation of law', *Yale Law Journal*, 98 (8): 1631–51.

Greenspan, A. (1998) 'Statement before the Committee on Banking and Financial Services, U.S. House of Representatives, October 1', *Federal Reserve Bulletin*, 84: 1046–50.

Greenwald, B. and Stiglitz, J. (1990) 'Asymmetric information and the new theory of the firm: financial constraints and risk behavior', *American Economic Review: Papers and Proceedings*, 80: 160–5.

Grogan, C., Feldman, R., Nyman, J. and Shapiro, J. (1994) 'How will we use clinical guidelines? The experience of Medicare carriers', *Journal of Health Politics, Policy and Law*, 19 (1): 7–26.

Groves, T. (1979) 'Efficient collective choice when compensation is possible', *Review of Economic Studies*, 227–41.

Hajer, M. (1997) *The Politics of Environmental Discourse*. Oxford: Oxford University Press.

Halpern, S. A. (2004) *Lesser Harms: the morality of risk in medical research*. Chicago: University of Chicago Press.

Hammack, J. B. and Raines, M. L. (1981) *Space Shuttle Safety Assessment Report*. Johnson Space Center, Safety Division, 5 March. Washington, DC: National Archives.

Hancock, S. F. (1994) 'The role of the judge in medical treatment decisions', *Albany Law Review*, 57: 647–54.

Hanley, M. (2002) 'The great protector', *CFO Europe*, 29 (34), February.

Harkness, J., Lederer, S. and Wikler, D. (2001) 'Laying ethical foundations for clinical research', *Bulletin of the World Health Organization*, 79 (4): 65–8.

Harrison, J. M. and Kreps, D. M. (1979) 'Martingales and arbitrage in multiperiod securities markets', *Journal of Economic Theory*, 20: 381–408.

Harrison, J. M. and Pliska, S. R. (1981) 'Martingales and stochastic integrals in the theory of continuous trading', *Stochastic Processes and their Applications*, 11: 215–60.

Harrison, P. (1997) 'A history of an intellectual arbitrage: the evaluation of financial economics', in John B. Davis (ed.) *New Economics and its History: history of political economy, annual supplement to vol. 29*. Durham, NC: Duke University Press, pp. 172–87.

Harvard Business School (2003) *Harvard Business Review on Motivating People*. Cambridge, MA: Harvard Business School Press.

Hastings, K. (1993) 'A view from the agency for health care policy and research: the use of language in clinical practice guidelines', *Joint Commission Journal of Quality Improvement*, 19 (8): 335–41.

Hawkins, K. O. (1984) *Environment and Enforcement: regulation and the social definition of enforcement*. New York: Oxford University Press.

Heal, G. and Kunreuther, H. (2003) 'You only die once: managing discrete interdependent risks'. NBER Working Paper 9885. Cambridge MA: National Bureau of Economic Research.

Health and Safety Commission (HSC) (1998) Press release C56:98.

(1999) 'Train accident at Ladbroke Grove Junction, 5 October 1999: First HSE Interim Report, October 1999'.

Health and Safety Executive (HSE) (1999) *Railway Safety: HM Chief Inspecting Officer of Railways' annual report on the safety record of the railways in Great Britain during 1998/99*. London: HSE Books.

Heclo, H. and Wildavsky, A. (1974) *The Private Government of Public Money*. London: Macmillan.

Heimer, C. A. (1988) 'Social structure, psychology and the estimation of risk', *Annual Review of Sociology*, 14: 491–519.

(1992) 'Your baby's just fine: certification procedures, meetings and the supply of information in neonatal intensive care units', in J. F. Short and L. Clarke (eds.) *Organizations, Uncertainties, and Risk*. Boulder, CO: Westview Press.

(1999) 'Competing institutions: law, medicine, and family in neonatal intensive care', *Law and Society Review*, 33 (1): 17–66.

Heller, J. (1972) 'Syphilis victims in the U.S. study went untreated for 40 years', *New York Times*, 26 July, pp. 1, 8.

Hershey, J., Asch, D., Thumasathit, T., Meszaros, J. and Waters, V. (1994) 'The roles of altruism, free riding, and bandwagoning in vaccination decisions', *Organizational Behavior and Human Decision Processes*, 59: 177–87.

Herzberg, F. (1987) 'Workers' needs: the same around the world', *Industry Week*, 21 September.

Hidden, A. (1989) *Investigation into the Clapham Junction Railway Accident*. London: HMSO.

Hilts, P. J. (2001) 'Drug's problems raise questions on warnings', *New York Times, Science Times*, 21 August, D1–D2.

(2003) *Protecting America's Health: the FDA, business, and one hundred years of regulation.* New York: Alfred A. Knopf.

Hoch, S. and Kunreuther, H. (2001) *Wharton on Making Decisions.* New York: Wiley.

Hölmström, B. (1982) 'Moral hazard in teams', *Bell Journal of Economics,* 13 (2): 324–40.

Hölmström, B. and Milgrom, P. (1991) 'Multi-task principal-agent analysis: incentive contracts, asset ownership, and job design', *Journal of Law, Economics and Organization,* Special Issue, 7: 24–52.

Holzer, B. and Millo, Y. (2004) *From risks to second-order dangers in financial markets: unintended consequences of risk management.* Discussion Paper 29. London: ESRC Centre for Analysis of Risk and Regulation, London School of Economics and Political Science.

Hood, C. (1996) 'Control over bureaucracy: cultural theory and institutional variety', *Journal of Public Policy,* 15 (3): 207–30.

(2002) 'The risk game and the blame game', *Government and Opposition,* 37 (1): 15–37.

Hood, C. and Jones, D. K. C. (1996) (eds.) *Accident and Design.* London: UCL Press.

Hood, C., James, O., Scott, C., Jones, G. W. and Travers, T. (1999) *Regulation Inside Government: waste watchers, quality police, and sleaze-busters.* Oxford: Oxford University Press.

Hood, C., Rothstein, H. and Baldwin, R. (2001) *The Government of Risk.* Oxford: Oxford University Press.

Horlick-Jones, T. (1996) 'Is safety a by-product of quality management?', in Hood, C. and Jones, D. K. C. (eds.) (1996).

http://www.bseinquiry.gov.uk

Hughes, E. (1958) *Men and Their Work.* Glencoe, IL: Free Press.

Hull, J. C. (2000) *Options, futures, & other derivatives.* Upper Saddle River, NJ: Prentice-Hall.

Hunt, B. (2003) *The Timid Corporation.* Chichester: John Wiley & Sons.

Hurwitz, B. (1999) 'Legal and political considerations of clinical practice guidelines', *British Medical Journal,* 318 (7184): 661–4.

Hutter, B. (1988) *The Reasonable Arm of the Law? The law enforcement procedures of environmental health officers.* Oxford: Clarendon Press.

Hutter, B. M. (1992) 'Public accident inquiries: the case of the railway inspectorate', *Public Administration,* 70: 177–92.

(1997) *Compliance: regulation and environment.* Oxford: Clarendon Press.

(1999) *Socio-legal Reader in Environmental Law.* Oxford: Clarendon Press.

(2001) *Regulation and Risk: occupational health and safety on the railways*. Oxford: Clarendon Press.

(2004) 'Risk management and governance', in P. Eliadis, M. M. Hill and M. Howlett (eds.) *Designing Government: from instruments to governance*. Montreal: McGill-Queen's University Press.

Hutter, B. M. and Lloyd-Bostock, S. (1990) 'The power of accidents: the social and psychological impact of accidents and the enforcement of safety regulations', *British Journal of Criminology*, 30: 453–65.

Hyams, A. L., Shapiro, D. W. and Brennan, T. A. (1996) 'Medical practice guidelines in malpractice litigation: an early retrospective', *Journal of Health Politics, Policy and Law*, 21 (2): 289–313.

Institute of Medicine, Committee on Clinical Practice Guidelines (1992) *Guidelines for Clinical Practice: from development to use*. Washington, DC: National Academy Press.

Institute of Medicine, Committee to Advise the Public Health Service on Clinical Practice Guidelines (1990) *Clinical Practice Guidelines: directions for a new program*. Washington, DC: National Academy Press.

Ip, G. and Zuckerman, G. (2001) 'Treasury sale averts a crisis in "repo" market', *Wall Street Journal*, 5 October, C1 and C12.

Jackall, R. (1988) *Moral Mazes: the world of corporate managers*. New York and Oxford: Oxford University Press.

Jasanoff, S. (1986) *Risk Management and Political Culture*. New York: Russell Sage Foundation.

(1994) *Learning From Disaster: risk management after Bhopal*. Philadelphia, PA: University of Pennsylvania Press.

(1995) 'Product, process, or programme: three cultures and the regulation of biotechnology', in M. Bauer (ed.) *Resistance to New Technology*. Cambridge: Cambridge University Press, pp. 311–31.

(1997) 'Civilization and madness: the great BSE scare of 1996', *Public Understanding of Science*, 6: 221–32.

(2005) *Designs on Nature: science and democracy in Europe and the United States*. Princeton, NJ: Princeton University Press.

Jorian, P. (2000) 'Value, risk and control: the call for integration', in J. Pickford (ed.) *Mastering Risk, Volume 1: Concepts*. London: Financial Times / Prentice Hall.

Joyce, K. A. (2000) 'The transparent body: magnetic resonance imaging, knowledge, and practices', PhD thesis, Department of Sociology, Boston College.

Kagan, R. (2000) 'The consequences of legal adversarialism', in R. Kagan and L. Axelrad (eds.) *Regulatory Encounters*. Berkeley, CA: University of California Press, pp. 372–413.

Kahneman, D. and Tversky, A. (1979) 'Prospect theory: an analysis of decision under risk', *Econometrica*, 47 (2).

Kalelkar, A. (1988) 'Investigation of large-magnitude incidents: Bhopal as a case study', http://www.bhopal.com/infoarch.htm

Kasperson, J. X., Kasperson, R. E., Pidgeon, N. and Slovic, P. (2003) 'The social amplification of risk: assessing fifteen years of research and theory', in N. Pidgeon, R. Kasperson and P. Slovic (eds.) *The Social Amplification of Risk*. Cambridge: Cambridge University Press, pp. 13–46.

Kerr, S. (1995) 'On the folly of rewarding A while hoping for B', *Academy of the Management Executive*, 9 (1): 7–14.

Kleindorfer, P., Kunreuther, H. and Schoemaker, P. (1993) *Decision Sciences, an Integrative Perspective*. Cambridge: Cambridge University Press.

Kleindorfer, P. R., Belke, J. C., Elliott, M. R., Lee, K., Lowe, R. A. and Feldman, H. I. (2003) 'Accident epidemiology and the US chemical industry: accident history and worst-case data from RMP', *Risk Analysis*, 23 (5): 865–81.

Knight, F. (1921) *Risk, Uncertainty and Profit*. Boston: Houghton Mifflin Co.

Knorr Cetina, K. and Bruegger, U. (2002) 'Global microstructures: the virtual societies of financial markets', *American Journal of Sociology*, 107: 905–51.

Kohn, A. (1993) 'Why incentive plans cannot work', *Harvard Business Review*, September–October: 54–63.

Kolata, G. (1997) 'Safeguards urged for researchers', *New York Times*, 17 April, section D, p. 23.

Kreps, D. (1990) *A Course in Microeconomic Theory*. Princeton, NJ: Princeton University Press, Chapter 16.

Krimsky, S. and Golding, D. (1992) (eds.) *Social Theories of Risk*. Westport CT: Praeger.

Kuhn, T. (1962) *The Structure of Scientific Revolutions*. Chicago: University of Chicago Press.

Kunreuther, H. and Heal, G. (2003) 'Interdependent security: the case of identical agents', *Journal of Risk and Uncertainty*, 26: 231–49.

Kunreuther, H., McNulty, P. and Kang, Y. (2002) 'Improving environmental safety through third party inspection', *Risk Analysis*, 22: 309–18.

Kunreuther, H., Onculer, A. and Slovic, P. (1998) 'Time insensitivity for protective measures', *Journal of Risk and Uncertainty*, 16: 279–99.

La Porte, T. (1994) 'A strawman speaks up', *Journal of Contingency and Crisis Management*, 4: 60–72.

Lam, J. (2000) 'Enterprise-wide risk management and the role of the chief
    risk officer', *Erisk Magazine*, 25 March.
    (2003) *Enterprise Risk Management – from incentives to controls*.
    London: John Wiley.
Latour, B. (1987) *Science in Action*. Cambridge, MA: Harvard
    University Press.
Lazear, E. (2000) 'Performance pay and productivity', *American Economic
    Review*, 90 (5): 1346–61.
Lederer, S. E. (1995) *Subjected to Science: human experimentation in
    America before the Second World War*. Baltimore: Johns Hopkins
    University Press.
Lee, C. R. (2000) 'Chief Risk Officer stepping up', *Risk Management*,
    September: 23–7.
Lempert, R. and Sanders, J. (1986) *An Introduction to Law and Social
    Science: desert, disputes, and distribution*. Philadelphia, PA: University
    of Pennsylvania Press.
Levine, R. J. (1991) 'Informed consent: some challenges to the universal
    validity of the western model', *Law, Medicine & Health Care*,
    19 (3–4): 207–13.
Lieberman, J. K. (1981) *The Litigious Society*. New York: Basic Books.
Lofquist, W. S., Cohen, M. A. and Rabe, M. A. (1997) (eds.) *Debating
    Corporate Crime*. Highland Heights, KY: Academy of Criminal Justice
    Sciences, Northern Kentucky University.
Loft, A. (1988) 'Understanding accounting in its social and historical
    context: the case of cost accounting in the UK, 1914–1925', *Accounting,
    Organizations and Society*, 13 (2): 137–69.
Loue, S., Okello, D. and Kawuma, M. (1996) 'Research bioethics in the
    Ugandan context: a program summary', *Journal of Law, Medicine, and
    Ethics*, 24: 47–53.
Lowenstein, R. (2000) *When Genius Failed: the rise and fall of Long-Term
    Capital Management*. New York: Random House.
Luhmann, N. (1993) *Risk: a sociological theory*. Berlin: de Gruyter.
Macgregor, D. G. (2003) 'Public response to Y2K', in N. F. Pidgeon et al.
    (eds.) *The Social Amplification of Risk*. Cambridge: Cambridge
    University Press.
MacKenzie, D. (2000) 'Fear in the markets', *London Review of Books*,
    13 April, pp. 31–2.
    (2003a) 'Long-Term Capital Management and the sociology of arbitrage',
    Economy and Society, 32: 349–80.
    (2003b) 'An equation and its worlds: bricolage, exemplars, disunity and
    performativity in financial economics', *Social Studies of Science*,
    33: 831–68.

MacKenzie, D. and Millo, Y. (2003) 'Constructing a market, performing theory: the historical sociology of a financial derivatives exchange', *American Journal of Sociology*, 109: 107–45.

Manley, J. E. (2001) 'The changing environment of professional work: the case of health care accreditation'. Unpublished. Paper presented at the American Sociological Association annual meeting.

March, J. and Shapira, Z. (1987) 'Managerial perspectives on risk and risk taking', *Management Science*, 23 (11): 1404–18.

Marcus, A. (1988) 'Risk, uncertainty, and scientific judgment', *Minerva*, 2: 138–52.

(1995) 'Managing with danger', *Industrial Environment Crisis Quarterly*, 9: 139–51.

Marks, H. M. (1988) 'Notes from the underground: the social organization of therapeutic research', in R. Maulitz and D. Long (eds.) *Grand Rounds*. Pittsburgh, PA: University of Pennsylvania Press, pp. 297–336.

(1997) *The Progress of Experiment: science and therapeutic reform in the United States, 1900–1990*. Cambridge: Cambridge University Press.

Marshall, D., Simpson, K., Norton, E., Biddle, A. and Youle, M. (2000) 'Measuring the effect of clinical guidelines on patient outcomes', *International Journal of Technology Assessment in Health Care*, 16 (4): 1013–23.

Marx, G. T. (1984) 'Notes on the discovery, collection, and assessment of hidden and dirty data', in J. W. Schneider and J. I. Kitsuse (eds.) *Studies in the Sociology of Social Problems*. Norwood NJ: Ablex Publishing, pp. 78–113.

Matthews, R. J. (1999) 'Practice guidelines and tort reform: the legal system confronts the technocratic wish', *Journal of Health Politics, Policy and Law*, 24: 275–304.

McCarthy, M. (2001) 'A century of US Army yellow fever research', *Lancet*, 357 (9270): 1772.

McClelland, G., Schulze, W. and Coursey, D. (1993) 'Insurance for low-probability hazards: a bimodal response to unlikely events', *Journal of Risk and Uncertainty*, 7: 95–116.

McDonough, W. J. (1998) 'Statement before the Committee on Banking and Financial Services, U.S. House of Representatives, October 1', *Federal Reserve Bulletin*, 84: 1050–4.

McNulty, P. J., Barrish, R. A., Antoff, R. C. and Schaller, L. C. (1999) 'Evaluating the use of third parties to measure process safety management in small firms'. Unpublished. Paper presented at the Annual Symposium, Mary Kay O'Connor Process Safety Center, Texas A&M University.

Meisel A. and Kabnick, L. D. (1980) 'Informed consent to medical treatment: an analysis of recent legislation', *University of Pittsburgh Law Review*, 41: 407–564.

Mello, M. (2001) 'Of swords and shields: the role of clinical practice guidelines in medical malpractice litigation', *University of Pennsylvania Law Review*, 149: 645–710.

Merry, S. E. (1990) *Getting Justice and Getting Even: legal consciousness among working-class Americans*. Chicago: University of Chicago Press.

Merton, R. C. (1973) 'Theory of rational option pricing', *Bell Journal of Economics and Management Science*, 4: 141–83.

Merton, R. K. (1936) 'The unanticipated consequences of purposive social action', *American Sociological Review*, 1: 894–904.

(1940) 'Bureaucratic structure and personality', *Social Forces*, 17: 560–68.

(1949) 'The self-fulfilling prophecy', in *Social Theory and Social Structure*. New York: Free Press, pp. 179–95.

(1968) *Social Structure and Social Theory*. New York: Free Press.

Merz, S. (1993) 'Clinical practice guidelines: policy issues and legal implications', *Joint Commission Journal of Quality Improvement*, 19 (8): 306–12.

Meulbroek, L. (2000) 'Total strategies for company-wide risk control', in J. Pickford (ed.) *Mastering Risk, Volume 1: Concepts*. London: Financial Times / Prentice Hall.

Meyer, J. W. and Rowan, B. (1977) 'Institutionalized organizations', *American Journal of Sociology*, 83: 340–63.

Meyer, J., Boli, J., Thomas, G. and Ramirez, F. (1997) 'World society and the nation state', *American Journal of Sociology*, 103: 144–81.

Miccolis, J., Hively, K. and Merkley, B. (2001) *Enterprise Risk Management: trends and emerging practices*. Altamonte Springs, FL: Institute of Internal Auditors Research Foundation.

Millenson, M. (1999) *Demanding Medical Excellence: doctors and accountability in the information age*. Chicago: University of Chicago Press.

Miller, F. G., Rosenstein, D. L. and Derenzo, E. G. (1998) 'Professional integrity in clinical research', *Journal of the American Medical Association*, 280 (16): 1449–54.

Miller, J. L. (2002) 'The board as monitor of organizational activity: the applicability of agency theory to non-profit boards', *Nonprofit Management and Leadership*, 12 (4): 429–50.

Ministry of Agriculture, Fisheries and Food (MAFF) (1989) *Report of the Working Party on Bovine Spongiform Encephalopathy* (Southwood Committee Report). London: HMSO.

Modigliani, F. and Miller, M. H. (1958) 'The cost of capital, corporation finance and the theory of investment', *American Economic Review*, 48: 261–97.

Moreno, J. D. (1999) 'Lessons learned: a half-century of experimenting on humans', *Humanist*, 59 (5): 9–15.

Morgan, G. and Engwall, L. (1999) 'Regulation and organizations: an introduction', in G. Morgan and L. Engwall (eds.) *Regulations and Organizations*. London: Routledge.

Morin, K. (1998) 'The standard of disclosure in human subject experimentation', *Journal of Legal Medicine*, 19: 157–221.

Mulrow, C. D. and Lohr, K. N. (2001) 'Proof and policy from medical research evidence', *Journal of Health Politics, Policy and Law*, 26 (2): 249–66.

Nagel, T. (1989) *The View From Nowhere*. Oxford: Oxford University Press.

National Commission for the Protection of Human Subjects of Biomedical and Behavioral Research (1978) *The Belmont Report: ethical principles and guidelines for the protection of human subjects of research*. Washington, DC: US Government Printing Office, OS78–0012.

Nelkin, D. (ed.) (1985) *The Language of Risk: conflicting perspectives on occupational health*. Beverly Hills CA: Sage Publications.

Nelkin, D. and Brown, M. S. (1984) *Workers at Risk: voices from the workplace*. Chicago: University of Chicago Press.

Niskanen, W. (1971) *Bureaucracy and Representative Government*. New York: Aldine-Atherton.

Noble, D. F. (1977) *America by Design: science, technology and the rise of corporate capitalism*. New York: Oxford University Press.

O'Brien, J., Jacobs Jr., L. and Pierce, D. (2000) 'Clinical practice guidelines and the cost of care: a growing alliance', *International Journal of Technology Assessment in Health Care*, 16 (4): 1077–91.

O'Connell, J. (1979) *The Lawsuit Lottery*. New York: Free Press.

Oberholzer-Gee, F. (1998) 'Learning to bear the unbearable: towards an explanation of risk ignorance'. Unpublished. Wharton School, University of Pennsylvania.

Orléan, A. (1998) 'Informational influences and the ambivalence of imitation', in J. Lesourne and A. Orléan (eds.) *Advances in Self-organization and Evolutionary Economics*. London: Economica, pp. 39–56.

Ostrom, E. (1990) *Governing the Commons: the evolution of institutions for collective action*. Cambridge: Cambridge University Press.

Ostrovsky, A. and Wiggins, J. (2001) 'Investors show resilience with orderly sell-off', *Financial Times*, 4 October, p. 4.

Paese, L. L. and Paese, G. (1999) 'Changes in tide for healthcare decision-making: the expansion of liability and the resulting adjustments ahead for healthcare delivery', *Journal of Medicine and Law*, 27: 43–73.

Parker, C. (2002) *The Open Corporation: effective self-regulation and democracy*. Cambridge: Cambridge University Press.

Pearce, F. and Tombs, S. (1990) 'Ideology, hegemony, and empiricism', *British Journal of Criminology*, 30 (4): 423–43.

Pentland, B. (1993) 'Getting comfortable with the numbers: auditing and the micro-production of macro-order', *Accounting, Organizations and Society*, 18 (7/8): 605–20.

Perold, A. (1999) *Long-Term Capital Management*. Boston, MA: Harvard Business School Publishing.

Perrow, C. (1984) *Normal Accidents: living with high risk technologies*. New York: Basic Books.

Phillips, D. F. (2000) 'IRBs search for answers and support during a time of institutional change', *Journal of the American Medical Association*, 283 (6): 729–30.

Phillips, Lord (2000) *The Inquiry into BSE and Variant CJD in the United Kingdom*. London: HMSO.

Phimister, J. R., Oktem, U., Kleindorfer, P. R. and Kunreuther, H. (2003) 'Near-miss management systems in the chemical process industry', *Risk Analysis*, 23 (3): 445–59.

Picinic, N. J. (1997) 'Physicians bound and gagged: federal attempts to combat managed care's use of gag clauses', *Seton Hall Legislative Journal*, 21: 567–620.

Pidgeon, N. F. and O'Leary, M. (2000) 'Man-made disasters: why technology and organizations (sometimes) fail', *Safety Science*, 34: 15–30.

Pidgeon, N. F., Kasperson, R. K. and Slovic, P. (2003) (eds.) *The Social Amplification of Risk*. Cambridge: Cambridge University Press.

Pinch, T. and Bijker, W. (1984) 'The social construction of facts and artefacts: or how the sociology of science and the sociology of technology might benefit each other', *Social Studies of Science*, 14: 399–441.

Pollnac, R. B., Poggie, J. J. and VanDusen, C. (1995) 'Cultural adaptation to danger and the safety of commercial oceanic fishermen', *Human Organisation*, 54 (2): 153–9.

Porter, T. (1995) *Trust in Numbers: the pursuit of objectivity in science and public life*. Princeton, NJ: Princeton University Press.

Posner, R. (2004) 'The 9/11 report: a dissent', *New York Times, Sunday Book Review*, 29 August.

Powell, W. W. (2001) 'The capitalist firm in the twenty-first century: emerging patterns in western enterprise', in P. DiMaggio (ed.) *The Twenty-First Century Firm*. Princeton, NJ: Princeton University Press, pp. 33–68.

Powell, W. W. and DiMaggio, P. J. (1991) *The New Institutionalism in Organizational Analysis*. Chicago: University of Chicago Press.

Power, M. (1997) 'Expertise and the construction of relevance: accountants and environmental audit', *Accounting, Organizations and Society*, 22 (2): 123–46.

(2000) *The Audit Implosion: regulating risk from the inside*. London: Institute of Chartered Accountants in England and Wales.

(2003) 'Risk management and the responsible organization', in R. Ericson and A. Doyle (eds.) *Risk and Morality*. Toronto: University of Toronto Press, pp. 145–64.

(2004a) *The Risk Management of Everything*. London: Demos.

(2004b) 'Enterprise risk management and the organization of uncertainty in financial institutions', in K. Knorr Cetina and A. Preda (eds.) *The Sociology of Financial Markets*. Oxford: Oxford University Press, pp. 250–68.

(2005) 'The invention of operational risk', *Review of International Political Economy*, 12 (4): 577–99.

Poynter, K. (2004) 'Risk and value management', *Risk & Regulation*, 7 (Summer), magazine of the ESRC Centre for Analysis of Risk and Regulation, London: London School of Economics and Political Science.

Preda, A. (2004) 'Informative prices, rational investors: the emergence of the random walk hypothesis and the nineteenth-century "science of financial investments"', *History of Political Economy*, 36 (2).

Prendergast, C. (1999) 'The provision of incentives in firms', *Journal of Economic Literature*, 37 (1).

Rees, J. (1988) *Reforming the Workplace: a study of self-regulation in occupational safety*. Philadelphia, PA: University of Pennsylvania Press.

(1997) 'Development of communitarian regulation in the chemical industry', *Law & Policy*, 19 (4): 177.

Rees, J. V. (1994) *Hostages of Each Other: the transformation of nuclear safety since Three Mile Island*. Chicago: University of Chicago Press.

Rehbinder, E. (1991) 'Reflexive law and practice: the corporate officer for environmental protection as an example', in A. Febbrajo and G. Teubner (eds.) *State, Law, Economy as Autopoetic Systems: regulation and autonomy in a new perspective*. Milan: Guiffré, pp. 579–608.

Reiss, A. J. (1984) 'Selecting strategies of social control over organisational life', in K. Hawkins and J. M. Thomas (eds.) *Enforcing Regulation*, Dordrecht: Kluwer-Nijhoff, pp. 23–35.

Reverby, S. M. (2001) 'More than fact and fiction: cultural memory and the Tuskegee syphilis study', *Hastings Center Report*, 31 (5): 22–8.

Richardson, G. M., Ogus, A. I. and Burrows, P. (1983) *Policing Pollution: a study of regulation and enforcement*. Oxford: Clarendon Press.

Roberts, K. H. and Libuser, C. (1993) 'From Bhopal to banking', *Organizational Dynamics*, 21: 15–26.

Rolt, L. T. C. (1986) *Red for Danger: the classic history of railway disasters*. London: Pan Books.

Rosoff, A. (2001) 'Evidence-based medicine and the law: the courts confront clinical practice guidelines', *Journal of Health Politics, Policy and Law*, 26 (2): 327–68.

Ross, S. A. (1987) 'Finance', in J. Eatwell, M. Milgate and P. Newman (eds.) *The New Palgrave Dictionary of Economics*, vol. 2. London: Macmillan, pp. 322–36.

(2001) 'Neoclassical and alternative finance'. Unpublished. Keynote address, European Financial Management Association Meetings.

Rothman, D. J. (2000) 'The shame of medical research', *New York Review of Books*, 47 (19): 60–4, 30 November.

Rothstein, H. (2003) 'Neglected risk regulation: the institutional attenuation phenomenon', *Health, Risk and Society*, 5 (1): 85–103.

Rubinstein, M. (1985) 'Nonparametric tests of alternative option pricing models using all reported trades and quotes on the 30 most active CBOE option classes from August 23, 1976 through August 31, 1978', *Journal of Finance*, 40: 455–80.

(1994) 'Implied binomial trees', *Journal of Finance*, 49: 771–818.

Ruggie, M. (1992) 'The paradox of liberal intervention: health policy and the American welfare state', *American Journal of Sociology*, 97 (4): 919–44.

Sagan, S. D. (1993) *The Limits of Safety: organizations, accidents, and nuclear weapons*. Princeton, NJ: Princeton University Press.

Schelling, T. (1978) *Micromotives and Macrobehavior*. New York: Norton.

Schlesinger, M., Dorwart, R. A. and Epstein, S. S. (1996) 'Managed care constraints on psychiatrists' hospital practices: bargaining power and professional autonomy', *American Journal of Psychiatry*, 153: 256–60.

Schmidt, K. M. (1997) 'Managerial incentives and product market competition', *Review of Economic Studies*, 64: 191–213.

Schuck, P. (1986) *Agent Orange on Trial: mass toxic disasters in the courts*. Cambridge, MA: Harvard University Press.

Schulman, P. R. (1993) 'The analysis of high reliability organizations', in K. H. Roberts (ed.) *New Challenges to Understanding Organizations*. New York: Macmillan.

Scott, J. C. (1998) *Seeing Like a State*. New Haven, CT: Yale University Press.

Scott, W. R., Martin, R., Mendel, P. J. and Caronna, C. A. (2000) *Institutional Change and Healthcare Organizations: from professional dominance to managed care*. Chicago: University of Chicago Press.

Seeger, P. (1955) 'Where Have All the Flowers Gone?'

Selznick, P. (1980) *Law, Society, and Industrial Justice*. New Brunswick NJ: Transaction Books.

Shapin, S. (1995) 'Cordelia's love: credibility and the social studies of science', *Perspectives on Science*, 3 (3): 255–75.

Sheehan, R. (1996) 'Mission accomplishment as philanthropic effectiveness: key findings from the excellence in philanthropy project', *Nonprofit and Voluntary Sector Quarterly*, 25 (1): 110–23.

Sheen, Sir Barry (1987) *MV Herald of Free Enterprise: report of Court no. 8074 formal investigation*. London: HMSO for Department of Transport.

Sheetz, M. (1997) 'Toward controlled clinical care through clinical practice guidelines: the legal liability for developers and issuers of clinical pathways', *Brooklyn Law Review*, 63 (4): 1341–80.

Shiller, R. J. (2003) *The New Financial Order: risk in the 21st century*. Princeton, NJ: Princeton University Press.

Shleifer, A. (2000) *Inefficient Markets: an introduction to behavioral finance*. Oxford: Oxford University Press.

Shleifer, A. and Vishny, R. W. (1997) 'The limits of arbitrage', *Journal of Finance*, 52: 35–55.

Short, J. (1992) '*Defining, explaining and managing risk*', in J. Short and L. Clarke (eds.), *Organizations, Uncertainties and Risk*. Boulder, CO: Westview Press, pp. 3–23.

Short, J. F. and Clarke, L. (1992) (eds.) *Organizations, Uncertainties, and Risk*. Boulder CO: Westview Press.

Shubik, M. (ed.) (1991) *Risk, Organizations and Society*. Dordrecht: Kluwer.

Sieber, S. D. (1981) *Fatal Remedies: the ironies of social intervention*. New York: Plenum Press.

Sigler, J. A. and Murphy, J. E. (1988) *Interactive Corporate Compliance: an alternative to regulatory compulsion*. New York: Quorum Books.

Silverman, W. A. (1980) *Retrolental Fibroplasia: a modern parable*. New York: Grune and Stratton.

Sitkin, S. B. and Bies, R. J. (1994) 'The legalization of organizations: a multi-theoretical perspective', in S. B. Sitkin and R. J. Bies (eds.) *The Legalistic Organization*. Thousand Oaks, CA: Sage, pp. 19–49.

Sklair, L. (2002) *Globalization: capitalism and its alternatives*, Oxford: Oxford University Press.

Slovic, P. (1992) 'Perception of risk: reflections on the psychometric paradigm', in S. Krimsky and D. Golding (eds.) *The Social Theories of Risk*. Westport, CT: Praeger.

(2002) 'Terrorism as hazard: a new species of trouble', *Risk Analysis*, 22 (3): 425–6.

Snider, L. (1987) 'Towards a political economy of reform, regulation and corporate crime', *Law and Policy*, 9 (1): 37–68.

Snook, S. A. (2000) *Friendly Fire: the accidental shoot-down of U.S. Black Hawks over northern Iraq*. Princeton, NJ: Princeton University Press.

Star, S. L. and Gerson, E. (1987) 'The management and dynamics of anomalies in scientific work', *Sociological Quarterly*, 28: 147–69.

Starr, P. (1982) *The Social Transformation of American Medicine*. New York: Basic Books.

Stein, M. (2000) 'The risk taker as shadow: a psychoanalytic view of the collapse of Barings Bank', *Journal of Management Studies*, 37 (8): 1215–30.

Stone, C. (1975) *Where the Law Ends: the social control of corporate behaviour*. Prospect Heights, IL: Waveland Press.

Suchman, L. A. (1987) *Plans and Situated Actions*. New York: Cambridge University Press.

Tanenbaum, S. (1994) 'Knowing and acting in medical practice: the epistemological politics of outcomes research', *Journal of Health Politics, Policy and Law*, 19 (1): 27–44.

Tillinghast Towers Perrin (2002) *Enterprise Risk Management in the Insurance Industry: 2002 benchmarking survey report*. http://www.towersperrin.com/tillinghast/default.htm

Tolbert, P. S. and Zucker, L. G. (1983) 'Institutional sources of change in the formal structure of organizations: the diffusion of civil service reform, 1880–1935', *Administrative Science Quarterly*, 28: 22–39.

Topper, J. (1997) 'The United States Army Yellow Fever Commission and the Spanish-American War: science and politics in Latin America, 1898–1904', http://www.med.virginia.edu/hs-library/historical/yelfev/tabcon.html

Turner, B. A. (1978) *Man-made Disasters*. London: Wykeham.

Turner, B. A. and Pidgeon, N. F. (1997) *Man-made Disasters*. Second edition. Oxford: Butterworth-Heinemann.

Uff, J. (2000) *The Southall Accident Inquiry Report*. London: HSC.

US Environmental Protection Agency (EPA) (2001) *Third party audit pilot project in the Commonwealth of Pennsylvania, final report U.S. EPA region III*. Philadelphia, PA: EPA, February.

Van Maanen, J. and Pentland, B. (1994) 'Cops and auditors: the rhetoric of records', in S. B. Sitkin and R. J. Bies (eds.) *The Legalistic Organization*. Thousand Oaks, CA: Sage, pp. 53–90.

Vaughan, D. (1996) *The Challenger Launch Decision: risky technology, culture and deviance at NASA*. Chicago: University of Chicago Press.

(1997) 'The trickle-down effect: policy decisions, risky work, and the *Challenger* tragedy', *California Management Review*, 39: 2.

(1998) 'Rational choice, situated action, and the social control of organisations', *Law & Society Review*, 32 (1): 23–61.

(1999) 'The dark side of organizations: mistake, misconduct, and disaster', *Annual Review of Sociology*, 25: 271–305.

(2002) 'Signals and interpretive work: the role of culture in a theory of practical action', in Karen A. Cerulo (ed.) *Culture in Mind: toward a sociology of culture and cognition*. New York: Routledge, pp. 28–54.

(2003) 'History as Cause: *Columbia* and *Challenger*', Report, Columbia Accident Investigation Board, Vol. 1, Chapter 8, August.

(2004) 'Public sociologist by accident', in M. B. Burawoy, W. Gamson, C. Ryan, S. Pfohl, D. Vaughan, C. Derber and J. Schor, 'Public sociologies: a symposium from Boston College', *Social Problems*, 51: 103–30.

(2005) 'NASA revisited: theory, analogy, and public sociology'. Unpublished.

(in progress) *Dead Reckoning: air traffic control in the early 21st century*. Chicago: University of Chicago Press.

Visvanathan, S. (with Kothari, R.) (1985) 'Bhopal: the imagination of a disaster', *Lokayan Bulletin*, 3: 48–76.

Vogel, D. (1986) *National Styles of Regulation*. Ithaca, NY: Cornell University Press.

Walker, R. D., Howard, M. O., Lampert, M. D. and Suchinsky, R. (1994) 'Medical malpractice guidelines', *Western Journal of Medicine*, 161 (1): 39–44.

Walter, C. (1996) 'Une histoire du concept d'efficience sur les marchés financiers', *Annales HSS*, 4 (July–August): 873–905.

Ward, S. (2001) 'Exploring the role of corporate risk manager', *Risk Management – An International Journal*, 3 (1): 7–25.

Waring, A. and Glendon, A. I. (1998) *Managing Risk: critical issues for survival and success into the 21st century*. London: Thompson Learning.

Weait, M. (1993) 'Icing on the cake? The contribution of the compliance function to effective financial regulation', *Journal of Asset Protection and Financial Crime*, 1 (1): 83–90.

Weber, M. (1946) *From Max Weber: essays in sociology*, translated and edited by H. H. Gerth and C. W. Mills. New York: Oxford University Press.

Weick, K. (1995) *Sensemaking in Organizations*. Thousand Oaks, CA: Sage.

(1998) 'Foresights of failure: an appreciation of Barry Turner', *Journal of Contingencies and Crisis Management*, 6 (2): 72–5.

Weick, K. E. (1990) 'The vulnerable system', *Journal of Management*, 16: 571–93.

Wells, C. (1996) 'Criminal law, blame and risk: corporate manslaughter', in C. Hood and D. K. C. Jones (eds.) *Accident and Design*. London: UCL Press.

(2001) *Corporations and Criminal Responsibility*. Second edition. Oxford: Clarendon Press.

Whitley, R. (1986a) 'The rise of modern finance theory: its characteristics as a scientific field and connections to the changing structure of capital markets', *Research in the History of Economic Thought and Methodology*, 4: 147–78.

(1986b) 'The transformation of business finance into financial economics: the roles of academic expansion and changes in U.S. capital markets', *Accounting, Organizations and Society*, 11: 171–92.

Wiggins, J. and Boland, V. (2001) 'Treasury market recovery will be slower than equities', *Financial Times*, 19 September, p. 32.

Wildavsky, A. (1988) *Searching for Safety*. New Brunswick, NJ: Transaction Books.

Wildavsky, A. and Drake, K. (1990) 'Theories of risk perception: who fears what and why?', *Daedalus*, 119 (4).

Willman, P., Fenton-O'Creevy, M., Nicholson, N. and Soane, E. (2002) 'Traders, managers and loss aversion in investment banking: a field study', *Accounting, Organizations and Society*, 27 (1/2): 85–98.

Wilson, J. Q. (1989) *Bureaucracy: what government agencies do and why they do it*. New York: Basic Books.

Wilthagen, T. (1993) 'Reflexive rationality in the regulation of occupational health and safety', in R. Rogowski and T. Wilthagen (eds.) *Reflexive Labour Law*. Boston: Kluwer-Nijhoff.

Winner, L. (1986a) 'On not hitting the tar-baby', in L. Winner (1986b), pp. 138–54.

(1986b) *The Whale and the Reactor: a search for limits in an age of high technology*. Chicago: University of Chicago Press.

Wood, D. (2002) 'From cop to CRO', *Erisk.com* (March).

Woodward, B. (1999) 'Challenges to human subjects, protections in US medical research', *Journal of the American Medical Association*, 282 (20): 1947–52.

Wynia, M. K., Cummins, D. S., VanGeest, J. B. and Wilson, I. B. (2000) 'Physician manipulation of reimbursement rules for patients: between a rock and a hard place', *Journal of the American Medical Association*, 283 (14): 1858–65.

Wynia, M. K., VanGeest, J. B., Cummins, D. S. and Wilson, I. B. (2003) 'Do physicians not offer useful services because of coverage restrictions?', *Health Affairs*, 22 (4): 190–7.

Wynne, B. (1988) 'Unruly technology: practical rules, impractical discourses, and public understanding', *Social Studies of Science*, 18: 147–67.

Yeager, P. C. (1991) 'Structural bias in regulatory law enforcement: the case of the U.S. Environmental Protection Agency', *Social Problems*, 34 (4): 330–44.

Zussman, R. (1992) *Intensive Care: medical ethics and the medical profession*. Chicago: University of Chicago Press.

Name index

Subject index